JAN RICHARDSON & MICHÈLE

THE NEXT STEP FORWARD IN
WORD STUDY
AND PHONICS

📖 SCHOLASTIC

In memory of Dr. Marie Clay, who changed the lives
of millions of children through her work in Reading Recovery.
Her wisdom and guidance continue to inspire and challenge us.

Classroom photos (cover and interior) ©: Heather Rush. Stock photos ©: 23: crayons and throughout: GWImages/Shutterstock, mop and throughout: cunaplus/Shutterstock, fly and throughout: jbd30/Shutterstock, socks and throughout: vlalexander/iStockphoto, fox and throughout: jimfeng/iStockphoto; 35: duck and throughout: Max2611/iStockphoto, rose bush: Chiyacat/Shutterstock, cat and throughout: Mila May/Shutterstock, mannequins and throughout: Massimo Lama/Dreamstime, sun and throughout: Sumroeng Chinnapan/Dreamstime, ship: Anton Balazh/Shutterstock, baby chicken and throughout: Toa55/Shutterstock, frog: Artur Synenko/Shutterstock; 54: zipper: Nomadsoul1/Shutterstock, camel: Nowak Lukasz/Shutterstock, moon: Anson/Shutterstock, nest: Mohd Hafez Abu Bakar/Dreamstime; 89: turtle: Kjeld Friis/Shutterstock, boys: Tomsickova Tatyana/Shutterstock, moon: Anson_shutterstock; 90 bat: Gucio_55/Shutterstock; 91: boy and girl: Jupiterimages/Getty Images, penguin: Hakat/Shutterstock, nest: Mohd Hafez Abu Bakar/Dreamstime; 92: breakfast: Africa Studio/Shutterstock, bat: Gucio_55/Shutterstock; 93: web: max2you/iStockphoto, playing: Pavel L Photo and Video/Shutterstock; 94: rose bush: Chiyacat/Shutterstock, camel: Nowak Lukasz/Shutterstock; 95: Zoonar RF/Getty Images, zipper: Nomadsoul1/Shutterstock; 98: poligonchik/iStockphoto; 121 ship: Anton Balazh/Shutterstock; 122: panutc/Shutterstock; 124: Kittijaroon/Dreamstime, Tomsickova Tatyana/Shutterstock, frog: Artur Synenko/Shutterstock; 125: iwka/Shutterstock.

Illustrations for Cookies and Scout series by Estelle Corke and Woodland Animals series by Amanda Enright, © Scholastic Inc.

Text and images from: *Busy Clarence, We Like Sunglasses, The Three Little Pigs, The Lion and the Mouse, Dinosaurs and Fossils, A World of Worms, Oki and the Polar Bear,* and *Beneath the Ocean Waves* copyright © Pioneer Valley Books. Used by permission of Pioneer Valley Books; *Puffins* by Agnes Land copyright © 2018 by Scholastic Inc. Published by Scholastic Inc.; *The Little Red Fort* text copyright © 2018 by Brenda Maier, illustrations copyright © 2018 by Sonia Sánchez. Used by permission of Scholastic Inc.; *When Marian Sang* text copyright © 2002 by Pam Muñoz Ryan, illustrations copyright © 2002 by Brian Selznick. Used by permission of Scholastic Inc. All Rights Reserved.

Publisher/Content editor: Lois Bridges
Editorial director: Sarah Longhi
Editor-in-chief/Development editor: Raymond Coutu
Senior editor: Shelley Griffin
Assistant editor: Molly Bradley
Art director: Brian LaRossa
Interior designer: Maria Lilja

CONTENTS

VIDEOS

Go to scholastic.com/NSFWordStudy to access this book's full menu of professional videos. Watch the authors teach and discuss word study activities at every reading stage, pre-A to fluent.

ACKNOWLEDGMENTS

This book grows out of many years of learning from teachers and children. The experiences we have accumulated from being classroom teachers, reading teachers, and Reading Recovery® teacher leaders have dramatically impacted our theories about how children learn to read. Together, we have observed, researched, and reflected on how best to help children become lifelong readers and writers. Of special importance has been the help of two very patient and smart men—our husbands, Cecil and Bob—who encouraged us, pushed our thinking, and prodded us to get it right!

A talented Scholastic team has contributed hugely to this effort. We want to thank our amazing publisher, Lois Bridges, for her insightful advice and contributions of research, and Ray Coutu, editor-in-chief, for his skilled and meticulous work on our manuscript. We also thank Sarah Longhi, editorial director; Shelley Griffin, senior editor; Molly Bradly, assistant editor; Brian LaRossa, art director; and Maria Lilia, interior designer. They gave us expert support, encouragement, and suggestions. We asked for a beautiful book, and they certainly delivered!

Additionally, we thank the teachers and administrators who helped us make this book relevant and practical. We want to recognize Karen Cangemi and the team of teachers at High Point Elementary School for field-testing the new assessments and procedures. We also want to thank Kelsey Holloway for allowing Michèle into her classroom to pilot new ideas and help us plan the independent learning centers. We are grateful to the teachers and administrators from Frontier Regional School District, Massachusetts, who hosted the videotaping. Many thanks to Louise Law, Director of Elementary Education, for skillfully interviewing us on video. We also thank Benjamin Barshefsky, Sunderland Elementary principal; Judith Shilling, Reading Recovery® teacher; and the school staff for rearranging their schedules, shuttling children to various classrooms, and making sure the children came to us with smiles on their faces. And a big thank you to Kevin Carlson and Lynne Graves for helping us catch those smiles on video and in photographs, and to Heather Rush from Pioneer Valley Books for all the other wonderful photos that appear throughout the book.

Finally, we want to acknowledge the thousands of precious children who have taught us to be better reading teachers. You are the reason we do what we do and why we love doing it.

A NOTE FROM JAN AND MICHÈLE

Teaching reading is a magical experience for any teacher. There's something beyond wonderful about seeing a child understand and respond to a story. It's one of the many reasons we teachers are so passionate about our profession.

In this book we aim to do three things:

1. State as clearly as possible the advantages of making word study an integral part of every guided reading program.

2. Present a simple and practical method for teaching word study skills, especially phonics. After those skills are taught, they should immediately be practiced in reading and writing. This book will show you how to do that.

3. Offer instructional guidance and sample lesson plans to make word study easy to implement and effective. It will be our joy to someday hear that this book's lessons are being widely and successfully used in classrooms throughout America.

Let's begin by sharing an inspirational story from Stacy, who witnessed a radical transformation in one of her students.

Tempest was a shy third-grader who liked to hide behind her long, beautiful hair. Despite being in reading intervention for years, she was reading at a kindergarten level. I had never worked with a student so far behind. Although Tempest had been taught phonics and knew her letters and sounds, she could barely read at all.

After attending a training session with Dr. Jan Richardson, I decided to try her guided reading framework with Tempest. At first, progress was slow. It would take days for her to learn a single sight word. We worked hard on building her phonics skills and prompting her to use what she had learned in word study to decode unfamiliar words. Imagine my delight when, after only one year of daily guided reading lessons, Tempest was reading at Level L—two years' growth!

Tempest didn't just grow as a reader, she grew into a confident, happy child. I also grew; I learned that close observation, appropriate word study instruction, and carefully selected books changed everything—for me and for Tempest!

Stacy Smith
Reading Specialist
Lake Geneva, Wisconsin

Footholds in Print

"Early in the lesson, the teacher helps the child gain footholds in print. The child learns some letters and begins to work with some simple words. The teacher asks herself, 'What detail in print is this child already attending to?'"

—Marie Clay (2005)

Imagine taking a driver's education course that doesn't require driving a car. Learning the rules of the road is important, but learning how to use the brake, steering wheel, and accelerator is more important. It's the same with word study and phonics. No matter how dedicated we teachers are to teaching both, students still need to "get behind the wheel" and use their word study and phonics skills in strategic ways while reading and writing.

In the story on page 7, Tempest had been taught phonics. In fact, she had worked through several phonics workbooks and computer programs. But merely learning phonics didn't teach her how to read. She needed to "get behind the wheel" and apply a variety of word study skills to texts at her instructional level.

UNDERSTANDING THE PLACE OF PHONICS AND SPELLING IN WORD STUDY

Word study, phonics, and spelling are critical parts of any literacy program. So it's important to understand what they are and how they work together.

Phonics

This book is about word study, which includes phonics and spelling. Phonics is learning the alphabetic code—the relationship between sounds and letters—in order to decode words. Word study is broader than that. It is about teaching children to study words in order to learn how they work. In addition to phonics, it includes phonemic awareness, high frequency word recognition, and understanding spelling patterns, word structures, vocabulary, and morphology. Phonics instruction teaches beginning readers the alphabetic code so they can decode words. Word study goes beyond the rote memorization of letters and sounds. It teaches readers how to apply their knowledge of letters, sounds, and words in order to read and spell. As Fountas and Pinnell remind us, word study aims to make word learning generative—to support students in developing "powerful systems…as well as giving them many opportunities to use their word study understandings in action while reading for meaning" (2017, p. 420).

> **RESEARCH NOTE**
>
> Children may benefit from considering not only how a word sounds, but also how it looks, what it means, and even where it comes from (Rasinski & Zutell, 2010, p. 14). Letter patterns play an important role in how we pronounce words—for example, *right - flight - tighten*. But meaning also impacts how words are spelled. Many words that we pronounce the same way are spelled differently to represent different meanings—for example, *sale* and *sail*. History has also played a part in how we pronounce a word—for example, the three different pronunciations of *ch*—in *child* (Old English), in *chef* (French), and in *chorus* (Greek). Children enjoy learning about why our language is so complicated!

Most phonics programs are built around a scope and sequence using one of the approaches listed in the chart below.

Approaches to Teaching Phonics	
Approach	**Instructional Method**
Synthetic phonics	Students first learn how to convert letters into sounds. They then blend the sounds together to form words.
Analytic phonics	Students learn to analyze letter/sound relationships in familiar words and apply those relationships to figure out new words. They do not pronounce sounds in isolation.
Analogy-based phonics	Students learn to use known words, word parts, and word families to read unknown words with similar features.
Phonics through spelling	Students learn to segment words into phonemes and then write the letters that represent the phonemes.
Embedded phonics	Students are taught letter/sound relationships while reading connected text.
Onset-rime phonics	Students learn to break words at the onset and rime.

We believe children should learn multiple strategic actions for decoding and encoding words. Consequently, we incorporate elements of *all* the phonics approaches listed above in our guided reading lessons, and we encourage students to apply those strategic actions when they encounter challenges during reading or writing. For example:

Learn letter/sound relationships and use sounds to blend short words. If the student stumbles on the word *fast*, the teacher might prompt him to blend the sounds together (synthetic phonics).

Analyze letter/sound relationships in known words and apply these relationships to new words. The teacher might show the student how to use /st/ from the known word *stop* and /ump/ from the known word *jump* to read the new word *stump* (analytic phonics).

Use known words to read unknown words. If a student struggles to read or write the word *shook*, the teacher might show her how to use *look* (a known word) to read or write *shook* (analogy-based phonics).

Hear and record sounds in words during writing. If the student is writing the word *lamp*, the teacher might prompt him to say the word slowly and record each sound (phonics through spelling).

Discover and learn letter/sound relationships. The teacher might write the word *action*, a word from the book. Then the student discovers how to pronounce the suffix (*tion*) and apply it to other words, such as *fraction* and *subtraction* (embedded phonics).

Learn to break words at the onset and rime to decode words. The student might use magnetic letters to break the word *stand* into *st* and *and* (onset-rime phonics).

Key Terms

Phoneme The smallest unit of sound

Phonemic Awareness The ability to hear and manipulate individual sounds in spoken words

Phonological Awareness A broad skill that features four levels of sound—word, syllable, onset-rime, and phoneme awareness

Syllable A part of a word that contains one vowel sound

Root Word The basic part of a word that holds the meaning. Also called the base word.

Morpheme The smallest part of a word that carries meaning. Prefixes, suffixes, and roots are morphemes.

Affix A word added to the beginning of a root word (prefix) or to the end (suffix)

Inflectional Ending A group of letters added to the end of a word to change its meaning

High Frequency Word A word that appears frequently in English texts

Sight Word A word that the reader recognizes immediately and does not have to decode

Spelling Programs

Like phonics, spelling is an integral part of word study. During word study, students learn to spell words that will be useful to them in reading and writing. To be good spellers, students need the following skills:

Phonetic Spelling Most English words follow regular phonetic rules. Children attend to the sounds in words and write the letters that make those sounds.

Visual Spelling Many English words, like *said* and *they*, are not spelled phonetically. Children need to remember what those words look like.

Analogy Spelling The same spelling patterns appear in many English words. Students need to hear similarities in words and word parts and use familiar patterns to spell new words.

If you need a weekly spelling program, consider the following approach:

- Choose different words for each guided reading group.

- Assign five to ten words each week. Take into consideration the sight words and phonics skill you have been teaching the group. See the chart below for a typical spelling list for a group reading at Level D. It includes three high frequency words that are often found in Level D books and three words that include digraphs, the target skill focus for Level D.

High Frequency Words	Words With the Target Skill Focus: Digraphs
down	with
away	ship
looking	that

- Establish independent routines for practicing spelling words. For example, students could make their spelling words with magnetic letters or write them on dry-erase boards. They could create a personal picture dictionary, or they could write sentences or stories using their spelling words. You could even create simple games that require students to spell or write their weekly spelling words.

- Review words for several weeks. Help students store words in their long-term memory by adding a few previously assigned words to the test each week. Revisit the words during sight word review at the beginning of each guided reading lesson.

See Appendix CC for a sample weekly spelling program by reading level.

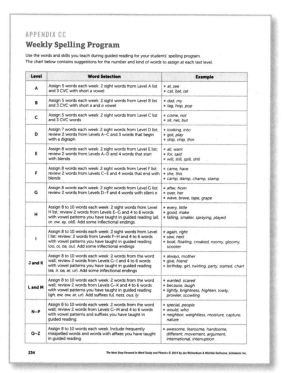

The Next Step Forward in Word Study and Phonics

WHAT'S THE BEST WAY TO TEACH WORD STUDY?

Because every reader progresses at a different pace, we see no benefit in teaching word study to the entire class. Our years of working with children and teachers tell us that the perfect time to teach word study is during a guided reading lesson. Word study, including phonics, should be taught in small groups and based on the developmental needs of individual students.

For that reason, this book provides instructions for how to plan and teach developmentally appropriate word study lessons as part of a guided reading program. We explore how students solve words, how to assess students' word study needs, and what materials and activities to use to help them become proficient word-solvers. The key phrase is "developmentally appropriate," not one size fits all. The focus must always be on individual students and their individual needs.

Areas of Learning

In this book, we address the following areas of learning and show you how to use engaging, hands-on activities to teach those areas of learning explicitly.

Areas of Learning	Key Concepts
Phonological Awareness	Identify and manipulate sounds (hear individual letters, word parts, rhyming words, and syllables)
Letter Knowledge	Learn letter names and a key word for each letter sound
Letter/Sound Relationships	Identify letter sounds and hear sounds in words
Spelling Patterns	Learn common spelling patterns and make analogies between similar words
High Frequency Words	Quickly recognize words that are commonly used in reading and writing
Word Meaning/ Vocabulary	Extend vocabulary by recognizing affixes and using them to infer the meanings of words
Word Structures	Change letters, letter clusters, inflectional endings and larger word parts to make new words
Word Solving	Take strategic action to problem-solve unknown words in reading and writing

HOW TO USE THIS BOOK

In Chapter 1, we show you how to embed word study in a guided reading lesson. Chapter 2 describes ten short, engaging activities for teaching word study to students reading texts at Levels A–Z. To view videos of us teaching the activities and discussing them with Louise Law, director of elementary education, Frontier Regional School District, Massachusetts, visit scholastic.com/NSFWordStudy.

Chapters 3 to 7 focus on teaching word study at each reading stage: pre-A, emergent, early, transitional, and fluent. Each of those chapters follows the Assess-Decide-Guide framework for planning and teaching lessons. The Appendices include assessments that target specific skills, printable leveled books, and resources to help you plan and teach your own word study lessons.

The ideas and activities presented between the covers of this book will help you become a better teacher. Follow them faithfully, and you'll see your students growing into thoughtful, proficient readers who can't wait to read another book!

Louise Law interviews Jan and Michèle about word study activities.
Go to scholastic.com/NSFWordStudy.

CHAPTER 1

Word Study:
An Essential Component of Guided Reading

"The goal of all forms of word analysis for the reader is to be able to take words apart, on the run, while reading unexpected known words, partially familiar words still being learned, and new, unknown words."

—Marie Clay (2016)

Guided reading is a small-group approach to reading instruction that allows teachers to meet the various instructional needs of their students. Usually group members are reading at or close to the same text level. After they are briefly introduced to the book, students read it independently while the teacher confers with each of them. Equipped with astute observation skills and an understanding of the reading process, the teacher prompts students to apply a network of strategic actions that help them improve their reading skills. After students have read the book, the teacher engages them in a short conversation that builds comprehension. It doesn't make sense to teach word study the same way to every child. Children enter school with different literacy experiences and competencies. Some have so much knowledge of letters and sounds that they are ready to learn how to decode multisyllabic words; others have almost no knowledge of letters and sounds.

Teach developmentally appropriate and needs-based word study lessons during guided reading, using the chart below as a guide. In a guided reading lesson, students with similar needs are grouped together, which makes it easier to provide appropriate instruction. While it takes a bit more time to plan word study lessons for multiple guided reading groups, teaching to the level at which each student is reading increases that student's engagement and allows him or her to progress more rapidly in understanding how letters, sounds, and words work. It also allows students to apply their newly learned skills immediately.

Word Study Skills by Text Level and Reading Stage				
Text Level	Reading Stage	Skill Focus		
A	Emergent	• Initial consonants	• Long vowels	
B		• Initial and final consonants	• Short *a* and *o*	
C		• All short vowels	• CVC words	
D	Early	• Digraphs	• Onset-rime	
E		• Initial blends	• Onset-rime	
F		• Final blends	• Onset-rime	
G		• Initial and final blends	• Silent *e*	• Onset-rime
H		• Silent *e*	• Vowel patterns	• Inflectional endings
I		• Silent *e*	• Vowel patterns	• Inflectional endings

Word Study Skills by Text Level and Reading Stage		
Text Level	**Reading Stage**	**Skill Focus**
J–K	Transitional	• Silent *e* • Inflectional endings • Compound words • Vowel patterns with spelling changes • *r*-controlled vowels
L–M		• Vowel patterns • Inflectional endings • Prefixes • *r*-controlled vowels with spelling changes • Suffixes • Compound words
N–P		• Vowel patterns • Inflectional endings • Prefixes with spelling changes • Suffixes
Q–Z	Fluent	• Affixes and roots

Word study lessons should prepare students to tackle the decoding challenges they will encounter as they read and write. Reading and writing should happen as soon

VIDEO LINK scholastic.com/NSFWordStudy

Jan and Michèle talk about why word study is best taught during guided reading.

after the word study activities as possible. That's why, even though the activities described in this book can be used in any small-group context, we recommend using them in the integrated lesson framework described in *The Next Step Forward in Guided Reading* (Richardson, 2016). The framework provides developmental and explicit instruction in reading, word study, and writing. It allows you to prompt students to use their newly acquired word study skills immediately, while they're engaged in reading and writing.

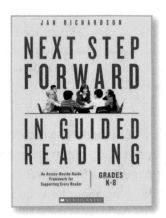

A Next Step lesson typically takes about 20 minutes a day for two days (emergent and early) or three days (transitional and fluent). The lessons are structured as follows.

Emergent and Early Plan Levels A–I		Transitional and Fluent Plan Levels J–Z		
20 minutes each day		20 minutes each day		
Day 1	**Day 2**	**Day 1**	**Day 2**	**Day 3**
Sight Word Review	Sight Word Review	Introduce a New Book	Read the Book With Prompting	Guided Writing
Introduce and Read a New Book With Prompting	Reread the Book With Prompting	Read the Book With Prompting	Discuss and Teach	
Discuss and Teach	Discuss and Teach	Discuss and Teach	Word Study	
Word Study	Guided Writing			

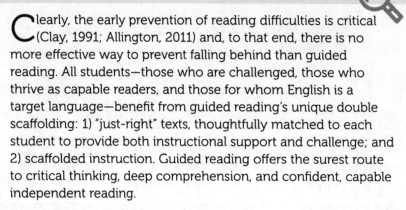

RESEARCH NOTE

Clearly, the early prevention of reading difficulties is critical (Clay, 1991; Allington, 2011) and, to that end, there is no more effective way to prevent falling behind than guided reading. All students—those who are challenged, those who thrive as capable readers, and those for whom English is a target language—benefit from guided reading's unique double scaffolding: 1) "just-right" texts, thoughtfully matched to each student to provide both instructional support and challenge; and 2) scaffolded instruction. Guided reading offers the surest route to critical thinking, deep comprehension, and confident, capable independent reading.

Although time is specifically allotted for word study, seize every opportunity to do word study during other parts of the guided reading lesson. The chart on the following page describes each component of guided reading and how it can support students in learning about letters, sounds, and words.

Weaving Word Study Into a Guided Reading Lesson		
Lesson Component	**Description**	**Benefit to Students**
Sight Word Review *(optional after Level I)*	• Students write three high frequency words they have been learning.	• Builds a sight word vocabulary, which increases reading and writing fluency
Book Introduction	• The teacher introduces new or unusual words and language structures.	• Applies decoding skills to problem-solve challenging words and construct meaning
Read With Prompting	• Each student reads the book independently while the teacher provides on-the-spot, targeted instruction to strengthen the student's processing system.	• Monitors and applies known skills to solve unknown words, and thereby increase fluency and phrasing
Discuss the Text	• The teacher engages students in a conversation about the text to enhance and extend comprehension.	• Practices using new vocabulary
Follow-Up Teaching Points	• The teacher demonstrates a word-solving action based on student processing needs.	• Develops strategic actions for decoding unfamiliar words
Word Study	• The teacher selects a new sight word to teach *(optional after Level I)*. • The teacher then provides students with a short, hands-on word study lesson based on the students' needs.	• Builds a core of known words • Develops a system for remembering words • Learns developmentally appropriate skills to use in decoding and encoding new words • Expands vocabulary strategies by analyzing unfamiliar words with affixes
Guided Writing	• Students write about the text with teacher support. The teacher may provide instruction in constructing new words by using Sound Boxes, Breaking Words, and Analogies.	• Applies skills that have been taught—hearing and recording sounds, using onsets and rimes to write new words, adding inflectional endings, and writing multisyllabic words

THE ASSESS-DECIDE-GUIDE FRAMEWORK FOR WORD STUDY

Use this framework to plan and teach targeted, developmentally appropriate word study lessons.

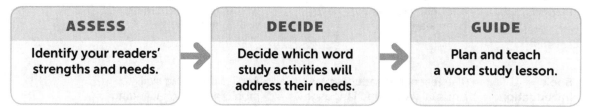

ASSESS	DECIDE	GUIDE
Identify your readers' strengths and needs.	Decide which word study activities will address their needs.	Plan and teach a word study lesson.

Assess

Formal and informal assessments play a critical role in helping you plan powerful word study activities. We have created leveled assessments for each reading stage: pre-A, emergent, early, transitional, and fluent. They will help you identify word study needs and monitor progress. You will find the assessments in Chapters 3 to 7 and in the Appendix.

Decide

Use your assessments to decide which skill to teach and the word study activity that will help students develop that skill and apply it to their reading and writing.

Guide

Teach word study skills in every guided reading lesson. Doing so allows students to apply those skills immediately. In Chapters 3 to 7, we have included a series of word study lessons for each reading stage. However, as you become more proficient with the procedures, you will be able to design lessons to meet the specific needs of your students.

RESEARCH NOTE

Unfortunately, the teaching of phonics has been politicized (Scharer, 2019), but our stance remains unchanged. In keeping with the Reading Recovery community of which we are both part, we stand by the research (Hurry & Fridkin, 2018; Doyle, 2018) that has demonstrated again and again that one-size-fits-all instruction does not work. Children need phonics, yes, but they also need meaningful reading experiences with books they love to read and opportunities to express themselves through writing for their own compelling purposes. As Scharer notes, "Quality word study begins with developing an appreciation, curiosity, and love of words." Successful teachers build on that curiosity and love through targeted and intentional instruction.

IF YOU WORK WITH ENGLISH LEARNERS

Some of you are working with English learners whose phonological system differs somewhat—or substantially—from English. While an English learner may control phonological awareness in his or her first language, that control may not automatically transfer to English. For example, the /ch/ and /sh/ sounds may not be part of their home language. What do we recommend for teaching word study to English learners? Emphasize meaning and practice flexibility!

First, center word study on meaning. Embed the analysis of words in meaningful text such as a story, poem, or song. This will help your English learners become familiar with English sounds, inflections, and vocabulary. For some English learners, it is easier to focus on chunks of meaning such as prefixes, suffixes, and root words rather than individual phonemes. Since English words have been borrowed from several languages, point out similarities in words that exist in both languages. These are called cognates. For example, the word *action* is *acción* in Spanish.

Be flexible in your expectations. Accept different dialects and pronunciation patterns, especially for children who are just learning English. Vowels can be especially tricky. Help the children hear the different English sounds, but don't expect them to correctly produce those sounds right away. It will take time for new sounds to be assimilated into their speech. Additionally, inflectional endings can be quite challenging for English learners. When a child says *look* for *looked*, it may appear she is not paying attention to the end of the word, but this could be a language-related error. If students do not control the verb tenses in their oral language, don't expect that structure when they are reading.

Ultimately, learning how to solve words is a fluid process; carefully observe your English learners as you do all your students so you can track their progress and know what elements of word study they are ready to learn next. Support them in their journey to successful, independent reading.

THE GOAL OF WORD STUDY

The ultimate goal of word study is for students to apply what they learn about letters, sounds, and words as they read and write. When you teach targeted, developmentally appropriate word study lessons, you operate in the student's zone of proximal development (Vygotsky, 1978), that sweet spot where students actually learn what you are teaching.

In the next chapter, we present ten powerful, engaging word study activities for students reading at Levels A–Z.

CHAPTER 2

Word Study Activities

"Word solving is not just about word learning. Its power lies in the discovery of the principles underlying the construction of words that make up written language."

—Gay Su Pinnell and Irene Fountas (2017)

In this chapter we present ten word study activities you can use for guided reading lessons at text Levels A–Z. Some are appropriate for emergent and early readers; others are better suited for transitional or fluent readers. Each activity will fully engage your students, while teaching them to apply phonics skills to their reading and writing. The following chart lists the text level ranges we recommend for each activity and the materials you will need.

Word Study Activity	Levels	Materials
Sight Word Review	A–I	• Dry-erase boards, markers, and erasers
Teach a New Sight Word	A–I	• Magnetic letters on trays • Dry-erase boards, markers, and erasers
Picture Sorting	A–E	• Picture cards for initial consonants, medial vowels, digraphs, and blends
Sound Boxes	A–G	• Sound Box templates inserted in write-on plastic sleeves • Dry-erase markers and erasers

Word Study Activity	Levels	Materials
Making Words	**A–J**	• Magnetic letters on trays
Breaking Words	**D–P**	• Magnetic letters on trays
Analogy Charts	**G–P**	• Analogy Charts inserted in write-on plastic sleeves • Dry-erase markers and erasers
Make a Big Word	**J–P**	• Magnetic letters on trays
Writing Big Words	**J–P**	• Dry-erase boards, markers, and erasers
Working With Affixes	**Q–Z**	• Magnetic letters on trays • Dry-erase boards, markers, and erasers • Affix word cards

WORD STUDY MATERIALS

Gather the following materials and organize them near your guided reading table. You will need a tabletop easel or large dry-erase board to model procedures. The student forms are available at scholastic.com/NSFWordStudy. You can purchase teaching tools at Pioneer Valley Books: www.pioneervalleybooks.com.

Picture Cards

Collect and organize picture cards for teaching initial consonants, medial vowels, digraphs, and blends. You will need six to eight cards for each letter or letter combination.

Magnetic Letters on Trays

Each student will need a set of magnetic letters organized on a small metal tray. You can purchase trays designed for teaching, or simply use a small cookie tray. Write the letters on the trays with permanent marker. Doing so will save you preparation time and help students replace the letters after the lesson. Also, be sure to have a box for organizing additional letters.

Dry-Erase Boards

We recommend small dry-erase boards to maximize space on the guided reading table.

Sound Box Templates

We recommend inserting the Sound Box template into a heavy-duty plastic sheet protector so students can write on it and erase easily. See Appendices R and T for Sound Box templates.

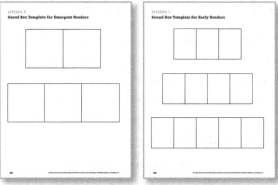

Analogy Charts

You will need two- and three-column Analogy Charts inserted into heavy-duty plastic sheet protectors. See Appendices U and W for Analogy Charts.

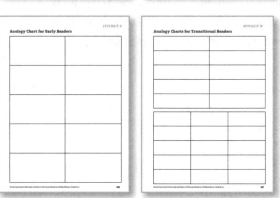

Affix Word Cards

At scholastic.com/ NSFWordStudy, you will find six word cards for each affix we teach during fluent guided reading lessons. Print out the cards and organize them by affix in a 3-x-5-inch file box.

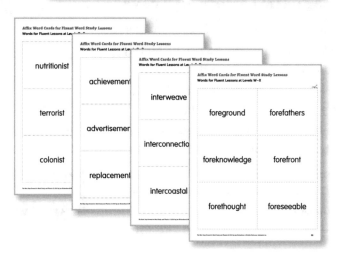

WORD STUDY ACTIVITIES

We've used these word study activities in thousands of classrooms and found them to be engaging and effective. Choose the ones that best meet your students' needs, and follow the steps below.

Teaching Sight Words (Recommended for Levels A–I, optional thereafter)

Students will automatically acquire some new words as they read books and write stories and other texts. Most, however, will need explicit teaching and guided practice to remember words. Having a bank of words they can identify quickly supports fluency and saves cognitive space for problem-solving other words. Our research and experience have taught us that most students can learn about ten words at each text level. In Appendix D, we recommend words for each text level, but you might want to make your own list from your collection of leveled books. Find the words that show up again and again. Whichever words you decide to teach, use the Sight Word Review and Teach a New Sight Word to help students build a system for remembering words.

> *"Learning to write many different words (at least 40) provides the child with enough generative power to build a much larger writing vocabulary."*
>
> **—Marie Clay (2016)**

Sight Word Review

Spend a minute or less at the beginning of each guided reading lesson reviewing words you've taught in previous guided reading lessons. Dictate three words for students to write on a dry-erase board. One should be the word you taught in the previous lesson. The other two should be familiar words that appear in the new book for that day. This review supports fluency and helps children anchor their reading. Marie Clay (2005) refers to those words as "footholds in print." Don't let students copy words from the word wall or your easel. Instead, have them do their best to retrieve the words from memory. By writing the words, they are held accountable for knowing and producing them. It also helps them build a memory trace. Clay states, "One way of remembering a word in all its details is to write it. This requires one to have learned a little program (like a computer program) that produces the word from beginning to end, with all its parts in the right order" (Clay, 2016, p. 71).

After you dictate a word, support students who need help writing it. Don't treat this as a spelling test. The goal is for every student to write the word accurately with correct letter formation. The chart below contains suggestions for prompting and scaffolding instruction when students have difficulty.

VIDEO LINK scholastic.com/NSFWordStudy

A group of students reviews sight words.

Prompts and Teaching Moves for Students Who Struggle With Sight Words		
Behavior	**Prompt**	**Teaching Move**
Student writes a letter backwards.	*Check your alphabet chart.*	Point to the letter on the chart and model how to write it.
Student writes the wrong letter.	*How does this word look?* Erase the incorrect letter and ask, *What's missing?*	Write the word on the easel for the student to copy.
Student can't recall the first letter or other easy-to-hear sounds.	*Say it slowly. What do you hear first (or next, or last)?*	Say the word with the student and emphasize the sound the student is missing.
Student forgets how to spell the word or confuses it with another word.	*What does it look like? What's the second letter?*	Give the student a way to remember the word (e.g., They *has* the *in* it. There *is* like *where*).

Monitoring Progress

Use the Sight Word Checklists in Appendix E to monitor progress. Place a checkmark under the student's name if he or she was able to write the word without help. We've found that once a child writes the word six times (on different days), the word has been stored in long-term memory. Use the checklists to help you select words that need to be reviewed and taught.

Teach a New Sight Word

After students read the new book, spend two to three minutes teaching them a new sight word, preferably one that is in the new book. By teaching the word after they have read the book, you give students the opportunity to read the word several times before teaching them to write it, which makes it easier for them to learn it.

The following four activities provide for a gradual release of responsibility and build visual memory. Do each of them every day in order. Once students become familiar with the routine, it will go smoothly and quickly. (In fact, they will let you know if you miss a step!)

1. What's Missing?

This activity is about looking and attending to the details, letter by letter. Write the word on a dry-erase board or make it with magnetic letters. Tell students the word and ask them to look at each letter as you slowly slide an index card left to right across the word. The purpose of this brief procedure is to help students develop a system for remembering words. This includes attending to the left-to-right sequence of letters within a word.

Erase or remove a letter and ask, "What's missing?" When a student tells you the missing letter, place it back in the word. Repeat the process several times, removing different letters, calling on a student each time to tell you "What's missing?" Because children think it's a game, they will pay attention and look closely at the word. When you get to the last student, erase the entire word and ask the student to spell it. This is the only time you will have students spell the word. (Spelling a word is not an efficient way to learn sight words. In fact, it will slow the rate at which students acquire them.) You want students to remember sight words as a complete unit.

2. Mix and Fix

Have students take magnetic letters off their trays to make a sight word. Although most students should be able to construct the word easily, they can use a model you provide, if necessary. Teach students how to check the word by sliding their finger under the letters as they read it. This helps them develop synchrony, the process of coordinating and integrating auditory and visual information. Students should hear and say what they see in a word. Make sure each student is looking at the letters as he or she says the word.

Have the students mix up and remake (fix) the word several times. After the final mix and fix, have each student cover the word with an index card.

3. Table Writing

Students write the word on the table with their finger as they say the word in a natural way. Do not encourage them to segment the sounds. Let them peek under the card if they forget how to write the word. This tactile activity helps them build a memory trace for the word (Myers, 1978).

4. Write and Retrieve

Students write the word on a small dry-erase board or at the bottom of an alphabet chart. (We use the alphabet chart if students need support with letter formation.) Immediately intervene if a student begins to misspell a word. When a child writes a word incorrectly, the word becomes difficult for them to unlearn. If they need help, they can lift the index card and look at the magnetic letters. Do not allow students to spell or sound out the word. You want them to learn the word as a complete unit. At first you may want them to say the word slowly in a natural way as they write it. Listening for the sounds will help them remember the letter sequence. Later, when they have developed a system for remembering, they will not need to do that.

Have students erase the word and write a different word, one they know well. Have them erase, then dictate the new word again for students to write. This step helps students build a long-term memory process for depositing and retrieving words.

After students learn a new sight word, it is important for them to practice the word in a variety of ways. Review the word for several days at the beginning of each lesson by having them write the word on a dry-erase board. Observe each student, checking to see if he or she quickly remembers the word. If students need extra help, they can say the word slowly and listen for sounds, but the goal is for them to write the word without having to say it.

During guided writing, expect correct spelling of the sight word. If students misspell a word you have taught, write it on a practice page in their journal and have them write it several times to build automaticity. Then have them write the word in their piece.

 VIDEO LINKS scholastic.com/NSFWordStudy

- A group of students uses the four steps to learn a new word.

- Jan and Michèle explain the four steps of teaching a new sight word.

Teaching Word Study Lessons

Spend about three to five minutes a day doing a word study lesson that teaches some aspect of phonics and phonemic awareness. Follow these three steps:

1. Select a Skill Focus

Use the word study assessments that match your students' reading stage (described in Chapters 3–7) and your daily observations during guided reading to identify a skill focus for your lesson. Most students will need the level-specific skills we identify in the following chart. Nevertheless, you may have some students who can read at higher text levels but still need to work on the target skills listed for lower text levels. Choose the skill that best fits the reader's needs.

	Word Study Skill Focus and Activities by Text Level		
Text Level	**Reading Stage**	**Skill Focus**	**Word Study Activities**
A	Emergent	• Initial consonants • Long vowels	• Picture Sorting • Making Words • Sound Boxes
B		• Initial and final consonants • Short *a* and *o*	• Picture Sorting • Making Words • Sound Boxes
C		• All short vowels • CVC words	• Picture Sorting • Making Words • Sound Boxes
D	Early	• Digraphs • Onset-rime	• Picture Sorting • Making Words • Sound Boxes • Breaking Words
E		• Initial blends • Onset-rime	• Picture Sorting • Making Words • Sound Boxes • Breaking Words
F		• Final blends • Onset-rime	• Making Words • Sound Boxes • Breaking Words

Word Study Skill Focus and Activities by Text Level

Text Level	Reading Stage	Skill Focus	Word Study Activities
G	Early *continued*	• Initial and final blends • Silent *e* • Onset-rime	• Making Words • Sound Boxes • Breaking Words • Analogy Charts
H		• Silent *e* • Vowel patterns • Inflectional endings	• Making Words • Breaking Words • Analogy Charts
I		• Silent *e* • Vowel patterns • Inflectional endings	• Making Words • Breaking Words • Analogy Charts
J–K	Transitional	• Silent *e* • Vowel patterns • *r*-controlled vowels • Inflectional endings with spelling changes • Compound words	• Breaking Words • Analogy Charts • Make a Big Word • Writing Big Words
L–M		• Vowel patterns • *r*-controlled vowels • Inflectional endings with spelling changes • Compound words • Prefixes • Suffixes	• Breaking Words • Analogy Charts • Make a Big Word • Writing Big Words
N–P		• Vowel patterns • Inflectional endings with spelling changes • Prefixes • Suffixes	• Breaking Words • Analogy Charts • Make a Big Word • Writing Big Words
Q–Z	Fluent	• Affixes and roots	• Working With Affixes

2. Choose a Word Study Activity

For each text level, we provide several activities for teaching word study skills. Each activity teaches a different aspect of word study and guides students to apply the target skill as they read and write. The following chart explains the purpose of the activities and how they help students transfer word study skills.

Word Study Activities			
Activity	**Level**	**Purpose**	**Transfer to Reading and Writing**
Picture Sorting	A–E	Hear sounds and link sounds to letters.	• Use sounds to predict what makes sense and monitor for visual and auditory match. • Cross-check visual information (letters and sounds) with meaning and structure to solve unknown words in reading.
Making Words	A–I	Visually scan words to check for letter/sound accuracy.	• Notice reading errors by monitoring for visual/auditory match and then self-correcting their errors. • Break words at the onset and rime to read and write unknown words.
Sound Boxes	A–G	Hear and record sounds in sequence.	• Write unknown words through sound analysis. • Check for accuracy by sliding a finger under a word to see if it looks and sounds right.
Breaking Words	D–P	Attend to parts of words.	• Solve unknown words by breaking the word at the onset and rime. • Take apart words in flexible ways. • Notice similarities in words.
Analogy Charts	G–P	Notice patterns in known words to read and write unknown words.	• Use analogies to solve unknown words during reading and writing.
Make a Big Word	J–P	See and hear syllable breaks. Learn inflectional endings, prefixes, and suffixes.	• Take apart unknown words. • Write multisyllabic words by hearing and recording parts.
Writing Big Words	J–P	Learn common prefixes and suffixes.	• Use known words to read and write unknown words with prefixes and suffixes.
Working With Affixes	Q–Z	Learn to use common affixes to infer the meanings of words.	• Improve word recognition, spelling, and vocabulary knowledge.

3. Follow Word Study Procedures

This section describes in detail the activities for teaching word study skills and scaffolding students who need support.

Picture Sorting

This activity teaches phonemic awareness, an important skill in learning to read (National Institute of Child Health and Human Development). Hearing phonemes in spoken words and linking them to letters helps students read and write more effectively. Each student needs three to four picture cards.

Follow these steps:

1. Choose the skill focus—two sounds for students to sort. You might have students sort pictures by initial consonants (*g* and *m*), medial vowels (short *i* and short *u*), digraphs (*ch* and *sh*), or blends (*sl* and *sp*). When sorting blends, always choose two blends that begin with the same letter. This forces students to attend to the second letter in the blend, which is the challenging sound to hear.

2. Pass out three or four picture cards to each student. Tell the students what the pictures are. On the easel, write the two sounds you want them to hear.

3. Have each student sort a picture by:

    - Saying the picture name (*ship*).
    - Saying the target sound (/sh/).
    - Saying the letter (or letters) that make that sound (*s-h*).
    - Putting the picture card under the correct letter or letters.

Students sort picture cards for blends.

Picture Sorting Lessons by Text Level

Text Level	Skill Focus	Examples	
A	Initial consonants	*d*	*h*
B	Initial and final consonants Short *a* and *o*	*a*	*o*
C	All short vowels	*i*	*u*
D	Initial digraphs	*sh*	*ch*
E	Initial blends	*fl*	*fr*

VIDEO LINKS scholastic.com/NSFWordStudy

- A group of students sorts initial blends.
- Jan and Michèle explain Picture Sorting.

Making Words

The sounds students hear in a word must match the letters they see. Making Words teaches students how to monitor for a visual and auditory match. This process is called synchrony. Students who lack synchrony tend to make errors such as saying *had* for the word *have* or saying *came* for *come* without noticing their mistake. Making Words also teaches left-to-right visual scanning across a word.

Each student will need a magnetic letter tray to make a series of words you dictate. Each word in the series should differ by a letter or letter cluster. Asking students to create a new word by making minimal changes draws their attention to the letter/sound sequences in words.

Follow these steps:

1. Create your own series of words that teach the target skill, or use one of the lessons in Chapter 4 or 5.

2. Tell students the letters they will need and have them remove those letters from their tray. Call out the letters in alphabetical order so students can quickly find them on their trays.

3. Dictate a word for the students to make and tell them how many letters they will need.

4. After students make the word with the magnetic letters, tell them to check the word by saying it slowly as they run their finger underneath it. This should help them notice their errors or confirm their accuracy.

5. Dictate a new word that differs by one letter (or letter cluster if you are targeting blends).

6. Before students reach for the letters to exchange, teach them to say the new word slowly as they slide their finger under the current word. This helps them decide which letter or letters they will need to change to make the new word.

At first you will have to tell students which letter to change, but they will soon be able to make changes without your help. The process students use to determine the mismatch between a sound and a letter is the same process they will use later to self-correct during reading.

When students do Making Words at text Level D and higher, have them break the magnetic letters at the onset and say each part.

d r o p

Making Words Lessons by Text Level

Text Level	Skill Focus	Example
A	• Initial consonants	*dad-had-sad-lad*
B	• Initial and final consonants • Short *a* and *o*	*can-cap-map-man-pan* *hot-hop-hog-log-lot*
C	• All short vowels • CVC words	*hop-hip-sip-sap-sat-hat*
D	• Digraphs	*hop-shop-ship-chip-chin*
E	• Initial blends	*rim-brim-slim-slam-slap-clap*
F	• Final blends	*went-wept-west-pest-past-pant*
G	• Initial and final blends	*band-brand-bland-blank-blink*
H	• Silent *e* • Vowel patterns	*rip-ripe-gripe-grip-grim-grime* *down-drown-frown-crown-clown*
I	• Vowel patterns	*coat-coast-boast-boat-goat-gloat*

 VIDEO LINKS scholastic.com/NSFWordStudy

- A group of students engages in Making Words.
- Jan and Michèle explain Making Words.

Sound Boxes

In this activity students learn how to say a word slowly to hear and write sounds in sequence. Each student needs a Sound Boxes template in a plastic write-on sleeve, a dry-erase marker, and an eraser.

Students use the Sound Boxes template.

Follow these steps:

1. Dictate a word for students to write in the boxes. Tell them how many boxes to use. Don't waste time asking students to figure out the number of boxes they will use.

2. Have students say the word slowly and run their finger under the boxes.

3. Have students say the word again slowly and write the letter or letters for each phoneme in one box. When students write a word with a digraph (*ch, sh, th*), both letters go in the same box because they are one phoneme. When they write words with a blend, each letter is written in a separate box because blends contain two or more phonemes.

Sound Boxes Lessons by Text Level		
Text Level	**Skill Focus**	**Examples**
A	Initial consonants Long vowels	g o m e
B	Initial and final consonants Short *a* and *o*	a m h o p
C	All short vowels CVC words	d i m c u t
D	Digraphs	th i n m a sh
E	Initial blends	c l a p
F	Final blends	l a s t
G	Initial and final blends	s t a m p

VIDEO LINKS scholastic.com/NSFWordStudy

- A group of students uses Sound Boxes to hear sounds in words.
- Jan and Michèle explain Sound Boxes.

Breaking Words

In this activity students learn how to break words at the onset and rime. Research shows that breaking a word at the onset and rime is a more effective and efficient way to decode a word than sounding out letter by letter (Moustafa, 1996). The onset is the beginning consonant letter or letter cluster, while the rime is the part of the word that begins with the vowel. For example, in the word *slick*, *sl* is the onset and *ick* is the rime. Begin using the Breaking Words procedure at about Level D, after you have taught the target skill using Picture Sorting, Making Words, and Sound Boxes.

> ### RESEARCH NOTE
>
> Children are natural pattern seekers—they find patterns in nature, art, music, and numbers. So it's no surprise that children will search for patterns in language and words. They can be taught to use onset-rime patterns in words they know in order to figure out how to pronounce words they don't know (Moustafa, 1996, Zinke, 2016). For example, they can use the *st* from the known word *stop* and the *ump* from the known word *jump* to read the new word *stump*.

Early Breaking Words. Students learn to break apart one-syllable words. Follow these steps:

1. Select three words that have the same rime. In the following example we use *stop*, *chop*, and *drop*. Write the first word (*stop*) on a dry-erase board. Do not say the word—and tell the students not to say the word.

2. Tell students to take the letters off their trays to make the word.

3. Tell students to break the word before the vowel.

s t   o p

4. Have students say each part chorally. (/st/ /op/)

5. Have students put the word back together and read it. (*stop*)

6. Tell students to change the onset to make a new word. For example, *Take away the* st *and put* ch. (*chop*)

7. Repeat steps 3 to 5: break it (*ch op*), say it (/ch/ /op/), make it (*chop*).

8. Write another word that has the same rime and have students read it (*drop*). If they need help, underline the rime.

Breaking Words is even more effective if you use it to teach a challenging word in the book students are reading in guided reading. For instance, perhaps the new word *quill* is in the book. Your Breaking Words activity might begin with *will* (a known word), move to *still*, and then *quill*.

 VIDEO LINK scholastic.com/NSFWordStudy
A group of students engages in Breaking Words.

Advanced Breaking Words. Begin these procedures at about text Level G, once students understand how to break one-syllable words. At this advanced stage, students work with words that have the same rime but different onsets and inflectional endings. Follow these steps:

1. On a dry-erase board, write a word with an inflectional ending. Do not say the word and do not have the students say the word (e.g., *spinning*).

2. Have students take the letters off their trays to make the word. (You will need to provide duplicate letters.)

3. Tell students to take off the ending and break the word before the vowel (*sp inn ing*).

4. Ask students to say each part chorally (/sp/ /in/ /ing/). Explain that if a word has a two-letter rime with a short vowel (e.g., *ap, at, op, un*), you double the final consonant before you add *-er, -ed,* or *-ing.*

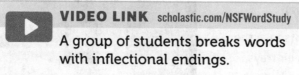

5. Have the students put the word back together and read it (*spinning*).

6. Tell students to change the onset. For example, say, "Change the *sp* to *gr* to make a new word." Do not say the word and do not have the students say the new word (*spinning – grinning*).

7. Repeat steps 3 to 5: break it (*gr inn ing*), say it (/gr/ /in/ /ing/), make it (*grinning*).

8. Write another example on the dry-erase board and have students read it (*thinning*). If they need help, underline the rime. When the activity becomes easy, change both the onset and the ending (*thinner*).

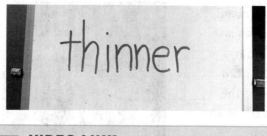

VIDEO LINK scholastic.com/NSFWordStudy
A group of students breaks words with inflectional endings.

As students progress, use the Advanced Breaking Words procedure with affix words. Follow these steps:

1. Write a word on the easel and have students make it with magnetic letters (e.g., *nervous*).

2. Have students break the word and read the parts with you.

3. Write another word for them to read (e.g., *wondrous*).

VIDEO LINK scholastic.com/NSFWordStudy
Jan and Michèle explain Breaking Words.

Analogy Charts

At first, use this activity to teach vowel patterns such as the silent-*e* feature and vowel clusters (e.g., *ee*, *ow*, *ai*). As your students progress, use it to teach them how to add inflectional endings.

Teaching vowel patterns. Because this is an auditory sort, always select two patterns with different sounds, such as *oa* and *igh*. Choose two vowel patterns from the book or use one of the lessons in Chapter 5 or 6. Follow these steps:

1. Distribute an Analogy Chart, a dry-erase marker, and an eraser to each student.

2. Tell students they are going to use the two-column chart to write words that have similar patterns.

3. At the top of the chart, write a key word for each of the two vowel patterns. The key words should be ones the children recognize. Students copy those words at the top of their own charts and underline the pattern in each word. Appendix X contains key words for each vowel pattern.

l<u>oo</u>k	d<u>ay</u>
h<u>oo</u>k	pl<u>ay</u>
sh<u>oo</u>k	st<u>ay</u>
br<u>oo</u>k	pr<u>ay</u>

4. Discuss the sound each vowel pattern makes. Then say a new word that has the same vowel pattern as one of the key words. Tell students to listen to the vowel sound in the word and find the key word that has the same sound. Have them write the new word under the matching key word and underline the vowel pattern.

5. Repeat the procedure with four to six words.

6. After students read the words in each column, write a new word that has one or both of the vowel patterns and have students read it.

7. As students become more proficient in hearing the vowel patterns, dictate words with inflectional endings.

c**ar**	f**or**
st**ar**t	f**or**t
c**ar**toon	st**or**my
ch**ar**ming	rec**or**ded

VIDEO LINK scholastic.com/NSFWordStudy

A group of students uses an Analogy Chart during word study.

Teaching spelling changes when adding inflectional endings. Select a feature such as doubling (e.g., *stopping*), e-drop (e.g., *hiking*), or changing the *y* to *i* (e.g., *cried*). Select a word from the story or use a lesson from Chapter 4. Follow these steps:

1. Distribute an Analogy Chart, a dry-erase marker, and an eraser to each student. (A two-column chart introduces the skill, and a three-column chart increases the challenge by combining skills. See examples on the next page.)

2. At the top of your chart, write a key word without and with inflectional ending(s) (e.g., *hop, hopping; love, loving, lovely*). Students copy those words at the top of their own charts.

3. Discuss the spelling rule.

   Doubling the consonant. If a word has a two-letter rime with a short vowel (e.g., *ap, at, op, un*), you double the final consonant before you add *-ing, -er,* or *-ed* (e.g., *spinning, stopper, slipped*).

   Dropping the final e. If a word ends in the silent *e*, you drop the *e* if you add an ending that begins with a vowel (*-ing, -er, -ed*). You do not drop the *e* if the ending begins with a consonant (*-ly, -ful*).

   Changing the y to i. If a word ends in *y* and is preceded by a consonant, you change the *y* to *i* before you add *-ed, -es* (e.g., *try–tries, carry–carried*).

hop	hopping
run	running
stop	stopped

love	loving
care	caring
hope	hoping

1. Dictate a word for students to write in the first column. Then say the word with an inflectional ending for students to write in the second column.

2. After you have dictated four to six words, have students read the words in each column.

3. To increase the challenge, use a three-column chart. Here are two examples.

Word	Double	Don't Double
hop	hopping	
jump		jumping
stop	stopper	

Word	Double	e Drop
run	running	
love		loved
trap	trapper	

Students use an Analogy Chart for ai and oa.

 VIDEO LINKS scholastic.com/NSFWordStudy

- A group of students uses a three-column Analogy Chart during word study.

- Jan and Michèle explain Analogy Charts.

Make a Big Word

This activity helps students write multisyllabic words by hearing the parts. Select a multisyllabic word from the new book or use a word study lesson from Chapter 6. Follow these steps:

1. Distribute the magnetic letter trays and tell students which letters they will need. Dictate the letters in alphabetical order to help students quickly find the letters on the trays.

2. Say the big word and have students clap each syllable.

3. Have students use the magnetic letters they removed from the tray to construct the word.

4. Once they make the word correctly, have them break it into parts, and then remake the word.

dan   ger ous   noc tur nal

A student makes a big word with magnetic letters.

 VIDEO LINKS scholastic.com/NSFWordStudy

- A group of students makes a big word during word study.

- Jan and Michèle explain Make a Big Word.

Writing Big Words

After you teach an affix, have students write several words that contain that affix. From the text, select a multisyllabic word that contains the target affix, or use a lesson from Chapter 6. Follow these steps:

1. Distribute dry-erase boards, markers, and erasers.

2. Dictate a word for students to write. Have them underline the target affix (e.g., _dis_cover).

3. Dictate other words that have the same prefix or suffix and have students write them (e.g., _dis_cover, _dis_agree, _dis_appear).

4. Discuss the meaning of any unfamiliar words.

A student writing a big word on a dry-erase board.

 VIDEO LINKS scholastic.com/NSFWordStudy

- A group of students writes big words during word study.
- Jan and Michèle explain Writing Big Words.

Working With Affixes

This activity is most beneficial to fluent readers because they are encountering many multisyllabic words. The goals are to teach students how to recognize an affix and to use the affix to infer the meanings of words. Select an affix that appears in a word from the story, or use a lesson from Chapter 7. Follow these steps:

Day 1: Make an Affix Word

1. Introduce the suffix or prefix and define it. For example, if you choose the affix *mis-*, you would introduce a familiar word that contains that prefix (e.g., *misbehave*) and explain that *mis* means *wrong* or *bad*. Misbehave *means "to behave badly."*

2. Select another word for students to make out of magnetic letters (*misfortune*). Dictate the letters in alphabetical order as students remove the letters from their trays. Have students clap the word before they make it with the letters. Then have them break the word so they can see the parts in the word. Be sure to discuss the meaning of the word.

Day 2: Write an Affix Word

1. Review the meaning of the affix.

2. Dictate three words with the same affix for students to write. Have them underline the affix in each word (e.g., <u>mis</u>inform, <u>mis</u>understand, <u>mis</u>place). Discuss the meaning of each word.

Day 3: Read an Affix Word

1. Review the meaning of the affix.

2. Give each student one of the affix word cards from scholastic.com/NSFWordStudy.

3. Have students read their word and explain what it means and use it in a sentence.

 VIDEO LINKS scholastic.com/NSFWordStudy
- A group of students works with affixes during word study.
- Jan and Michèle explain Working With Affixes.

CHAPTER 3

Word Study for the Pre-A Reader

"Children need a wide variety of direct experiences that help them learn how to look at letters and connect them with the letter names and sounds."

—**Gay Su Pinnell and Irene Fountas (2017)**

An increasing number of children are coming to school having limited experience with print or speaking a language other than English. The lessons and procedures described in this chapter provide opportunities for those children—children who know fewer than 40 upper- and lowercase letters—to learn letters and sounds, concepts of print, and phonemic awareness. Most important, they will discover that the print carries a message.

Word Study Goals for Pre-A Readers

- Identify 40 or more upper- and lowercase letters by name.
- Learn 8+ letter sounds.
- Hear and identify the initial consonant sound in a word.
- Write his or her name.
- Learn correct letter formation.

TEXT CONSIDERATIONS FOR PRE-A READERS

Texts for pre-A readers need to provide both support and challenge. To support students who are learning one-to-one matching, the spaces between words needs to be wide, and the font needs to be simple. Only one line of print should appear on each page. Stories should contain familiar concepts, engaging themes, and plots that appeal to a beginning reader. Illustrations and photographs should support and extend the story's meaning.

Busy Clarence (Level A) by Michèle Dufresne is an example of a very simple text (see sample pages below). Notice that each spread contains one line of print and an illustration that supports the story.

In the Appendices, pages 245–282, and at scholastic.com/NSFWordStudy, you will find several printable books you can use with pre-A readers.

I am sleeping.

I am jumping.

Pages from Busy Clarence

Working With Pre-A English Learners

English learners need opportunities to learn letters, sounds, and language. Build flexibility with letters and sounds by singing alphabet songs; sorting magnetic letters by name, shape, and color; and playing with sounds through poems and songs. Immerse students in English structures and vocabulary through engaging picture books. Because letter learning often begins with students' first names, it makes sense to use their names and the names of their classmates to teach letters and sounds.

THE ASSESS-DECIDE-GUIDE FRAMEWORK

Use this framework to plan and carry out instruction.

Assess: Determine your pre-A readers' word study strengths and needs

The Letter Name/Sound Checklist is the only assessment you need for planning pre-A lessons. It will tell you the letter names and sounds the student knows and the ones you need to teach. The Letter Name/Sound Checklist must be administered individually. For this assessment, you will need the Letter Name/Sound Recognition Student Form, Letter Name/Sound Teacher Recording Form, and Letter Name/Sound Checklist.

Follow these steps:

1. Show the student the Letter Name/Sound Recognition Student Form.

2. Point to the first uppercase letter and say, "Start here and tell me the names of the letters you know." The student should name the letters left to right.

3. Have the student point to each letter as he or she reads it. If this is too difficult, you can point to the letters. If the student struggles with the first few letters, ask him or her to scan the row and name any letters he or she recognizes. Record responses on the Letter Name/Sound Teacher Recording Form.

4. Repeat with the lowercase letters.

5. Point to the lowercase letters again, but this time ask the student to say the sound for each letter. Record responses on the Letter Name/Sound Teacher Recording Form.

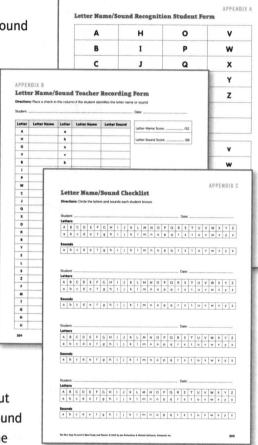

Appendices A–C, pages 203–205

6. Transfer information from the Teacher Recording Form to the Letter Name/Sound Checklist. Highlight or circle the letters and sounds the student knows on the Letter Name/Sound Checklist. Record the number of known letters and sounds for each student.

Decide: Prepare for your pre-A lessons

Form groups of three or four according to your pre-A students' letter knowledge. Write their names on the Letter Name/Sound Checklist and highlight or circle the letters and sounds each student knows. Having that data readily available on one form will make it easier for you to plan your lessons. Update the group checklist whenever you administer the Letter Name/Sound Checklist to individual students. (We recommend administering it weekly.) You should also use it during your lessons to record letters and sounds students are beginning to recognize.

Gather Texts and Materials

You will need a collection of Level A books—books with short, repetitive patterns, one line of text per page, and engaging illustrations. In the Appendices, pages 245–282, you'll find printable books you can use in your pre-A lessons. Gather the following materials and organize them near your guided reading table.

Reading Materials		
Prepare	**Directions**	**Example**
Name Templates	Print each student's first name on a sheet of white paper and insert it into a plastic sheet protector.	
Alphabet Chart	Make a photocopy of the Alphabet Chart in Appendix P for each student, or download copies at scholastic.com/NSFWordStudy.	

Reading Materials		
Prepare	**Directions**	**Example**
Name Puzzles	Print each student's first name on a strip of tag board. Write the child's name on an envelope and insert the strip.	
Personal Letter Bags	Put the lowercase magnetic letters the student knows and the letters of the student's name into a small plastic bag and label it with his or her name. If the student knows fewer than ten letters, include two of each letter he or she knows and two of each letter in his or her name. Add new letters as they are learned.	
Picture Cards	Collect six to eight pictures that begin with each consonant sound (excluding *x*).	

Guide: Teach word study lessons

Children can learn a lot through shared reading, read-alouds, and interactive writing, but pre-A students' needs are best met with individual and small-group instruction. We recommend daily tracing of an alphabet book and a daily pre-A small-group lesson.

Tracing an Alphabet Book

Have each student trace an alphabet book daily with a tutor (e.g., a teaching assistant, classroom volunteer, or upper-grade student). Choose a simple alphabet book with an easy-to-trace font in upper- and lowercase letters and one simple picture on each page. Do not use an alphabet book with words, as it distracts students from focusing on the picture and letter.

Tracing should be done one-on-one, outside of the small-group lesson. The child uses his or her pointing finger to trace each upper- and lowercase letter, saying the letter name and identifying the accompanying picture (e.g., *A*, *a*, *apple*). The tutor sits next to the student and provides support. The goals for tracing the alphabet book are to teach the name of each letter (upper- and lowercase), create a picture link to the letter sound, and teach correct letter formation.

If students know fewer than ten letters by name, have them trace only the letters they know and the letters in their first name until they learn ten letters. Then they should trace the entire alphabet book. If after four weeks of tracing, the student still knows fewer than ten letters by name, have him or her trace the entire book once a day with a tutor. Students will learn letters through tracing, whole-group instruction, and pre-A lessons. Our research shows that once a student can identify 17 to 20 letters, he or she will learn about ten more letters a week through the tracing activity and the pre-A small-group lesson described below.

A student traces the letter k.

 VIDEO LINK scholastic.com/NSFWordStudy

A student traces letters in an alphabet book.

Teaching a Pre-A Small-Group Lesson

A daily 20-minute pre-A lesson provides enhanced opportunities to learn letters and sounds, develop phonemic awareness, learn letter formation, experience books, and write with support. Each component supports early literacy behaviors and teaches foundational skills. The following chart summarizes the activities and word study opportunities for each component. The sooner you begin these lessons, the more rapidly students will develop the needed foundational literacy skills to begin emergent guided reading lessons.

Component	Activity
1	Working With Names (2–3 minutes)
2	Working With Letters (2–3 minutes)
3	Working With Sounds (2–3 minutes)
4	Working With Books (5–6 minutes)
5	Interactive Writing and Cut-Up Sentence (5 minutes)

LESSON WALK-THROUGH

The following pre-A lesson plan has been annotated to show how word study skills can be taught and practiced throughout a lesson. The plan is based on the book *Busy Dogs* by Michèle Dufresne.

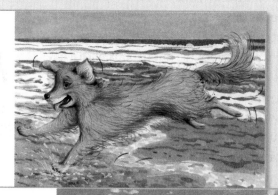

I can run.

1

I can jump.

3

Pages from Busy Dogs

❶ Working With Names

Point to the known letters in their name and ask students to name them. Say a letter in their name and have them point to it.

❷ Working With Letters

Review known and partially known letters and sounds. Build letter-picture and letter-sound links.

❸ Working With Sounds

Help students segment the the initial consonant sound for each picture. Link the sound to the correct letter name.

❹ Working With Books

Support vocabulary as students talk about the pictures. Students can locate known letters in the book.

❺ Interactive Writing and Cut-Up Sentence

Segment the initial sound in each word and link to the letter name. Practice letter formation. As students make the cut-up sentence, have them segment the first sound in each word and find the word card on the table.

Pre-A Lesson Plan: *Busy Dogs*

APPENDIX DD

Pre-A Lesson Plan (<40 letters)	
Date: 10/9	Students: Kayla, Tim, Kia, and Zephyr

Components	Activity
① **Working With Names** (2–3 minutes)	Choose one: ☒ Name Puzzle ☐ Magnetic Letters ☐ Rainbow Writing
② **Working With Letters** (2–3 minutes)	Choose one: ☒ Match letters in the bag ☐ Match letters to an ABC chart ☐ Name letters left to right ☐ Find the letter on an ABC chart ☐ Name a word that begins with that letter ☐ Find the letter that makes that sound ☐ Name the letter that begins that word
③ **Working With Sounds** (2–3 minutes)	Choose one: ☒ Clapping Syllables ☐ Hearing Rhymes ☐ Sorting Pictures *Clap the syllables in the students' names.*
④ **Working With Books** (5 minutes)	Title: *Busy Dogs* *Discuss the pictures and support oral language.* *Help students point to each word as they read.*
	Follow-Up Teaching Points (choose one or two) ☒ One-to-one matching ☐ Concept of a word ☐ First/last word ☐ Concept of a letter ☐ First/last letter ☐ period ☐ Upper/lowercase
⑤ **Interactive Writing and Cut-Up Sentence** (5 minutes)	Dictated Sentence: *I can swim.* Letter Formation: *I*
Next Steps	Letters and Names: *Reassess each student's letter knowledge and add new letters each identifies to his or her letter bag.* / Sounds: *Sort pictures that begin with K and Z.*

Books: *Continue to work on one-to-one matching.*	Writing: *Include known letters and sounds in the dictated sentence.*

The Next Step Forward in Word Study and Phonics © 2019 by Jan Richardson & Michèle Dufresne, Scholastic Inc.   **235**

See Appendix DD, page 235, for the lesson plan template.

APPENDIX DD

Teacher Notes and Observations for Pre-A Readers (< 40 letters)

Anecdotal notes, observations, and teaching points	Next Steps
Student: __Kayla__ Very quiet – encourage more talking during the lesson. Help her create a complete sentence about a picture in the book. Pair her with Zephyr as a talking buddy during read-aloud time.	☐ Clap Syllables ☐ Hear Rhymes ☐ Hear Initial Consonants ☐ Attend to Print ☐ One-to-One Matching ☐ Use Pictures ☒ Oral Language ☐ Other:
Student: __Tim__ Needs to look at print. Make a simple book that uses the names of the children in the group. Tim likes to_____. Kia likes to _____. Zephyr likes to_____. Kayla likes to _____.	☐ Clap Syllables ☐ Hear Rhymes ☐ Hear Initial Consonants ☒ Attend to Print ☐ One-to-One Matching ☐ Use Pictures ☐ Oral Language ☐ Other:
Student: __Kia__ Guessed the initial sound during Picture Sorting. Use a mirror to show her how to make the initial sound. Link sound to picture in ABC book. Sort pictures that begin with a *K* and link to her name.	☐ Clap Syllables ☐ Hear Rhymes ☒ Hear Initial Consonants ☐ Attend to Print ☐ One-to-One Matching ☐ Use Pictures ☐ Oral Language ☐ Other:
Student: __Zephyr__ Needs help with letter formation. Try out some pencil grips. Reading books: Have her frame each word with two fingers so she sees the spaces between words. Put large spaces between the words in the cut-up sentence.	☐ Clap Syllables ☐ Hear Rhymes ☐ Hear Initial Consonants ☐ Attend to Print ☒ One-to-One Matching ☐ Use Pictures ☐ Oral Language ☐ Other:

236   *The Next Step Forward in Word Study and Phonics* © 2019 by Jan Richardson & Michèle Dufresne, Scholastic Inc.

Pre-A Lesson Components, Activities, and Word Study Goals		
Component	**Activities**	**Word Study Goals**
1. Working With Names	Choose one: • Complete a name puzzle • Make name with magnetic letters • Trace name over a template	• Develop visual memory for first name • Identify and discriminate letters • Learn correct letter formation • Learn to write first name
2. Working With Letters	Choose one: • Find matching letters in the bag • Match letters to an alphabet chart (Appendix P) • Name letters from left to right • Find a letter on the chart • Name a word that begins with a letter • Name the first letter of a word • Find a letter that makes that sound	• Identify letters by name and sound • Link letters to sounds • Link sounds to letters • Link letters to anchor pictures • Develop flexibility with letters and sounds
3. Working With Sounds	Choose one: • Clap syllables • Work with rhymes • Sort pictures by first letter	• Phonological awareness (syllables and rhymes) • Phonemic awareness (segmenting initial sound and linking to a letter)
4. Working With Books	• Discuss pictures in book • Read book together • Encourage pointing to each word • Teach concepts of print	• Attend to print • Learn the concept of a word • Identify known letters in print • Understand the concept of upper- and lowercase letters
5. Interactive Writing and Cut-Up Sentence	• Write a sentence together • Remake a cut-up sentence	• Hear initial consonant sounds • Link sounds to letters • Learn correct letter formation • Learn concepts of letters and words • Locate a word by the first sound

In each lesson, students should do a letter activity, name activity, and sound activity. They should also read a book together and write a sentence interactively.

1. Working With Names

A student's name is a powerful place to begin developing his or her knowledge of letters and sounds. Spend two to three minutes on one of the following activities.

- Construct their names with a puzzle
- Make their names with magnetic letters
- Trace their names with different color markers (rainbow writing)

Discontinue the activity when students can write their names quickly and easily on their own.

VIDEO LINK scholastic.com/NSFWordStudy

A group of students does name activities.

RESEARCH NOTE

Gay Su Pinnell and Irene Fountas write, "The most powerful and effective way for children to begin learning the complex process of learning about letters is by writing their own names" (2011). Young children are naturally enamored with their own names, which makes children's names a powerful learning and teaching resource. Children will enjoy finding their names on a chart, naming the letters in their names, using magnetic letters to spell their names, and noticing one of "their" letters in another word.

Michèle's three-year-old granddaughter, Harper, makes an attempt to write her name and writes it perfectly...backwards!

2. Working With Letters

For this component, do one of the following seven activities. The first three require the personal letter bags described on page 54, and the last four require the alphabet chart (Appendix P).

- **Match two sets of the same letters.**
- **Match letters to the alphabet chart and name the letter.**
- **Name the letters in their bag.** Have students choose letters from their bag and place the letters in a line. Have them name each letter as they line it up.
- **Find the letter on an alphabet chart.** Name a letter and ask students to find it on the chart. Have students say the letter name and the picture.
- **Name a word that begins with that letter.** Name a letter, have students find it on the alphabet chart, and ask them to think of a word that begins with that letter.
- **Find the letter on the alphabet chart that makes that sound.** Say a letter sound and have students find the matching letter.
- **Name the first letter of a word.** Say a word and ask students to name the beginning letter. Have them refer to the alphabet chart if they have trouble connecting the first sound to a letter name.

The goal of these activities is to recognize and name letters quickly, and to use letter and sound knowledge flexibly.

A child matches letters to an alphabet chart.

 VIDEO LINK scholastic.com/NSFWordStudy

A group of students does letter activities.

3. Working With Sounds

To build phonological awareness, choose one of the following activities each day.

- **Clap syllables.** Have students clap the syllables in their name and then clap syllables of objects in the room or on picture cards.

- **Listen for rhymes.** Beginning readers need to be taught to listen for rhymes so they can make connections between one-syllable words. If they know the word *can*, for example, and they've been taught to listen for rhymes, they can read and write *man*, *ran*, and *fan*. English is built on rhyming families. Not all languages have that feature (Cunningham & Zilbusky, 2014). To help students learn to hear rhymes, have them listen to two words and decide whether they rhyme. After you say the two words, ask the students to repeat them. If the words rhyme, students should give a thumbs-up. If the words do not rhyme, they should give a thumbs-down. If students struggle to hear the rhyming portion of the word, break the words at the onset and rime. For example, say, "B-at, c-at. Do they rhyme? Listen to the end of each word."

- **Sort pictures.** Use picture cards to teach students to segment the initial sound of a word and link it to a letter. The easiest sounds to learn are the ones with their sound in their letter name: *b, d, f, j, k, l, m, n, p, r, s, t, v, z*.

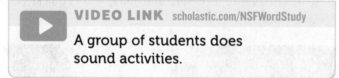

VIDEO LINK scholastic.com/NSFWordStudy

A group of students does sound activities.

4. Working With Books

This is a shared reading activity in which students chorally read a simple book along with you. The purpose of this activity is to support oral language skills, teach concepts of print, and encourage students to practice beginning reading strategies. Advanced pre-A readers may also start to recognize some sight words.

RESEARCH NOTE

The skill of quickly recognizing letter names and the sounds associated with the letters opens the gate to reading and provides key ingredients to learning to read. "Without deep knowledge of the English letters and an awareness that words are made up of sounds, students cannot learn to read"(Blevins, 2017). But children do not need to know all their letters and sounds before they begin reading and writing stories (Clay, 1991). The beginning reader has to give attention to visual information *and* the language and message from the story.

VIDEO LINK scholastic.com/NSFWordStudy
**A group of students reads
a book together.**

5. Interactive Writing and Cut-Up Sentence

During interactive writing, students help you write a sentence. Dictate a simple sentence that includes the sounds you sorted. On a sentence strip draw a line for each word. Then have students help you write each word. Teach them to say the word slowly and listen for a specific sound. Target easy-to-hear consonant sounds at the beginning or end of the word. Once they isolate a sound, have them locate the corresponding letter on their alphabet chart. Invite one student to write the letter on the sentence strip while the other students write the letter on their alphabet chart. You write the sounds students are not ready to learn. Student contributions will vary depending on their phonemic awareness skills.

Letter Formation

As described earlier, students learn correct letter formation by tracing an alphabet book with a tutor. You can also spend a few seconds teaching letter formation during interactive writing. Do not let students develop bad habits such as using poor pencil grip, writing a letter bottom to top, or forming letters with separate strokes. We suggest using movement, verbal directions, and visual form when teaching a new letter (Clay, 1991). Appendix Q contains verbal directions for teaching letter formation.

Follow these steps:

1. Use verbal directions for strokes: "Watch me write the letter *s*. Start like a *c*, then around like a snake."

2. Have students practice in the air: "Make it with me; start like a *c*, around like a snake."

3. Have students write it with their finger on the table or on their alphabet chart, saying to themselves, "Start like a *c*, then around like a snake."

4. Have them find the *s* on the alphabet chart.

5. Lastly, have them write the letter on the bottom of the alphabet chart.

Looking for a fun video on letter formation to share with your students? Try this one on YouTube, starring Jan and musician Jack Hartmann of the Kids Music Channel! Enter "Jan Richardson Jack Hartmann Letter Formation" into the search function.

Interactive writing teaches phonemic awareness in a meaningful way. Students segment a sound, link it to a letter, and write the letter in a sentence. This also provides a great opportunity to teach correct letter formation.

 VIDEO LINK scholastic.com/NSFWordStudy
A group of students writes and constructs a cut-up sentence interactively.

A student constructs a cut-up sentence.

When you finish writing the sentence with the students, have them reread it as you cut it into individual words. Place the word cards in random order on the table, or give a word to each student. Help them reconstruct the sentence on the table, putting a space between each word. Then have them read the sentence again as you point to each word. At the end of the lesson, you might want to collect the words, clip them together, and give them to a student to take home.

 VIDEO LINK scholastic.com/NSFWordStudy
Jan and Michèle explain phonemic awareness.

Word Study Lessons

In this section, you will find eight sample pre-A lesson plans with recommended word study activities for each component. Make adjustments based on the needs of your students. The first three lessons are for students who know fewer than 20 letters. You will find the books you can print and use for those lessons in the Appendices, pages 245–282. The last five lessons are for students who know more than 20 letters. Choose books from your leveled book collection for those lessons.

Lesson 1

Component	Procedures
Working With Names (2–3 minutes) **Name Puzzle**	1. Write each student's name on a strip of paper. Cut each name into two pieces (e.g., *Ke vin*). 2. Have students put their name puzzle together, using their printed name on the envelope as a model. 3. When they are successful, turn the envelope over and have them make their name without a model. 4. Cut the puzzle into more pieces and repeat the process.
Working With Letters (2–3 minutes) **Match the Letters in the Bag**	1. Give students two sets of known letters and the letters in their names. 2. Ask them to match the letters that are the same. Have them say the letter name as they line them up from left to right.
Working With Sounds (2–3 minutes) **Clap the Syllables**	1. Choose a student and clap the syllables in his or her name (e.g., *Ben-ja-min*). Have students clap with you. 2. Repeat with the names of other students or use pictures on the alphabet chart.
Working With Books (5–8 minutes) ***Busy Dogs*** (Appendices, pages 247–255)	1. Give each student an opportunity to talk about one of the pictures in *Busy Dogs*. Support those with limited oral language by modeling a sentence for them to repeat. 2. Read the book chorally, encouraging students to point to the words as they read. 3. After they discuss the book, teach the concept of a word. 4. Have them point to or frame each word on one page as you read the page together. 5. Choose another page and repeat the process.
Interactive Writing and Cut-Up Sentence (5–8 minutes) **I can swim.**	1. Dictate the sentence *I can swim* and draw three lines on a sentence strip. 2. Write the sentence with the students by saying a word and emphasizing a sound. Ask them to find the letter on their alphabet chart. 3. While one student writes the letter on the sentence strip, the others practice writing it on their chart. You will need to write the sounds the children aren't ready to learn. For this sentence, students will probably be able to help you write the underlined letters: I can swim. 4. Teach students how to write the letter or another letter they need to practice. Use the verbal directions in Appendix Q. 5. Cut up the sentence and put the words on the table. 6. Reconstruct the sentence with students.

Lesson 2

Component	Procedures
Working With Names (2–3 minutes) **Use Magnetic Letters**	1. Have students use the letters in their letter bags to make their first name. If they need a model, they can use the front of their name puzzle envelope. 2. Guide them to use left-to-right sequential construction and encourage them to say each letter as they make their name.
Working With Letters (2–3 minutes) **Match the Letters to the Alphabet Chart**	1. Have students match the letters in their letter bags to the ones on the alphabet chart. 2. Remind them to say the letter name and the picture as they place the magnetic letter on the chart.
Working With Sounds (2–3 minutes) **Work With Rhymes**	1. Say two words and have the students repeat them. If the words rhyme, they give a thumbs-up. If the words do not rhyme, they give a thumbs-down. Examples: *can – man*; *can – mop*; *dog – dig*; *dog – log*. 2. If needed, break the words at the onset and rime (*d-og*; *d-ig*) so students can hear the part that rhymes.
Working With Books (5–8 minutes) ***Looking for Dinner*** (Appendices, pages 256–264)	1. Give each student an opportunity to talk about one of the pictures in *Looking for Dinner*. Support students with limited oral language by modeling a sentence for them to repeat. 2. Read the book chorally, encouraging students to point to the words as they read. 3. After they discuss the book, teach the concept of first and last word: "Point to the first word on the page. Point to the last word. Let's do it again on another page."
Interactive Writing and Cut-Up Sentence (5–8 minutes) **I am a deer.**	1. Dictate the sentence *I am a deer* and draw four lines on a sentence strip. 2. Write the sentence with the students by saying a word and emphasizing a sound. Ask them to find the letter that makes that sound on their alphabet chart. 3. While one student writes the letter on the sentence strip, the others practice writing it on their chart. You will need to write the sounds the children aren't ready to learn. For this sentence, students will probably be able to help you write the underlined letters: I̲ am̲ a̲ de̲er̲. 4. Teach students how to write the letter *m* or another letter they need to practice. Use the verbal directions in Appendix Q. 5. Cut up the sentence and put the words on the table. 6. Reconstruct the sentence with the students.

Lesson 3

Component	Procedures
Working With Names (2–3 minutes) **Rainbow Writing**	1. Have students use a dry-erase marker to trace their name on their name template. 2. After they trace their name with one color, have them do it again with another color. 3. Work with individuals to teach correct letter formation.
Working With Letters (2–3 minutes) **Name the Letters in the Bag**	1. Have students randomly choose letters from their bags as they place them in a line. 2. Ask them to name the letters as they line them up.
Working With Sounds (2–3 minutes) **Picture Sorting**	1. Sort pictures that begin with the letters *s* and *m*. 2. Give each student three or four pictures to sort. 3. Write the two letters on the dry-erase easel and review the sound each letter makes. 4. Have each student choose one of their pictures and say the word, the first sound, and the letter. 5. If they need help, connect the sound to the picture on the alphabet chart.
Working With Books (5–8 minutes) **Playtime for Cookie and Scout** (Appendices, pages 265–273)	1. Give each student an opportunity to talk about one of the pictures in *Playtime for Cookie and Scout*. Support those with limited oral language by modeling a sentence for them to repeat. 2. Read the book chorally, encouraging students to point to the words as they read. 3. After they discuss the book, teach the concept of a letter: "Show me one letter. Show me two letters. Show me the biggest word. It has the most letters. Let's count the letters in that word. Find the smallest word. How many letters does it have?"
Interactive Writing and Cut-Up Sentence (5–8 minutes) **I see my mom.**	1. Dictate the sentence *I see my mom* and draw four lines on a sentence strip. 2. Write the sentence with the students by saying a word and emphasizing a sound. Ask them to find the letter on their alphabet chart. 3. While one student writes the letter on the sentence strip, the others practice writing it on their chart. You will need to write the sounds the children aren't ready to learn. For this sentence, students will probably be able to help you write the underlined letters: I̲ s̲ee m̲y m̲o̲m̲. 4. Teach students how to write the letter *s* or another letter they need to practice. Use the verbal directions in Appendix Q. 5. Cut up the sentence and put the words on the table. 6. Reconstruct the sentence with students.

Lesson 4

Component	Procedures
Working With Names (2–3 minutes) **Rainbow Writing**	1. Have students use a dry-erase marker to trace their name on their name template. 2. After they trace their name with one color, have them do it again with another color. 3. Work with individuals to teach correct letter formation.
Working With Letters (2–3 minutes) **Match the Letters to the Alphabet Chart**	1. Have students match the letters in their letter bags to the ones on the alphabet chart. 2. Remind them to say the letter name and the picture as they place the magnetic letter on the chart.
Working With Sounds (2–3 minutes) **Picture Sorting**	1. Use your Letter Name/Sound Checklist for pre-A groups to select two sounds to sort, beginning with letters the students know by name. 2. Give each student three or four pictures that begin with each letter. 3. Write the two letters on the dry-erase easel and review the sound each letter makes. 4. Have each student choose one of their pictures and say the word, the first sound, and the letter. 5. If they need help, connect the sound to the picture on the alphabet chart.
Working With Books (5–8 minutes)	1. Choose a Level A book from your collection. 2. Give each student an opportunity to talk about one of the pictures in the book. Support those with limited oral language by modeling a sentence for them to repeat. 3. Read the book chorally, encouraging students to point to the words as they read. 4. After they discuss the book, teach the concept of first and last letter: "Show me the first word on the page. Now frame the first letter of that word. Frame the last letter. Let's try this on the next word."
Interactive Writing and Cut-Up Sentence (5–8 minutes)	1. Come up with a sentence that follows the sentence pattern in the book and includes the sounds students sorted during Working With Sounds. 2. Dictate the sentence as you draw a line for each word on a sentence strip. Write the sentence with the students by saying a word and emphasizing a sound. Ask them to find the letter on their alphabet chart. 3. While one student writes the letter on the sentence strip, have the others practice writing it on their chart. You will need to write the sounds the children aren't ready to learn. 4. Teach students how to write a letter they need to practice. Use the verbal directions in Appendix Q. 5. Cut up the sentence and give each student a word. 6. Reconstruct the sentence with students.

Lesson 5

Component	Procedures
Working With Names (2–3 minutes)	1. Choose one of the name activities: Name Puzzle, Magnetic Letters, or Rainbow Writing (page 60). 2. If all the students can write their first name correctly without a model, discontinue this component.
Working With Letters (2–3 minutes) **Find a Letter on the Alphabet Chart**	1. Name a letter and ask students to find it on the alphabet chart. Have students say the letter name, sound, and the picture (e.g., M, /m/, monkey). 2. Repeat with other letters.
Working With Sounds (2–3 minutes) **Picture Sorting**	1. Use your Letter Name/Sound Checklist for pre-A groups to select two sounds to sort. Choose sounds most of the students need to learn. 2. Give each student three or four pictures that begin with each letter. 3. Write the two letters on the dry-erase easel and review the sound each letter makes. 4. Have each student choose one of their pictures and say the word, the first sound, and the letter. 5. If they need help, connect the sound to the picture on the alphabet chart.
Working With Books (5–8 minutes)	1. Choose a Level A book from your collection. 2. After students discuss the pictures, read the book chorally. Support students who need help by pointing to the words as they read. 3. If time permits, have them reread the book independently. 4. After they discuss the book, teach the period: "Show me the period. Show me the period on another page."
Interactive Writing and Cut-Up Sentence (5–8 minutes)	1. Come up with a sentence that follows the sentence pattern in the book and includes the sounds students sorted during Working With Sounds. 2. Dictate the sentence as you draw a line for each word on a sentence strip. Write the sentence with the students by saying a word and emphasizing a sound. Ask them to find the letter on their alphabet chart. 3. While one student writes the letter on the sentence strip, the others practice writing it on their chart. You will need to write the sounds the children aren't ready to learn. 4. Teach students how to write a letter they need to practice. Use the verbal directions in Appendix Q. 5. Cut up the sentence and give each student a word. 6. Reconstruct the sentence with students.

Lesson 6

Component	Procedures
Working With Names (2–3 minutes)	1. Choose one of the name activities: Name Puzzle, Magnetic Letters, or Rainbow Writing (page 60). 2. If all the students can write their first name correctly without a model, discontinue this component.
Working With Letters (2–3 minutes) **Name a Word That Begins With That Letter**	1. Name a letter and ask students to find it on the alphabet chart. Ask them to think of a word that begins with that letter. 2. Repeat with other letters.
Working With Sounds (2–3 minutes) **Picture Sorting**	1. Use your Letter Name/Sound Checklist for pre-A groups to select two sounds to sort. Choose sounds most of the students need to learn. 2. Give each student three or four pictures that begin with each letter. 3. Write the two letters on the dry-erase easel and review the sound each letter makes. 4. Have each student choose one of their pictures and say the word, the first sound, and the letter. 5. If they need help, connect the sound to the picture on the alphabet chart.
Working With Books (5–8 minutes)	1. Choose a Level A book from your collection. 2. Read it chorally, encouraging students to point to the words as they read. 3. If time permits, have them reread the book independently. 4. After they discuss the book, teach the concept of upper- and lowercase letters: "Find a capital letter. Show me a lowercase letter."
Interactive Writing and Cut-Up Sentence (5–8 minutes)	1. Come up with a sentence that follows the sentence pattern in the book and includes the sounds students sorted during Working With Sounds. 2. Dictate the sentence as you draw a line for each word on a sentence strip. Write the sentence with the students by saying a word and emphasizing a sound. Ask them to find the letter on their alphabet chart. 3. While one student writes the letter on the sentence strip, the others practice writing it on their chart. You will need to write the sounds the children aren't ready to learn. 4. Teach students how to write a letter they need to practice. Use the verbal directions in Appendix Q. 5. Cut up the sentence and give each student a word. 6. Reconstruct the sentence with students.

Lesson 7

Component	Procedures
Working With Names (2–3 minutes)	1. Choose one of the name activities: Name Puzzle, Magnetic Letters, or Rainbow Writing (page 60). 2. If all the students can write their first name correctly without a model, discontinue this component.
Working With Letters (2–3 minutes) **Find the Letter That Makes That Sound**	1. Say a letter sound and ask students to find the letter on the chart: "Find the letter that says /b/." 2. Repeat with other letters.
Working With Sounds (2–3 minutes) **Picture Sorting**	1. Use your Letter Name/Sound Checklist for pre-A groups to select two sounds to sort. Choose sounds most of the students need to learn. 2. Give each student three or four pictures that begin with each letter. 3. Write the two letters on the dry-erase easel and review the sound each letter makes. 4. Have each student choose one of their pictures and say the word, the first sound, and the letter. 5. If they need help, connect the sound to the picture on the alphabet chart.
Working With Books (5–8 minutes)	1. Choose a Level A book from your collection. 2. Read it chorally, encouraging students to point to the words as they read. 3. If time permits, have them reread the book independently. 4. After they discuss the book, teach a concept they need to learn, following the procedures described in the sample lessons above.
Interactive Writing and Cut-Up Sentence (5–8 minutes)	1. Come up with a sentence that follows the sentence pattern in the book and includes the sounds students sorted during Working With Sounds. 2. Dictate the sentence as you draw a line for each word on a sentence strip. Write the sentence with the students by saying a word and emphasizing a sound. Ask them to find the letter on their alphabet chart. 3. While one student writes the letter on the sentence strip, have the others practice writing it on their chart. You will need to write the sounds the children aren't ready to learn. 4. Teach students how to write a letter they need to practice. Use the verbal directions in Appendix Q. 5. Cut up the sentence and give each student a word. 6. Reconstruct the sentence with students.

Lesson 8

Component	Procedures
Working With Names (2–3 minutes)	1. Choose one of the name activities: Name Puzzle, Magnetic Letters, or Rainbow Writing (page 60). 2. If all the students can write their first name correctly without a model, discontinue this component.
Working With Letters (2–3 minutes) **Name the Letter That Begins That Word**	1. Say a word and ask students to look at the alphabet chart and find the letter that makes the sound at the beginning of the word. 2. Repeat with other letters.
Working With Sounds (2–3 minutes) **Picture Sorting**	1. Use your Letter Name/Sound Checklist for pre-A groups to select two sounds to sort. Choose sounds most of the students need to learn. 2. Give each student three or four pictures that begin with each letter. 3. Write the two letters on the dry-erase easel and review the sound each letter makes. 4. Have each student choose one of their pictures and say the word, the first sound, and the letter. 5. If they need help, connect the sound to the picture on the alphabet chart.
Working With Books (5–8 minutes)	1. Choose a Level A book from your collection. 2. Read it chorally, encouraging students to point to the words as they read. 3. If time permits, have them reread the book independently. 4. After they discuss the book, teach a concept they need to learn, following the procedures described in the sample lessons above.
Interactive Writing and Cut-Up Sentence (5–8 minutes)	1. Come up with a sentence that follows the pattern of the book. Include the two sounds students sorted during Picture Sorting. 2. Dictate the sentence as you draw a line for each word on a sentence strip. 3. Have students help you write each word. While one student writes a letter on the sentence strip, have the others practice writing that letter at the bottom of their alphabet chart. You will need to write the sounds the children aren't ready to learn. 4. Teach students how to write a letter they need to practice. Use the verbal directions in Appendix Q. 5. Cut up the sentence and give each student a word. 6. Reconstruct the sentence on the table.

The Next Step Forward in Word Study and Phonics

Optional Two-Day Pre-A Lesson

Here is an optional two-day lesson. Use it if you have less than 20 minutes for each guided reading lesson.

Day 1	Day 2
15 minutes each day	
Working With Names (3 minutes)	**Working With Letters** (3 minutes)
Working With Letters (3 minutes)	**Reread Familiar Books** (3 minutes)
Working With Sounds (3 minutes)	**Interactive Writing** (6 minutes)
Working With Books (6 minutes)	**Cut-Up Sentence** (3 minutes)

Monitor Progress

Assess students on their letter names and sounds once a week. Record their progress on the Letter Name/Sound Checklist. Students are ready to move to Level A guided reading lessons when they can:

- Write their first name without a model
- Identify at least 40 upper- and lowercase letters by name
- Demonstrate left-to-right directionality across one line of print
- Understand enough English to follow simple directions
- Identify at least eight letter sounds

Firm Up Knowledge During Independent Practice

Students can practice many of the pre-A lesson activities during independent work time. Here are some activities students can do by themselves or with a partner:

- **Partner Reading** Provide each student with several books they have read in their pre-A lessons. Have them reread those books to or with a partner. Partners do not need to be in the same reading group.
- **Picture Sorting** Select picture cards for the sounds the students have been learning and place the cards in a tub. Then add the magnetic letters that match the first letters of the pictures. Have students work in pairs to match the beginning sound of the pictures to the correct letters.

- **Tracing Letters** Download a tracing app to a digital device and have students practice tracing letters on it.

- **Make a Name** Laminate a card with a student's name and have that student use magnetic letters to make his or her name and colored markers to practice writing his or her name.

- **Matching Letters** Have the students match magnetic letters to a small alphabet chart.

- **Letter Search and Sort** Make two circles on a large magnetic dry-erase board. In each circle write two different letters students have been learning. Give them a tub of letters and have them find the correct letters and put them in the circles.

- **Names to Faces** Have students match the names of their classmates with their pictures.

SUPPORTING STRIVING READERS

In this section we discuss typical challenges in working with striving pre-A readers and offer advice on overcoming them.

Challenge: Students are confusing letters that look similar. It's difficult for students to learn similar-looking letters at the same time. Do not teach them in the same lesson. For example, don't teach the lowercase *d* and *b* together until students firmly know one of the letters.

Challenge: Students have trouble with letter formation. Intervene if you see a student writing a letter incorrectly. Use the three ways for learning letters: movement, verbal directions, and visual form (see page 63).

Challenge: Students are having difficulty remembering letter names. Students are often able to identify a letter without being able to name it. Use the following activity to get a clearer picture of what the student knows.

Put three magnetic letters in front of the student. Name one of the letters and ask the student to find it. If the student points to the correct letter, place it in the "known" pile and add another letter to the lineup. If the student points to the wrong letter, remove both the letter you asked for and the letter the student pointed to and place them in the "unknown" pile. Continue adding more letters for the student to identify. This simple assessment will tell you which letters they can identify but not name. Those are the letters they can most easily learn next. Focus on them.

Keep in mind, the first few letters a student learns will take more time. Once they can identify about 17 letters, they will learn at a faster rate. Remember also that learning letters in isolation can be boring. Reading and writing stories will make learning letters more relevant (and fun) for a beginning reader.

Challenge: Students have trouble with one-to-one matching. Model how to read a page while framing each word with your index fingers. Then have the students do it in their own book.

QUESTIONS TEACHERS ASK ABOUT PRE-A WORD STUDY

Should I start teaching sight words during pre-A lessons? Learning sight words is not a goal for the pre-A lesson, but some children will begin to notice words that appear in the books you read together. To encourage that behavior, after they read the story, you can ask them to find a word on the page, especially if it begins with a letter they know. Say, "Listen to the beginning sound in the word *me* (/m/). What letter makes that sound? /m/. Find the word *me*."

During interactive writing, you might see students trying to write the whole word. This is a sign that they are developing a visual memory and may be ready to move to the emergent lessons. Let them try writing the word and help them with any letters they miss.

My pre-A students know different letters. How do I help each student increase his or her letter knowledge? During Working With Letters, each student has a different letter bag that contains the letters he or she knows and the ones he or she almost knows. Add new letters to their bags as students learn them. During interactive writing, call on the students who know the letter and invite a student to write it on the sentence strip while the others practice it on their alphabet chart. During Working With Sounds, teach sounds that will be helpful to all or most of the students.

Some of my students know how to write their first names and some don't. Do I still do the Working With Names activity? Working With Names is an optional activity and can be omitted once students write their first names correctly without a model. For those who can write their first names while others can't, we suggest you have them do a name activity using their last names.

My lessons are taking longer than 20 minutes. What should I do? Record your lesson and watch or listen to the recording to determine which component is consuming your time. Perhaps your materials need to be better organized. Or maybe you are spending too much time on one component. It's also not uncommon for the problem to be teacher talk. Beginners get antsy or distracted when they have to listen for long periods of time. We find that students are much more engaged when they are reading, writing, and working with manipulatives. Most important, set your timer and change the activity about every five minutes.

CHAPTER 4

Word Study for the Emergent Reader: Levels A–C

"Learning about how words work makes an important contribution to students as both readers and writers."

—Patricia L. Scharer (2018)

As students transition from shared reading in pre-A lessons to reading books independently, it's time to teach them how to use letters, sounds, and words to read simple books. They will learn some words that appear frequently in books for emergent readers—words that provide "anchors." Learning them helps students monitor for comprehension (check that what they're reading makes sense) and get back on track when they notice something isn't quite right. In conjunction with using illustrations to problem-solve unknown words, emergent readers are also learning to use letters and sounds, most often initial consonants.

> ## Word Study Goals for Emergent Readers
>
> - Identify all consonants and short vowels by name and sound
> - Form letters correctly
> - Hear and record sounds in consonant-vowel-consonant (CVC) words
> - Read and write about 30 high frequency words
> - Use knowledge of letters, sounds, and words to read and write simple texts.

TEXT CONSIDERATIONS FOR EMERGENT READERS

Texts for emergent readers must provide a balance of support and challenge to help students develop phonics skills. Some support comes from the simplicity of the text. Emergent books have very few lines of print, repetitive sentences, natural language structures, and illustrations or photographs to help the reader understand that words convey meaning. Topics and concepts should be familiar and appealing. Emergent texts progress from one line of print to multiple sentences on one page.

By selecting the right guided reading book, you ensure that your students have an opportunity to apply the word study concepts you teach them. To provide the appropriate degree of challenge, books for emergent readers should contain both familiar and new sight words and an occasional change in sentence pattern (Dufresne, 2002). There should also be some words the students will not recognize but can figure out by using the illustrations and letter cues.

Level A Books

We Like Sunglasses by Michèle Dufresne is a good example of an emergent text at Level A (see sample pages below), with one line of print per spread and supportive illustrations. When introducing *We Like Sunglasses*, you can rehearse the sentence pattern and have students discuss the photographs. During the guided reading lesson, you may address the high frequency word *look* and prompt students to use the first letters in conjunction with the photographs to read the color words, as well as the word *sunglasses*, which is likely to be unfamiliar to students. Children reading at Level A must learn to use consonant sounds; otherwise, they will likely become dependent on the illustrations and ignore the print.

Pages from We Like Sunglasses

Level B and C Books

Like Level A books, books at Levels B and C have simple storylines and cover topics and concepts that are familiar and appealing to students. The text is still heavily supported by the illustrations. New challenges at Level C include more lines of text (three to five lines on some pages), less-patterned text, and some new high frequency words. Students need to learn to discriminate between similar looking words (e.g., *am/me, can/come, look/like, said/and*). The focus for emergent word study shifts from using only the first letter of a word to looking through the word and noticing medial vowels and final consonants.

The Three Little Pigs by Michèle Dufresne is a good example of a Level C text (see sample pages below). The story is familiar to most students, and the illustrations help them grasp the text's meaning. While there are still repetitive phrases in Level C texts, they are more complex than those in Level A and B texts. High frequency words are more complex, too (e.g., *here*, *is*, *look*, *my*, *like*, *said*, and *the*). Students should be able to figure out some unfamiliar words by using the illustrations, sentence structure, and letter sounds.

"Here is my house." said the little pig. "I like my house."

Oh, no! Here comes the big bad wolf. Look out, Little Pig. Look out!

"Yum, yum." said the big bad wolf.

In the Appendices, pages 245–282, and at scholastic.com/ NSFWordStudy, you will find several printable books you can use with emergent readers.

Pages from The Three Little Pigs

Working With Emergent English Learners

Books that contain repetitive patterns enable English learners to follow along with the text and join in orally with you and their peers. If possible, share books that feature culturally sensitive poetry and songs. A predictable book scaffolds English learners in powerful ways because it:

- features language that is often musical and rhythmical and, therefore, easy and pleasurable to follow.
- builds familiarity with particular topics.
- features illustrations that support and extend the written text.
- showcases natural language (i.e., demonstrates how people talk and use language) (Ascenzi, L. & Espinosa, C., in press).

THE ASSESS-DECIDE-GUIDE FRAMEWORK

Use this framework to plan and carry out instruction.

Assess: Determine your emergent readers' word study strengths and needs

Because students enter your classroom with a variety of literacy experiences, they will differ in their knowledge of letters, sounds, and words. Although formative assessments, such as running records, are extremely useful in analyzing how students process print, the Emergent Word Study Inventory (Appendix F) and the Sight Word Assessment (Appendix D) allow you to pinpoint quickly the word study skills you need to teach. Let these questions guide your observations and assessments:

- Which consonant sounds and short vowels can students hear and record?
- Which sight words can they read and write?
- Which letters can they form correctly? Which ones do they need to work on?
- Do they apply known phonics skills in reading and writing?

Emergent Assessments for Planning		
Assessment	**What it tells you**	**How to use it to plan lessons**
Emergent Word Study Inventory (A–C)	• The sounds the student can hear and record • The sounds he or she confuses • The letters he or she forms incorrectly	• Decide which skills to teach next • Decide which word study activity to use • Identify the known skills to expect students to use during reading and writing
Sight Word Assessment (A–C)	• The sight words the student can write • The words he or she partially knows	• Decide which sight words need a quick review • Decide which words to teach next • Identify the known words to expect students to use during reading and writing

Emergent Word Study Inventory (Levels A–C)

Purpose: The Emergent Word Study Inventory is a carefully designed list of words for students to write. The words are arranged to help you assess specific letter sounds:

Level A	Level B	Level C
Sounds assessed: *a, b, d, f, j, m, n, p, r, s, t, v*	**Sounds assessed:** *a, b, c, g, h, l, m, o, p, t, w, x, y, z*	**Sounds assessed:** *a, b, c, d, e, g, h, i, k, l, m, n, o, p, r, s, u*
bat	wax	run
jam	hog	leg
rap	yam	kid
sad	cob	sob
fat	zap	cap
van	lot	him

Directions: In small groups, give each student a blank sheet of paper. Then dictate the words for students to write. Say, "You don't know how to spell some of these words, but I want you to try. Say each word slowly, and write all the sounds you hear." Be sure students cannot see one another's papers.

Analyze and Reflect: On the Word Study Inventory, circle or highlight the sounds the student missed. Record your observations about individual students.

Appendix F, page 210

- Did the student pronounce each word slowly as he or she wrote it?
- Did the student reverse any letters?
- Did the student hear and record beginning, middle, and final sounds?
- Does the student need more work on letter formation?

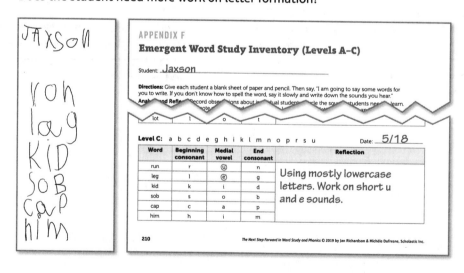

The Next Step Forward in Word Study and Phonics

Sight Word Assessment (Levels A–C)

Purpose: The Sight Word Assessment will tell you the sight words your students know how to write and the ones you should target in your lessons.

The chart to the right contains words that appear frequently in texts for emergent readers. Words at Levels A and B are easier for readers to learn because they are mostly phonetic. Assess students at their instructional reading level and one level below.

Directions: Give each student a blank sheet of paper. Then say, "I am going to say some words for you to write. You won't know how to spell some of these words, but I want you to try. Say each word slowly, and write all the sounds you hear." Be sure students cannot see one another's papers.

Analyze and Reflect: On the Sight Word Checklists (Appendix E), check the words the student wrote correctly. Count reversed letters as correct except *b/d* and *p/q*.

Sight Word List		
Level A	**Level B**	**Level C**
am	dad	and
me	he	are
at	in	come
can	it	for
go	look	got
is	mom	here
like	my	not
see	on	play
the	up	said
to	we	you

Appendix E, page 207

Emergent

RESEARCH NOTE

"New words are acquired through reading books and writing stories" (Clay, 2016). We need to create opportunities for students at the earliest stages of literacy to see the words they are learning in different settings, creating echoes from one part of the lesson to another part. Known words become a rich source of information from which we can grow our students' knowledge base.

Decide: Determine a skill focus and word study activity

Use information from the Emergent Word Study Inventory to select a skill focus for instruction. The word study lessons for each skill on pages 89–99 are organized by text level. If students can write most of the consonant sounds assessed at Level A, they may be ready to begin Level B word study lessons, which focus on harder to hear consonant sounds and some medial vowel sounds. If students can write the harder consonant sounds and some medial vowel sounds, they are probably ready to begin Level C word study lessons, which focus on learning all short vowel sounds.

Level	Skill Focus
A	• Initial consonants • Long vowels
B	• Initial and final consonants • Short a and o
C	• All short vowels • CVC words

Once you've chosen a skill focus, choose an activity: Picture Sorting, Making Words, or Sound Boxes. The following chart summarizes the purpose of each activity and when to use it.

Activity	Purpose	When to Use	Where to Find Teaching Guidelines
Picture Sorting	To hear initial consonants and short medial vowels and link sounds to letters	When introducing a new skill	Chapter 2, page 34
Making Words	To scan CVC words to check for letter/sound accuracy	When students need to transfer this skill to reading	Chapter 2, page 36
Sound Boxes	To hear and record CVC words in sequence	When students need to transfer this skill to writing	Chapter 2, page 38

The following chart summarizes the skill focus by level for the three activities.

Level	Skill Focus	Picture Sorting	Making Words	Sound Boxes
A	• Initial consonants • Long vowels	Students sort pictures by their initial consonant.	Students change initial consonant (e.g., *cat, hat, bat, fat*).	Students use 2 boxes to write CV words (e.g., *me, go, no, he*).
B	• Initial and final consonants • Short *a* and *o*	Students sort pictures by their initial consonant or medial vowel.	Students change final consonant (e.g., *hat, ham, had*). Students change initial and final consonant (e.g., *cat, can, fan, fat*).	Students use 2 or 3 boxes to write short *a* and *o* words (e.g., *at, on, am; hop, fan, mom, dad*).
C	• All short vowels • CVC words	Students sort pictures by their medial vowel.	Students change initial, middle, and final letters in CVC words (e.g., *hot, hat, ham, him*).	Students use 3 boxes to write CVC words (e.g., *pan, red, hit, hot, run*).

Use the Sight Word Checklists (Appendix E) to summarize data for each guided reading group. Write the students' names across the top, and check the words each student wrote correctly. Use the checklists to choose words to review at the beginning of the lesson. They should be words most of the students know how to write. As you dictate a word, add a check mark to the chart if a student writes the word correctly without your support. Also, select one new word to teach during the lesson. It is helpful if the new word appears in the book they will read that day.

Guide: Teach word study in an integrated lesson framework

Word study should be part of a guided reading lesson that

1. allows for developmental and explicit instruction not only in word study, but also in reading and writing.

2. invites students to use their newly acquired word study skills immediately, while they're engaged in reading and writing.

LESSON WALK-THROUGH

The following emergent guided reading plan has been annotated to show how word study skills can be taught and practiced throughout a lesson. The plan is based on the book *Fun at the Park* by Michèle Dufresne.

Pages from Fun at the Park

❶ Sight Word Review (Days 1 and 2)

Select three words you have taught. Prompt students to write each word quickly on the dry-erase board. This builds visual memory and automaticity.

❷ Book Introduction (Day 1)

During the introduction, have students locate a new sight word in the text. Have them check the letters and sounds by running their finger under the word and saying it slowly.

❸ Read With Prompting (Days 1 and 2)

Prompt students to figure out unknown words by crosschecking letters and sounds with meaning and structure (e.g., "Could it be *field* or *grass*? How do you know?").

❹ Follow-Up Teaching Points (Days 1 and 2)

Select a challenging word from the book and write it on an easel or make it with magnetic letters. Have students read the word. Model how to check a word to make sure it looks right by running your finger under it and saying it. Have students locate known sight words in the book.

❺ Teach One Sight Word (Days 1 and 2)

Use the four steps described on pages 29–30 to help students develop a process for learning new words.

❻ Word Study (Day 1)

Teach students how to use the sounds they know to construct, read, and/or write unknown words.

Guided Writing (Day 2)

Dictate a sentence that gives students an opportunity to practice the skills you have taught. Work with individual students at their point of need to help them apply the skills they have learned.

Emergent Guided Reading Plan: *Fun at the Park*

Emergent Guided Reading Plan (Levels A–C)

Students: Kelsey, Samantha, Reza, Miguel, Jenny, Jess   Date: 3/10-11   Title/Level: Fun at the Park/C

Word Study Focus	Strategy Focus	Comprehension Focus
Short vowels	Cross-checking	Making connections

	Day 1		Day 2		
①					

① Sight Word Review 1 minute | **Sight Word Review** 1 minute

like	can	here	said	go	is

Reading 8-10 minutes

②

Introduce and Read a New Book	**Reread Yesterday's Book**
Synopsis: Cookie and Scout have fun at the park. Let's find out what they do. New Vocabulary: fun(p.2), field(p.3)	(and other familiar books) Prompt students to stop pointing with their finger. Student to Assess: Kelsey

③

Read the book with prompting (use backside for recording observations and prompts)	*Read books with prompting (use backside for recording observations and prompts)*
Discussion Prompts: What did Cookie and Scout do at the park? What is your favorite thing to do at the park?	Discussion Prompts: What did this book remind you of? Why did they go in the house?

④

Follow-Up Teaching Points (choose 1 or 2 each day)

☐ Apply one-to-one matching   ☐ Take risks   ☐ Use meaning   ☐ Monitor for meaning
☐ Use letters and sounds   ☒ Cross-check M, S, V   ☐ Use known words   ☐ Visually scan
☐ Reread to problem-solve

Teaching Point for Day 1	**Teaching Point for Day 2**
p. 3 Did Cookie and Scout run on the grass or the field? How do you know?	Cover the picture and have students read the page. At difficulty, have them sound the first letter before you show the picture.

⑤

New Sight Word   What's Missing? • Mix and Fix • Table Writing • Write It & Retrieve It   (1-2 minutes)

said	said

⑥

Word Study (Day 1) 5-8 minutes	**Guided Writing (Day 2)** 8-10 minutes
☐ Picture Sorting ☒ Making Words ☐ Sound Boxes Letters needed: a, b, c, n, r, u can-ran-run-rub-cub-cab	☐ A: 3-5 words ☐ B: 5-7 words ☒ C: 7-10 words Scout said, "I like to go to the park. We can run and have fun at the park."

Next Steps	Text: Select another Level C book that has the word "said" and supports cross-checking	Next Goals: Cross-checking without prompting. Sound Boxes with short vowels	Students to Assess: Reza

The Next Step Forward in Word Study and Phonics © 2019 by Jan Richardson & Michèle Dufresne, Scholastic Inc.   **237**

See Appendix EE, page 237, for the lesson plan template.

APPENDIX EE

Teacher Notes and Observations for Emergent Readers (Levels A–C)

Monitoring and Word-Solving Prompts
- ☐ Point to each word. (One-to-one matching)
- ☐ Check the picture. What would make sense?
- ☐ Say the first sound. What would make sense?
- ☐ Show me the word _____. (Locate a sight word.)
- ☐ Check the word with your finger.
- ☐ Could it be _____ or _____? How do you know?
- ☐ What did you notice?
- ☐ What can you do to help yourself?

Fluency and Comprehension Prompts
- ☐ Read without pointing.
- ☐ Read it the way the character would say it.
- ☐ What did you read? Tell me about the book.
- ☐ What does this book remind you of?
- ☐ Have you ever felt like the character feels? When?
- ☐ What was the problem? How was it solved?
- ☐ What is your favorite part? Why?
- ☐ How is this book like another book you have read?

Anecdotal notes, running records, observations, and teaching points	Goals/Next Steps
Student: __Kelsey__ ✔ ✔ ✔ <u>grass</u> ✔ ✔ T: Are you right? Say the first sound. 　　　field (Day 2) ✔ ✔ <u>Cookie</u>　<u>said</u>　T: Reread and make it look right. 　　　　said　Cookie	☐ One-to-One Matching ☐ Use Pictures ☐ Use First Letters ☒ Cross-Check M, S, and V ☐ Visual Scanning ☐ Other:
Student: __Samantha__ ✔ <u>look</u> ✔ ✔ ✔ <u>the</u> ✔ ✔ ✔ T: Are you right? Does that make sense? 　 like　　　　　　　　　　Find the word "like." Check it with your finger. (Day 2) ✔ ✔ ✔ <u>park</u>/SC ✔ ✔ ✔ <u>on</u> ✔ ✔. 　　　　　slide　　　　　down T: "On" makes sense. Now check the first letter.	☐ One-to-One Matching ☐ Use Pictures ☐ Use First Letters ☒ Cross-Check M, S, and V ☐ Visual Scanning ☐ Other:
Student: __Reza__ ✔ ✔ ✔ ✔ ✔ ✔ ✔ ✔ ✔ ✔ ✔ ✔ ✔ (Accurate but slow) T: Don't point with your finger. ✔ ✔ ✔ ✔ ✔ ✔ ✔ ✔ ✔ ✔ ✔ ✔ ✔ (Good expression. Fast and fluent!) What did the dogs do at the park?	☐ One-to-One Matching ☐ Use Pictures ☐ Use First Letters ☐ Cross-Check M, S, and V ☐ Visual Scanning ☒ Other: move up?
Student: __Miguel__ ✔ ✔ ✔ <u>f-i-e-l-d</u>/A　T: What would make sense? 　　　field/T　　　Check the picture. (Day 2) ✔ ✔ ✔ <u>park</u>/SC ✔ ✔ ✔ <u>d</u> ✔ ✔ ✔ T: Praise 　　　　　slide　　　　down	☐ One-to-One Matching ☒ Use Pictures ☐ Use First Letters ☐ Cross-Check M, S, and V ☐ Visual Scanning ☐ Other:
Student: __Jenny__ ✔ ✔ ✔ ✔ ✔ ✔ <u>on</u>/SC ✔ ✔ T: Good checking. 　　　　　down　　　　What did you notice? ✔ ✔ ✔ ✔ ✔ ✔ <u>fort/h-home</u> T: Could it be home or 　　　　　house　　　house? How do you know?	☐ One-to-One Matching ☐ Use Pictures ☐ Use First Letters ☒ Cross-Check M, S, and V ☐ Visual Scanning ☐ Other:
Student: __Jess__ ✔ ✔ ✔ <u>f-</u>✔　✔ ✔ <u>r-un</u> ✔ ✔ ✔ 　　　field　　　run T: You made the first sound and that helped you figure out the word "field"! ✔ ✔ ✔ ✔ ✔ ✔ <u>playground</u>　T: Check the end of the word. 　　　　　park	☐ One-to-One Matching ☐ Use Pictures ☐ Use First Letters ☐ Cross-Check M, S, and V ☒ Visual Scanning ☐ Other:

Word Study Lessons

In this section, you will find a series of word study lessons to embed in your emergent guided reading lessons. Teach these lessons during the last five to eight minutes of Day 1. Because Picture Sorting teaches children sounds, use it before Making Words and Sound Boxes. As you become more proficient with the procedures, you will be able to design your own lessons.

There is no need to teach every lesson at each level. Choose the ones that best meet the needs of your students as identified by your assessments. Use the chart on this book's inside front cover to pinpoint specific lessons, based on your findings. The lessons at each level are sequenced so that the skill focus of Picture Sorting matches the skill focus of Making Words and Sound Boxes. Most students should move up a text level every three to four weeks. They will learn more about letters and sounds at each level.

Level A Word Study Lessons

These lessons teach and review these sounds: *a, b, d, e, f, g, h, j, l, m, n, o, p, r, s, t, w.* Make adjustments to match the needs of your students.

Lesson	Skills	Activity	Directions
1	Consonants: *s* and *t*	**Picture Sorting**	Distribute *s* and *t* picture cards. Write the letters *s* and *t* on the easel. Students take turns saying the picture, the first sound, and the letter. Then they place the card under the correct letter.
2	Consonants: *r* and *m*	**Picture Sorting**	Distribute *r* and *m* picture cards. Write the letters *r* and *m* on the easel. Students take turns saying the picture, the first sound, and the letter. Then they place the card under the correct letter.

3	Consonants: *m, r, s, t* Short vowel: *a*	**Making Words**	Students remove the following letters from their trays: **a m r s t** Dictate these words for students to make: *at, mat, rat, sat.* Have students check each word by sliding their finger left to right to determine which letter they should change to make the new word.
4	Consonants: *f* and *b*	**Picture Sorting**	Distribute *f* and *b* picture cards. Write the letters *f* and *b* on the easel. Students take turns saying the picture, the first sound, and the letter. Then they place the card under the correct letter. *f* *b*
5	Consonants: *f, m, n, r, t* Short vowel: *a*	**Making Words**	Students remove the following letters from their trays: **a f m n t r** Dictate these words for students to make: *man, fan, tan, ran.* Have students check each word by sliding their finger left to right to determine which letter they should change to make the new word.
6	Consonants: *g, n, s* Long vowel: *o*	**Sound Boxes** (2 boxes)	Distribute Sound Boxes, dry-erase markers, and erasers. Dictate the following words: *no, go, so.* Have students say the word slowly, running their finger under the two boxes. Then have them write one sound in each box as they say the word again slowly. After they write the word, have them check the letters with the sounds by saying the word slowly as they run their finger under the letters. | n	o	

| 7 | Consonants: *d* and *n* | **Picture Sorting** | Distribute *d* and *n* picture cards. Write the letters *d* and *n* on the easel. Students take turns saying the picture, the first sound, and the letter. Then they place the card under the correct letter. |

d *n*

| 8 | Consonants: *h, m, w*
Long vowel: *e* | **Sound Boxes**
(2 boxes) | Distribute Sound Boxes, dry-erase markers, and erasers. Dictate the following words: *me, he, we*.

Have students say the word slowly, running their finger under the two boxes. Then have them write one sound in each box as they say the word again slowly. After they write the word, have them check the letters with the sounds by saying the word slowly as they run their finger under the letters. |

m	e

| 9 | Consonants: *j* and *p* | **Picture Sorting** | Distribute *j* and *p* picture cards. Write the letters *j* and *p* on the easel. Students take turns saying the picture, the first sound, and the letter. Then they place the card under the correct letter. |

j *p*

| 10 | Consonants: *j, m, p, r, s* | **Making Words** | Students remove the following letters from their trays:

a   j   m   p   r   s

Dictate these words for students to make: *jam, Sam, Pam, ram*.

Have students check each word by sliding their finger left to right to determine which letter they should change to make the new word. |

| 11 | Consonants: b and *l* | Picture Sorting | Distribute *b* and *l* picture cards. Write the letters *b* and *l* on the easel. Students take turns saying the picture, the first sound, and the letter. Then they place the card under the correct letter. |

b   *l*

| 12 | Consonants: b, d, l, m, p, s | Making Words | Students remove the following letters from their trays: |

a b d l m p s

Dictate these words for students to make: *bad, lad, mad, pad, sad.*

Have students check each word by sliding their finger left to right to determine which letter they should change to make the new word.

Level B Word Study Lessons

These lessons teach and review these sounds: *a, b, c, d, f, g, h, l, m, n, o, p, r, s, t, w, x, y, z*.
Make adjustments to match the needs of your students.

Lesson	Skills	Activity	Directions
13	Consonants: *w* and *g*	Picture Sorting	Distribute the *w* and *g* picture cards. Write the letters *w* and *g* on the easel. Students take turns saying the picture, the first sound, and the letter. Then they place the card under the correct letter. **w** **g**
14	Consonants: *b, d, g, n, t* Short vowel: *a*	Making Words	Students remove the following letters from their trays: **a b d g n t** Dictate these words for students to make: *bag, bat, ban, bad*. Have students check each word by sliding their finger left to right to determine which letter they should change to make the new word.
15	Short vowels: *a* and *o*	Picture Sorting	Distribute the *a* and *o* picture cards. Write the letters *a* and *o* on the easel. Students take turns saying the picture, the medial vowel sound, and the letter. Then they place the card under the correct letter. **a** **o**
16	Consonants: *g, h, p, t* Short vowel: *o*	Making Words	Students remove the following letters from their trays: **g h o p t** Dictate these words for students to make: *hot, hop, hog*. Have students check each word by sliding their finger left to right to determine which letter they should change to make the new word.

| 17 | Consonants:
b, g, m, r, t, w

Short vowels:
a and *o* | **Sound Boxes**
(3 boxes) | Distribute Sound Boxes, dry-erase markers, and erasers. Dictate the following words: *ram, bog, got, wag*.

Have students say the word slowly, running their finger under the three boxes. Then have them write one sound in each box as they say the word again slowly. After they write the word, have them check the letters with the sounds by saying the word slowly as they run their finger under the letters. |

r	a	m

| 18 | Consonants:
c and *h* | **Picture Sorting** | Distribute the *c* and *h* picture cards. Write the letters *c* and *h* on the easel. Students take turns saying the picture, the first sound, and the letter. Then they place the card under the correct letter. |

c   *h*

| 19 | Consonants:
c, g, h, l, t

Short vowels:
a and *o* | **Making Words** | Students remove the following letters from their trays:

a   c   g   h   l   o   t

Dictate these words for students to make: *hat, cat, cot, lot, log*.

Have students check each word by sliding their finger left to right to determine which letter they should change to make the new word. |

| 20 | Consonants:
b, c, f, g, l, p, s, x

Short vowels:
a and *o* | **Sound Boxes**
(3 boxes) | Distribute Sound Boxes, dry-erase markers, and erasers. Dictate the following words: *fox, lap, cob, sag*.

Have students say the word slowly, running their finger under the three boxes. Then have them write one sound in each box as they say the word again slowly. After they write the word, have them check the letters with the sounds by saying the word slowly as they run their finger under the letters. |

f	o	x

| 21 | Consonants: y and z | **Picture Sorting** | Distribute the y and z picture cards. Write the letters y and z on the easel. Students take turns saying the picture, the first sound, and the letter. Then they place the card under the correct letter. |

y   **z**

| 22 | Consonants: b, d, g, p, t Short vowels: a and o | **Making Words** | Students remove the following letters from their trays:

a b d g o p t

Dictate these words for students to make: *dog, bog, bag, tag, tap, top.*

Have students check each word by sliding their finger left to right to determine which letter they should change to make the new word. |

| 23 | Consonants: b, g, l, p r, t, y, z Short vowels: a and o | **Sound Boxes** (3 boxes) | Distribute Sound Boxes, dry-erase markers, and erasers. Dictate the following words: *zag, yap, lot, rob.*

Have students say the word slowly, running their finger under the three boxes. Then have them write one sound in each box as they say the word again slowly. After they write the word, have them check the letters with the sounds by saying the word slowly as they run their finger under the letters. |

z	a	g

| 24 | Consonants: b, c, h, p Short vowels: a and o | **Making Words** | Students remove the following letters from their trays:

a b c h o p

Dictate these words for students to make: *cob, cab, cap, cop, hop.*

Have students check each word by sliding their finger left to right to determine which letter they should change to make the new word. |

Level C Word Study Lessons

These lessons teach and review all the short vowels and consonant sounds.
Make adjustments to match the needs of your students.

Lesson	Skills	Activity	Directions
25	Short vowels: *a* and *i*	Picture Sorting	Distribute *a* and *i* picture cards. Write the letters *a* and *i* on the easel. Students take turns saying the picture, the medial vowel sound, and the letter. Then they place the card under the correct letter.

a   *i*

| 26 | Consonants: *b, g, j, t*

Short vowels: *a, i, o* | Making Words | Students remove the following letters from their trays:

a b g i j o t

Dictate these words for students to make: *bat, bit, big, jig, jog.*

Have students check each word by sliding their finger left to right to determine which letter they should change to make the new word. |
| 27 | Consonants: *d, f, k, l, p, t, x*

Short vowels: *a, o, i* | Sound Boxes (3 boxes) | Distribute Sound Boxes, dry-erase markers, and erasers. Dictate the following words: *kit, fox, lid, tap.*

Have students say the word slowly, running their finger under the three boxes. Then have them write one sound in each box as they say the word again slowly. After they write the word, have them check the letters with the sounds by saying the word slowly as they run their finger under the letters. |

k	i	t

| 28 | Short vowels: *i* and *u* | **Picture Sorting** | Distribute *i* and *u* picture cards. Write the letters *i* and *u* on the easel. Students take turns saying the picture, the medial vowel sound, and the letter. Then they place the card under the correct letter. |

i   *u*

| 29 | Consonants: *f, g, h, t, x*

Short vowels: *i, o, u* | **Making Words** | Students remove the following letters from their trays:

f g h i o t u x

Dictate these words for students to make: *hug, hog, fog, fig, fit, fix.*

Have students check each word by sliding their finger left to right to determine which letter they should change to make the new word. |

| 30 | Consonants: *c, d, l, n, p, m, v*

Short vowels: *a, i, u* | **Sound Boxes**
(3 boxes) | Distribute Sound Boxes, dry-erase markers, and erasers. Dictate the following words: *cup, van, lid, mud.*

Have students say the word slowly, running their finger under the three boxes. Then have them write one sound in each box as they say the word again slowly. After they write the word, have them check the letters with the sounds by saying the word slowly as they run their finger under the letters. |

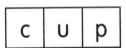

| 31 | Short vowels: *e* and *u* | **Picture Sorting** | Distribute *e* and *u* picture cards. Write the letters *e* and *u* on the easel. Students take turns saying the picture, the medial vowel sound and the letter. Then they place the card under the correct letter. |

e   *u*

| 32 | Consonants: *b, g, t, w, y*

Short vowels: *e* and *u* | **Making Words** | Students remove the following letters from their trays: |

b   e   g   t   u   w   y

Dictate these words for students to make: *bug, beg, bet, wet, yet.*

Have students check each word by sliding their finger left to right to determine which letter they should change to make the new word.

| 33 | Consonants: *g, n, p, r, t, w, y, z*

Short vowels: *a, e, i, u* | **Sound Boxes**
(3 boxes) | Distribute Sound Boxes, dry-erase markers, and erasers. Dictate the following words: *wig, zap, run, yet.*

Have students say the word slowly, running their finger under the three boxes. Then have them write one sound in each box as they say the word again slowly. After they write the word, have them check the letters with the sounds by saying the word slowly as they run their finger under the letters. |

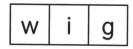

| 34 | Consonants: *b, d, g, m*

Short vowels: *a, e, u* | **Making Words** | Students remove the following letters from their trays: |

a   b   d   e   g   m   u

Dictate these words for students to make: *mad, mud, bud, bed, beg.*

Have students check each word by sliding their finger left to right to determine which letter they should change to make the new word.

35 | Consonants: | **Sound** | Distribute Sound Boxes, dry-erase markers, and erasers. Dictate the following words: *vet, pat, hip, log, cut.*

Consonants: *c, g, h, l, p, t, v*

Sound Boxes (3 boxes)

Short vowels: *a, e, i, o, u*

Distribute Sound Boxes, dry-erase markers, and erasers. Dictate the following words: *vet, pat, hip, log, cut.*

Have students say the word slowly, running their finger under the three boxes. Then have them write one sound in each box as they say the word again slowly. After they write the word, have them check the letters with the sounds by saying the word slowly as they run their finger under the letters.

v	e	t

36

Consonants: *b, d, g, h, j, k, m, p, s*

Sound Boxes (3 boxes)

Short vowels: *a, e, i, o, u*

Distribute Sound Boxes, dry-erase markers, and erasers. Dictate the following words: *sad, hem, kid, bop, jug.*

Have students say the word slowly, running their finger under the three boxes. Then have them write one sound in each box as they say the word again slowly. After they write the word, have them check the letters with the sounds by saying the word slowly as they run their finger under the letters.

s	a	d

Encourage Students to Apply Word Study Skills to Reading

It is important for students to understand, from an early age, that what they read must make sense. As students read, prompt them to use what they know about letters and sounds to help them make sense of the text. For example, if the text says *Look at the pony,* a student might see a horse in the picture and read, "Look at the horse." Praise the student for using the picture, and then guide him or her to use the letters and sounds to correct the miscue by saying, "Yes, *horse* makes sense, but look at the first letter." Show him the first letter of *pony* and say, "Make the first sound and reread it. Think about what would make sense and look right." This kind of prompting guides students to use their budding knowledge about letters, sounds, and words to read for meaning (Fountas & Pinnell, 1998). Use the following prompts to guide students to use word study skills to solve unknown words.

Word-Solving Goals and Prompts	
Word-Solving Goals	**Prompts for Strategic Action**
Cross-check first letter with meaning and structure (language syntax) cues	• Cover up the word and ask, *What letter would you expect to see at the beginning of...?* • *That makes sense, but look at the first letter.*
Use knowledge of letter/sound relationships to initiate an action at the point of difficulty	• *Read it again, and think about what makes sense and begins with that letter.* • *Do you know a word that starts with those letters?*
Self-correct using known high frequency words.	• *Find the word....* • *You said.... Were you right?* • *Where is the tricky word?*
Read high frequency words quickly	• *Find.... That's a word you know. Read it quickly.*

In guided reading lessons, teach students to apply the skills they are learning during word study to their reading. Short, targeted prompts and explicit demonstrations help students use initial and final letters and known words to monitor and self-correct.

Teach for Transfer

You should always expect and inspect skills you have taught. The following chart provides examples of how to prompt students to use their word study skills during reading and writing.

If...	Then...
Student miscues or omits a high frequency word you have taught	Ask the student to locate the word and quickly write it with their finger on the table.
Student uses the picture but ignores the first letter (e.g., says *dirt* for *mud*)	Use your finger to cover the word (*mud*) in the book. Ask, "What letter would you expect to see at the beginning of *mud*?" Then show the student that the first letter is *m*, not *d*. Ask, "Could it be *dirt* or *mud*? How do you know?"
Student misspells a word you have taught	Write the word at the top of the student's journal, and have him or her practice writing it before putting it in the text.
Student asks for help with a CVC word or misses a letter in it	Draw three boxes at the top of the journal. Have the student say the word slowly to hear and record each sound.
Student writes a letter backwards	Prompt the student to use an alphabet chart to form the letter correctly.

Emergent

Monitor Progress

It is important to monitor the progress students are making when learning letters, sounds, and words. The following formative assessments can help you determine when they are ready to tackle texts and skills at a higher level. They can be administered during your guided reading lessons.

Skill Focus	Assessment Tool	When to Administer
Sight Words	Sight Word Assessment (Appendix D, page 206)	At the beginning of each guided reading lesson.
Letters and Sounds	Emergent Word Study Inventory (Appendix F, page 210)	When you are considering moving students to a higher text level.
Strategic Actions	Running Records	At least once a week for striving readers, every two weeks for other students. This assessment can be done on Day 2, when students are reading familiar books.

Firm Up Knowledge During Independent Practice

While you are working with guided reading groups, the rest of the class should be engaged in purposeful practice activities. During independent practice, always have students read familiar books and write. In addition to reading and writing, the following activities will firm up the letter, sound, and word knowledge they have been learning in their guided reading lessons.

- **Picture Sorting** Select picture cards for the sounds the students have been learning and place them in a tub. Have students work in pairs to sort the pictures by their beginning consonant or medial vowel sound.

- **Sight Word Tracing** Laminate a card with the sight words you have taught the group and have students use dry-erase markers to trace the words. Students can also make them with magnetic letters.

- **Sight Word Game** Make a simple board game that has sight words printed in the spaces. When students roll the dice and land on a word, they read it and then write it on a recording form. The first student to reach the finish line wins the game.

- **Go Fish** Write the students' sight words on index cards, at least two cards for each word. For two players you will need between 15 and 20 word cards; for three or four players, you need about 30. A student deals five cards to each player. The remaining cards are placed facedown in a pile. The players then take turns asking one another for a word that matches one in their hand. ("Sarah, do you have the word *come?*") If Sarah has that card, she gives it to the student who asked. The student places the match faceup on the table and says a sentence with the word *come* in it. If Sarah doesn't have the word, she says, "Go Fish!" and the other player picks up a card from the pile. When a player runs out of cards or the pile is depleted, the student with the most word pairs is declared the winner.

- **Muffin Tin Toss** On small pieces of paper, write six CVC words (e.g., *can, got, mom, cat, map, bit*). Place one word inside each cup of a six-cup muffin tin. Students take turns tossing a small, plastic counter into the tin. When the counter lands inside a muffin cup, the student reads the word in the cup and gives a word that rhymes with it. For example, if the student tosses the counter into the cup with the word *can*, she might say, *man*. Students could also write the rhyming word on a sheet of paper.

- **Rhyming CVC Words** Make pairs of cards containing CVC rhyming words (e.g., *cat-rat, leg-beg, log-hog, bit-fit, map-lap, rug-hug*). Put all the cards out facing up. Students take turns finding a matching pair and then write a third word that rhymes with the pair of words (e.g., *cat-rat, mat*).

- **Word Chunk Connect 4** Make a Connect 4 board with two-letter phonograms (e.g., *ig*) you have been working on during word study. (See list of phonograms in Appendix S.) Create word cards in two different colors that match the phonograms on the board (e.g., *dig*, *wig*, *big*). A student picks a card and matches it to the phonogram on the board. The first student to get four in a row in any direction wins.

SUPPORTING STRIVING READERS

If a student is not progressing, make sure you are following the lesson procedures and teaching consistent daily lessons. Don't skip any components. If you have an intervention teacher, have him or her teach a second guided reading lesson that follows the same format with a different book. Sometimes another set of eyes will help. Ask a colleague to observe the student during a guided reading lesson. Share your observations with each other to determine what is interfering with the student's progress. Decide together what is needed to accelerate the student.

In this section we discuss typical challenges in working with striving emergent readers and suggest questions to ask yourself to overcome those challenges.

Challenge: Students are having trouble remembering the words you have taught.

Are you choosing the right words to teach? Choose a word that contains known letters. For instance, it is easier to learn the word *can* if the student already knows the letters *c*, *a*, and *n*. It is even more helpful if the student also knows the sounds of each letter, since *can* is a phonetically regular word. Avoid teaching similar-looking words in consecutive lessons. For example, don't teach *look* right after you teach *like*. Students will get them confused.

Wait until one word is firmly known before you teach another that looks similar. Don't teach all the two-letter words first. Teach some three- and four-letter words too.

Are you trying to teach too many words? The lesson plan tells you to teach the same sight word on Day 1 and Day 2. However, if the students are still not firm with that word, spend another lesson teaching it. Don't teach a new word until the previous one has been learned.

Are you giving ample opportunities for students to practice writing the words? Always include the new high frequency word in the dictated sentence. In fact, you might include it in dictated sentences for several lessons. Also, have students practice hard-to-remember words during sight word review.

Do students have opportunities to read outside of guided reading? During independent reading, students should reread the books they've read in guided reading. They can read with a buddy or on their own. They could also take the book home to read it with a parent or sibling.

Challenge: Students are having trouble hearing and recording sounds in words.

Are you choosing the best sounds for Picture Sorting? When you select the two letters for Picture Sorting, choose letters students already know by name but not sound. The following consonant sounds are easiest to learn because they have the sound in their letter name: *b, d, f, j, k, l, m, n, p, r, s, t, v, z*. Be sure to choose letters with distinctly different sounds. Don't have students sort *b* and *p*, *m* and *n*, or *d* and *t* in the same lesson. These sounds are easily confused. Once students learn one sound, you can pair it with a similar sound.

Are you using Sound Boxes? When doing Sound Boxes, use words that have sounds the children know. If they forget which letter makes a particular sound, provide a link to the alphabet chart or to a known word (/a/ like *apple*). If the student is receiving intervention from another teacher, be sure you both use the same alphabet chart.

Are students using the skills you've taught during reading? If students know their letters and sounds but aren't using them in reading, make sure you are following the procedures for Making Words. The Making Words activity teaches children to attend to print and monitor for a visual/auditory match. This is a great word study activity to use when children are not looking at print. When doing the Making Words activity, start with a known word and have students change one letter to make a new word. Be sure you have students say the word slowly as they check the letters and sounds with their finger before they reach for a new letter. This helps them notice the letter that needs to be changed.

Are students using the skills you've taught during writing? If a student knows the sounds but isn't using them in writing, the student probably isn't saying the word slowly.

Sometimes teachers make the mistake of saying the word for the students. Sound Boxes are a powerful tool for teaching children how to hear sounds. Insist that they say the word slowly while they move their finger below (or into) the boxes. You can share the task with them by saying the word as they push their finger into the boxes. Then have the student say the word as you push your finger into the boxes. The ultimate goal is for the student to both say the word and simultaneously slide his or her finger into the boxes. What they say needs to match what they hear and write.

Are students writing letters and sounds out of sequence? Intervene immediately. Show them the model for writing the word correctly. Never allow a student to write a word from right to left. If directionality is a challenge, draw an arrow or dot on the child's paper to show where to begin writing.

Are students struggling with letter formation? Teach correct letter formation during guided writing. Place an alphabet strip at the top of their writing journal and circle the letters the students reverse. Tell them to check the alphabet strip *before* they write those letters. Have them make the letter with large movements in the air before they practice writing the letter at the top of their journal.

Are students working too slowly? Encourage them to quickly read and write what they know, even at the emergent level. Also have them write quickly during the sight word review. If letter formation is getting in the way of fluent writing, spend a few seconds teaching letter formation during the sight word review or guided writing. (See letter formation tips, page 63.) Emergent readers need to attend to print, but when one-to-one matching is firm, tell the students to stop pointing at the words.

Emergent

QUESTIONS TEACHERS ASK ABOUT EMERGENT WORD STUDY

Do my students need to know all the high frequency words on the Level A list before they move to Level B? No. Students should know most of the words, but they don't need to know all of them. High frequency words should continue to be learned and reviewed at each level. Most of the words they are learning at Level A will also appear at text Levels B and C.

I think my students are ready to move to text Level C, but they aren't firm on all the consonant sounds. Should I use the word study lessons at Level C, or reteach the lessons at Levels A and B? The skills we have targeted at each text level are typical for most students. However, you may have some groups that are ready to read a Level C text but still need the word study lessons at Level B. It is important to get the consonant sounds firmly established. Then teach short *a* and *o* before you use the word study lessons listed for Level C.

Can my students practice word study procedures during center time? Yes! Independent work time provides a great opportunity for students to practice what they learned in guided reading. They can sort picture cards with a partner, practice Making Words with magnetic letters, or write words on dry-erase boards.

Should I use the high frequency words I've taught in guided reading as spelling words? Yes again! You can use the words they are learning in guided reading as spelling words. Each week, send home a list of five to seven words students can practice with their parent. These should be words you have already taught. You can also include word patterns that have been part of their word study lessons. For example, a weekly spelling list for a student reading at Level B might have three high frequency words you have taught in guided reading (e.g., *mom, look, up*) and four words that match the spelling pattern from word study (e.g., *man, hat, hop, log*). See Appendix CC for an example of a differentiated weekly spelling program.

CHAPTER 5

Word Study for the Early Reader: Levels D–I

"Word study is not a one-size-fits-all program of instruction that begins in the same place for all students within a grade level. One unique quality of word study lies in the critical role of differentiating instruction for different levels of word knowledge."

—Donald Bear, Marcia Invernizzi, Shane Templeton, and Francine Johnston (2016)

Early readers know their letters and sounds and an increasing number of high frequency words. However, they need to gain knowledge of word features such as digraphs, blends, inflectional endings, and some vowel patterns, while learning to apply that knowledge to read and write unfamiliar words. As such, word study at this level needs to teach students how to use parts of words, letter clusters, and familiar spelling patterns to read and write.

Word Study Goals for Early Readers

- Monitor for visual information. (*Does it look right?*)
- Check one source of information against another. (*Does it look right and make sense?*)
- Take two-syllable words apart (*to-day*).
- Recognize automatically a large number of high frequency words.
- Learn and use digraphs, blends, and vowel patterns to read and write new words.
- Break unfamiliar words at their onset and rime (*st-and, fl-ap*).
- Use known words to problem-solve unknown words (*day – stay, jump – stump*).

TEXT CONSIDERATIONS FOR EARLY READERS

Texts for early readers should be engaging, with a variety of sentence structures and challenging vocabulary. They should be longer than texts for emergent readers, with multiple lines of print per page and only a few unfamiliar concepts that you will need to introduce.

The Lion and the Mouse (Level F) by Michèle Dufresne is a good example of an early text (see sample pages on the next page). The story doesn't have an overwhelming number of characters, and the dialogue carries most of the plot. Readers encounter new high frequency words (*one, saw, was*) and words with inflectional endings (*sleeping, walking*). They also encounter words to take apart (*for-est, a-sleep*).

One day, a mouse
was walking in the forest.
He saw a sleeping lion.

"Look at the lion.
He is asleep."
said the little mouse.

Pages from The Lion
and the Mouse

The nonfiction book *Dinosaurs and Fossils* (Level H) by Michèle Dufresne contains text features, such as diagrams and photographs, that provide support for unfamiliar concepts (see sample pages below). There are also challenging words for students to decode (*spikes, teeth, their, small, meat, short, claws, prey*).

Pages from Dinosaurs
and Fossils

Working With Early English Learners

Some English learners will depend on memorization to learn words because that is what is required in their home language (e.g., Mandarin). Although visual memory is important for developing a sight vocabulary, English learners also need to become proficient at hearing rhymes in words. One-syllable rhyming words are quite common in English, but they are not common in other languages, such as Spanish. It's important to teach children to hear rhyming words so they can use their knowledge of one word (e.g., *cake*) to read and write similar words (e.g., *make, bake*).

THE ASSESS-DECIDE-GUIDE FRAMEWORK

Use this framework to plan and carry out instruction.

Assess: Determine your early readers' word study strengths and needs

To plan word study lessons for early readers, you need to know their strengths and needs and how they use phonics skills during reading and writing. Formal assessments and daily observations will play a critical role in your planning. Let these questions guide your observations and assessments:

- Which blends and digraphs can they hear and record?
- Which vowel patterns can they write?
- Do they use known vowel patterns to solve unknown words?
- Which inflectional endings can they write?
- Do they attend to endings when reading?
- Which high frequency words can they read and write?
- Do they apply known phonics skills in reading and writing?

Although running records and other formative assessments conducted during guided reading lessons are extremely beneficial in analyzing how students process print, the following assessments can help you more quickly pinpoint word study skills you need to teach.

Early Assessments for Planning		
Assessment	**What it tells you**	**How to use it to plan lessons**
Early Word Study Inventory (D–F and G–I)	• The sounds the student can hear and record	• Decide which skills to teach next • Decide which word study activity to use • Identify the known skills to expect students to use during reading and writing
Sight Word Assessment (D–I)	• The sight words the student can write • The words he or she partially knows • The words he or she is confusing	• Decide which words to review • Decide which words to teach next • Identify the known words to expect students to use in reading and writing

Early Word Study Inventory (Levels D–F and G–I)

Purpose: The Early Word Study Inventory is a carefully designed list of words for students to write. The words are sequenced to help you assess specific target skills:

- Level D: all short, medial vowels, initial and final digraphs (e.g., *sh*, *ch*, *th*)
- Level E: initial blends, digraphs
- Level F: initial and final blends, digraphs
- Level G: blends, silent *e*, inflectional endings
- Level H: blends, silent *e*, inflectional endings, simple vowel patterns (e.g., *all*, *ee*, *ar*, *or*, *ow*)
- Level I: blends, silent *e*, inflectional endings, more complex vowel patterns (e.g., *ay*, *oo*, *oi*, *oa*)

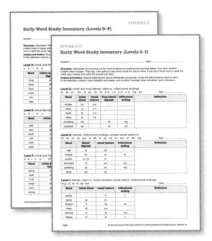

Appendix G, page 211
Appendix H, page 212

Directions: In small groups, give each student a blank sheet of paper. Then dictate the words for students to write. Say, "You don't know how to spell some of these words, but I want you to try. Say each word slowly, and write all the sounds you hear." Be sure students cannot see one another's papers.

Analyze and Reflect: On the Early Word Study Inventory, circle or highlight the words the student missed. Use the following questions to identify areas that need more instruction:

- Did the student pronounce each word slowly?
- Did the student hear and record the target skills being assessed?
- Does the student need to work more on letter formation?
- Which skills need to be taught next?

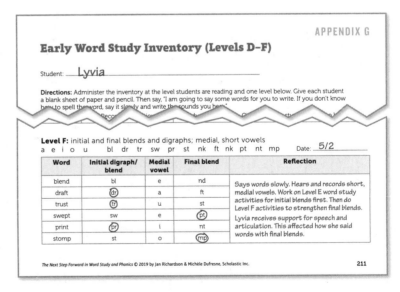

APPENDIX G

Early Word Study Inventory (Levels D–F)

Student: _____Lyvia_____

Directions: Administer the inventory at the level students are reading and one level below. Give each student a blank sheet of paper and pencil. Then say, "I am going to say some words for you to write. If you don't know how to spell the word, say it slowly and write the sounds you hear."

Level F: initial and final blends and digraphs; medial, short vowels
a e i o u   bl dr tr sw pr st nk ft nk pt nt mp   Date: ___5/2___

Word	Initial digraph/ blend	Medial vowel	Final blend	Reflection
blend	bl	e	nd	Says words slowly. Hears and records short, medial vowels. Work on Level E word study activities for initial blends first. Then do Level F activities to strengthen final blends. Lyvia receives support for speech and articulation. This affected how she said words with final blends.
draft	(dr)	a	ft	
trust	(tr)	u	st	
swept	sw	e	(pt)	
print	(pr)	i	nt	
stomp	st	o	(mp)	

The Next Step Forward in Word Study and Phonics © 2019 by Jan Richardson & Michèle Dufresne, Scholastic Inc.   211

Sight Word Assessment (Levels D–I)

Purpose: The Sight Word Assessment will tell you the sight words your students know how to write and the ones you should target in your lessons.

The following chart contains words that appear frequently in texts for early readers.

Sight Word List for Levels D–I					
Level D	**Level E**	**Level F**	**Level G**	**Level H**	**Level I**
day	all	came	don't	didn't	again
down	away	have	eat	does	because
into	back	help	from	every	could
looking	big	next	give	friend	knew
she	her	now	good	know	laugh
they	over	one	make	little	night
went	this	some	of	many	very
where	want	then	out	new	walk
will	who	was	saw	were	who
your	with	what	why	when	would

Directions: Give each student a blank sheet of paper. Dictate the sight words for their instructional text level and one level below.

Analyze and Reflect: On the Sight Word Checklist, check the words the student wrote correctly. Count reversed letters as correct except *b/d* and *p/q*.

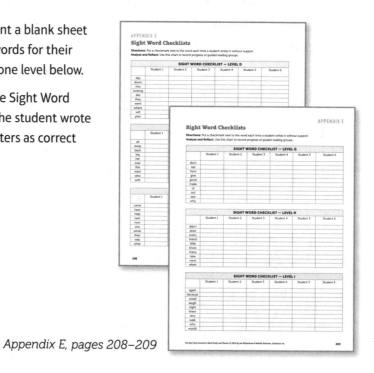

Appendix E, pages 208–209

Decide: Determine a skill focus and word study activity

Use information gained from the Early Word Study Inventory to select a skill focus for each group. The word study lessons for each skill on pages 121–135 are organized by text level. Because you will probably teach 10 to 15 guided reading lessons at each text level, you will have plenty of opportunities to address the needs of each group's students.

Level	Skill Focus
D	• Digraphs • Onset-rime
E	• Initial blends • Onset-rime
F	• Final blends • Onset-rime
G	• Initial and final blends • Silent *e* • Onset-rime
H	• Silent *e* • Vowel patterns • Inflectional endings
I	• Silent *e* • Vowel patterns • Inflectional endings

Once you've chosen a skill focus, choose an activity: Picture Sorting, Making Words, Sound Boxes, Breaking Words, or Analogy Charts. The following chart summarizes the purpose of each activity and when to use it.

Activity	Purpose	When to Use	Where to Find Teaching Guidelines
Picture Sorting	To hear digraphs and blends and link sounds to letters	When introducing a new skill	Chapter 2, page 34
Making Words	To scan visually words with blends and digraphs to check for letter/sound accuracy	When students need to transfer this skill to reading	Chapter 2, page 36
Sound Boxes	To hear and record digraphs and blends in sequence	When students need to transfer this skill to writing	Chapter 2, page 38
Breaking Words	To take words apart at the onset and rime when decoding unfamiliar words	When students need to break words at the onset, rime, and ending	Chapter 2, page 40
Analogy Charts	To use patterns in known words to read and write unknown words	When students would benefit from using an analogy to read and write unknown words	Chapter 2, page 43

The following chart summarizes the skill focus by level for the five activities.

Level	Skill Focus	Picture Sorting	Making Words	Sound Boxes	Breaking Words	Analogy Charts
D	• Digraphs (*sh, ch, th*) • Onset-rime	Sort pictures that begin with two different digraphs. *ch - th*	Make a series of words by changing the initial or final digraph. *bat-bath-math-mash-mush* Students break each word at the onset and rime.	3 boxes Write words with digraphs. *chat* *shop* *with*	Break each word at the onset and rime. *ch at* *th at*	N/A
E	• Initial blends • Onset-rime	Sort pictures of initial blends that begin with the same letter. *cl - cr*	Make a series of words by changing the initial blend. *stab-slab-grab-gram-slam-slim* Students break each word at the onset and rime.	4 boxes Write words with initial blends. *clam* *grin* *sled*	Break each word at the onset and rime. *gr ab* *sl ab*	N/A
F	• Final blends • Onset-rime	N/A	Make a series of words by changing the final blends. *went-wept-west-pest* Students break each word at the onset and rime.	4 boxes Write words with final blends. *film* *milk* *kept*	Break one-syllable words with final blends and digraphs. Change onset. *p ink* *w ink*	N/A
G	• Initial and final blends • Silent *e* • Onset-rime	N/A	Make a series of words with blends or short and long vowels (silent e). *rest-quest-chest-check-chick-quick* *pin-pine-pane-pan-plan-plane*	5 boxes Write words with initial and final blends. *draft* *plump* *stand*	Break one-syllable words with initial and final blends. Change onset. *bl ack* *sh ack*	Write words with short vowels and the silent *e* | **sick**	**like** | |---|---|
chick	spike
slick	quite	

Level	Skill Focus	Picture Sorting	Making Words	Sound Boxes	Breaking Words	Analogy Charts
H	• Silent *e* • Vowel patterns • Inflectional endings	N/A	Make a series of words with the same vowel pattern but different initial or final letters. *see-seed-greed-green*	N/A	Break two-syllable words with vowel patterns and inflectional endings *gr eet ing* *sl eet ing* *sw eet er*	Write words with similar vowel patterns. <table><tr><td>**ball**</td><td>**for**</td></tr><tr><td>small</td><td>sport</td></tr><tr><td>stall</td><td>storm</td></tr></table>
I	• Silent *e* • Vowel patterns • Inflectional endings	N/A	Make a series of words with the same vowel pattern but different initial or final letters. *boat-boast-coast-coach*	N/A	Break one-syllable words with silent e feature or vowel pattern. Change onset. *j oke* *ch oke* *br oke*	Write words with similar vowel patterns. Add endings. <table><tr><td>**moon**</td><td>**girl**</td></tr><tr><td>spoon</td><td>twirl</td></tr><tr><td>snoopy</td><td>firmly</td></tr></table>

Early

Use the Sight Word Checklists (Appendix E) to summarize the data for each guided reading group. Write the students' names across the top and check the words each student wrote correctly. Use these checklists to select words to review and teach. Select three words from the checklist to review at the beginning of each lesson—words most of the students know. Teach a new word during each lesson using the four steps described on pages 29–30. Monitor student progress by adding a checkmark each time a student writes a word correctly during the Sight Word Review.

Guide: Teach word study in an integrated lesson framework

Word study should be part of a guided reading lesson that:

1. allows for developmental and explicit instruction not only in word study, but also in reading and writing.

2. invites students to use their newly acquired word study skills immediately, while they're engaged in reading and writing.

LESSON WALK-THROUGH

The following early guided reading plan has been annotated to show how word study skills can be taught and practiced throughout a lesson. The plan is based on the book *Puffins* by Agnes Land.

Pages from Puffins

Puffins have white feathers and black feathers.

They have orange feet and a big orange beak.

Puffins dive, too! They dive to catch fish.

Puffins eat fish.

① Sight Word Review (Days 1 and 2)

Notice students are writing two words that begin with the same letters. The *th* words can be challenging. Review tricky words at the beginning of each lesson.

② Book Introduction (Day 1)

Have students locate challenging words before they read the book. Prompt them to run their finger under each word as they say it. This teaches them to crosscheck auditory (sounds) with visual information (letters).

③ Read With Prompting (Days 1 and 2)

Prompt students to take words apart when they get stuck. (e.g., "Cover the ending. Is there a part you know?")

④ Discussion Prompt

Encourage students to use the new vocabulary words you introduced.

⑤ Follow-Up Teaching Points (Days 1 and 2)

Select a challenging word from the book and write it on an easel or make it with magnetic letters. Demonstrate strategies for taking the word apart (e.g., "Use known parts. Use a known word with the same vowel pattern. Cover the ending.").

⑥ Teach One Sight Word (Days 1 and 2)

Use the four steps described on pages 29–30 to help students develop a process for learning new words. Continue to review and teach sight words through Level I.

⑦ Word Study (Day 1)

Use manipulatives to teach digraphs, blends, vowel patterns, and inflectional endings.

Guided Writing (Day 2)

Dictate one sentence that includes the new sight word and skills you taught that day. Students write more sentences. Differentiate your prompting as needed.

Early Guided Reading Plan: *Puffins*

Early Guided Reading Plan (Levels D–I)

Students: Charlotte, Sam, Raoul, Dante, Amy, Meli

Date: 12/9–10

Title/Level: Puffins/E

Word Study Focus	Strategy Focus	Comprehension Focus
Initial blends	Use known parts	Compare & Contrast

Day 1	Day 2
Sight Word Review 1 minute	**Sight Word Review** 1 minute

they	this	down	have	where	your

Reading 8–10 minutes

Day 1	Day 2
Introduce and Read a New Book Synopsis: Puffins are small black-and-white birds that live near the ocean. Read to find out how they live and care for their babies. New Vocabulary: feather, beak, their	**Reread Yesterday's Book** (and other familiar books) Running Record Student: Amy
Students read the book with prompting (use back side for recording observations and prompts)	*Students read books with prompting (use back side for recording observations and prompts)*
Discussion Prompts: What did you learn about puffins? How are puffin parents like your parents?	Discussion Prompts: How are puffins like penguins? How are they different?

Follow-Up Teaching Points (choose 1 or 2 each day)
☐ Use meaning ☐ Monitor for meaning ☐ Reread at difficulty
☐ Monitor for letters and sounds ☐ Attend to word endings ☐ Visually scan the word ☒ Use known parts
☐ Attend to contractions ☒ Use analogies ☐ Break apart words

Teaching Point for Day 1	Teaching Point for Day 2
Write "small" on the easel and underline "all." Write other "all" words for students to read (fall, taller, called).	Use magnetic letters to make the word "land." Break the word (l-and). Give each student one of the following letters (s, t, g, r, b, h). Have them help you make new words with and in them (hand, band, stand, grand, brand).

New Sight Word What's Missing? • Mix and Fix • Table Writing • Write It &Retrieve It (1–2 minutes)

have	have

Word Study (Day 1) (5–8 minutes)	Guided Writing (Day 2) (8–10 minutes)
☐ Picture Sorting ☐ Making Words ☐ Sound Boxes ☒ Breaking Words ☐ Analogy Charts Write "feed" and have students make it with magnetic letters: Break it – say it Make: weed Write and read: bleed, freed	☒ Dictated sentences ☐ B-M-E ☐ Problem-Solution ☐ SWBS ☒ New facts ☐ Other:_____ Puffins have to stay close to the water, so they have fish to eat. Write another fact about puffins.

Next Steps	Text: Move to Level F–fiction	Next Goals: Break at onset and rime during reading.	Students to Assess: Meli

The Next Step Forward in Word Study and Phonics © 2019 by Jan Richardson & Michèle Dufresne, Scholastic Inc.

239

See Appendix FF, page 239, for the lesson plan template.

APPENDIX FF

Teacher Notes and Observations for Early Readers (Levels D–I)

Monitoring and Word-Solving Prompts
☐ Reread and think what would make sense.
☐ Say the first part. Now look through the word.
☐ Check the end (or middle) of the word.
☐ Find the tricky part. What can you try?
☐ Show me a part you know.
☐ Do you know another word that looks like that?
☐ Use your finger to cover the ending.
☐ Break the word apart.

Fluency and Comprehension Prompts
☐ Can you read it quickly?
☐ How did you sound?
☐ What did you read? What's happened so far?
☐ What have you learned?
☐ Why did the character do (or say) that?
☐ Why…?
☐ What are you thinking?

Anecdotal notes, running records, observations, and teaching points	Goals/Next Steps

Student: Charlotte
 	
✔✔✔. ✔✔✔✔ <u>sm</u>✔✔. T: You noticed a part you know!
     small
 	
✔✔ <u>w-wings</u> - ✔✔✔.   T: Are you right? What would
  white feathers   make sense and look right?
	☒ Monitor
	☒ Word Solving
	☐ Visual Scanning
	☐ Fluency
	☐ Retell
	☐ Other:

Student: Sam ✔✔✔ <u>feather</u> ✔✔✔ <u>feather</u>. T: Check the end. feathers feathers T: Why do puffins live near the ocean?	☐ Monitor ☐ Word Solving ☒ Visual Scanning ☐ Fluency ☐ Retell ☐ Other:

Student: Raoul
✔✔ <u>n-nest</u> ✔✔.   T: That makes sense. Check the end.
  nests
 	
✔✔✔✔✔ <u>has</u>/SC ✔✔.   T: You noticed that didn't look right.
     have
            T: How do puffins take care of their babies?
	☐ Monitor
	☐ Word Solving
	☒ Visual Scanning
	☐ Fluency
	☐ Retell
	☐ Other:

Student: Dante
 	
✔ <u>puffins</u> ✔✔✔✔✔.
  puffin   T: That sounds right. Now check the end.
         Is it puffin or puffins?
T: What did you read about puffins?
	☐ Monitor
	☐ Word Solving
	☒ Visual Scanning
	☐ Fluency
	☐ Retell
	☐ Other:

Student: Amy <u>Then</u> ✔✔✔✔✔. T: You noticed the first part. Look through the word. They <u>So</u> ✔✔✔✔. T: Does it look right? Check it. Soon T: What does this book remind you of?	☐ Monitor ☐ Word Solving ☒ Visual Scanning ☐ Fluency ☐ Retell ☐ Other:
Student: Meli ✔✔✔. ✔✔✔✔✔. ✔✔✔. ✔✔✔✔✔. What other bird is like a puffin? How is it similar?	☐ Monitor ☐ Word Solving ☐ Visual Scanning ☒ Fluency ☐ Retell ☐ Other:

Word Study Lessons

In this section, you will find a series of word study lessons to embed in your early guided reading lessons. Teach these lessons during the last five to eight minutes of Day 1. There are ten lessons for each level. As you become more proficient with the procedures, you will be able to design your own lessons using the word lists in Appendices W, X, and Y.

There is no need to teach every lesson at each level. Choose the ones that best meet the needs of your students as identified by your assessments. Use the chart on this book's inside front cover to pinpoint specific lessons, based on your findings. The lessons at each level are sequenced so that the skill focus of Picture Sorting matches the skill focus of Making Words, Sound Boxes, and Breaking Words. That helps students become flexible with the skill and supports them in transferring the skill during reading and writing. Most students should move up a text level every three to four weeks. They will learn more about letters and sounds at each level.

Level D Word Study Lessons

These lessons teach digraphs and medial short vowels. Make adjustments to match the needs of your students.

Lesson	Skills	Activity	Directions
1	Initial digraphs: *ch* and *sh*	**Picture Sorting**	Distribute *ch* and *sh* picture cards. Write the letters *ch* and *sh* on the easel. Students take turns saying the picture, the sound, and the two letters. Then they place the card under the correct digraph.
2	Initial digraphs: *ch* and *sh*	**Making Words**	Students remove the following letters from their trays: a c h i p s t Dictate these words for students to make: *cat, chat, chap, chip, ship*. Have students check each word and then break apart the word at the onset and rime.

3	Initial digraphs: *ch* and *sh*	**Sound Boxes** (3 boxes)	Distribute Sound Boxes, dry-erase markers, and erasers. Dictate the following words for students to write: *chat*, *ship*, *chop*, *shut*. After you say each word, have students say the word slowly, running their finger under the three boxes. Then have students write one sound in each box as they say the word again slowly. After they write the word, have them check the letters with the sounds by saying the word slowly as they run their finger under the letters.

Note: A digraph is one phoneme, so the two letters go in one box.

ch	a	t

4	Initial digraphs: *ch* and *th*	**Picture Sorting**	Distribute *ch* and *th* picture cards. Write the letters *ch* and *th* on the easel. Students take turns saying the picture, the sound, and the two letters. Then they place the card under the correct digraph.

ch *th*

5	Initial digraphs: *ch* and *th*	**Making Words**	Students remove the following letters from their trays:

c h i n o p t

Dictate these words for students to make: *tin*, *thin*, *chin*, *chip*, *chop*. Have students check each word and then break apart the word at the onset and rime.

6	Initial digraphs: *ch* and *th*	**Sound Boxes** (3 boxes)	Distribute Sound Boxes, dry-erase markers, and erasers. Dictate the following words for students to write: *chin*, *that*, *chop*, *then*.

Note: A digraph is one phoneme, so the two letters go in one box.

ch	i	n

7	Initial digraphs: *th*, *sh*, *ch*	**Breaking Words**	Write *thin* on the easel and tell students to take the letters off their trays to make the word.
			Students break the word at the onset and rime (*th-in*) and read it.
			Tell them to change the *t* to an *s*. Students break and read the word *shin*.
			Write the word *chin* on the whiteboard. Students read the word.

8	Final digraphs: *th* and *sh*	**Making Words**	Students remove the following letters from their trays:
			a b h m s t
			Dictate these words for students to make: *bat*, *bath*, *bash*, *mash*, *math*. Have students check each word and then break apart the word at the onset and rime.

9	Final digraphs: *ch* and *sh*	**Sound Boxes** (3 boxes)	Distribute Sound Boxes, dry-erase markers, and erasers. Dictate the following words for students to write: *rich*, *rash*, *much*, *wish*.

r	i	ch

10	Final digraphs: *ch*, *sh*, *th*	**Making Words**	Students remove the following letters from their trays:
			a c h m s t u
			Dictate these words for students to make: *math*, *mash*, *mush*, *much*, *such*. Have students check each word and then break apart the word at the onset and rime.

11	Final digraph: *sh*	**Breaking Words**	Write *hash* on the easel and tell students to take the letters off their trays to make the word.
			Students break the word at the onset and rime (*h-ash*) and read it.
			Tell them to change the *h* to *g*. Students break and read the word *gash*.
			Write the word *cash* on the whiteboard. Students read the word.

Early

Level E Word Study Lessons

These lessons teach initial blends and digraphs. Make adjustments to match the needs of your students.

Lesson	Skills	Activity	Directions
12	Initial blends: *fl* and *fr*	**Picture Sorting**	Distribute *fl* and *fr* picture cards. Write the letters *fl* and *fr* on the easel. Students take turns saying the picture, the blend, and the two letters. Then they place the card under the correct blend.

fl   *fr*

Lesson	Skills	Activity	Directions
13	Initial blends: *sp* and *sl*	**Picture Sorting**	Distribute *sp* and *sl* picture cards. Write the letters *sp* and *sl* on the easel. Students take turns saying the picture, the blend, and the two letters. Then they place the card under the correct blend.

sp   *sl*

| 14 | Initial blends: *fl, sp, sl, sw* | **Making Words** | Students remove the following letters from their trays: |

a f l m o p s w

Dictate these words for students to make: *spam, swam, slam, slap, flap, flop*. Have students check each word and then break apart the word at the onset and rime.

| 15 | Initial blends: *fl, fr, sw, sk* | **Sound Boxes** (4 boxes) | Distribute Sound Boxes, dry-erase markers, and erasers. |

Dictate the following words for students to write: *flip, frog, swam, skin*.

f	l	i	p

16	Initial blends: *br, fl, sl*	**Breaking Words**	Write *slat* on the easel and tell students to take the letters off their trays to make the word.
			Students break the word at the onset and rime (*sl-at*) and read it.
			Tell them to change the *s* to *f*. Students break and read the word *flat*.
			Write the word *brat* on the easel. Students read the word.
17	Initial blends: *cl* and *cr*	**Picture Sorting**	Distribute *cl* and *cr* picture cards. Write the letters *cl* and *cr* on the easel. Students take turns saying the picture, the blend, and the two letters. Then they place the card under the correct blend.

cl   **cr**

18	Initial blends: *br, cl, cr, sl*	**Making Words**	Students remove the following letters from their trays:
			a b c i l m r s
			Dictate these words for students to make: *brim, slim, slam, clam, cram, crab*. Have students check each word and then break apart the word at the onset and rime.
19	Initial blends: *br, cl, sp, st*	**Sound Boxes** (4 boxes)	Distribute Sound Boxes, dry-erase markers, and erasers. Dictate the following words for students to write: *spin, clot, brag, step*.

| s | p | i | n |

20	Initial blends: *cr, sl, st*	**Breaking Words**	Write *stab* on the easel and tell students to take the letters off their trays to make the word. Students break the word at the onset and rime (*st-ab*) and read it.
			Tell them to change the *st* to *cr*. Students break and read the word *crab*.
			Write the word *slab* on the easel. Students read the word.
21	Initial blends: *br, dr, gl, pl*	**Making Words**	Students remove the following letters from their trays:
			a b d g l m p r u
			Dictate these words for students to make: *glum, plum, drum, drug, drag, brag*. Have students check each word and then break apart the word at the onset and rime.

Level F Word Study Lessons

These lessons teach final blends. Make adjustments to match the needs of your students.

Lesson	Skills	Activity	Directions
22	Final blends: *nd, ng, nt*	**Making Words**	Students remove the following letters from their trays: a b d g n p t u Dictate these words for students to make: *and, band, bang, pang, pant, punt*. Have students check each word and then break apart the word at the onset and rime.
23	Final blends: *nd, ng, nt, nk*	**Sound Boxes** (4 boxes)	Distribute Sound Boxes, dry-erase markers, and erasers. Dictate the following words for students to write: *fang, land, punt, pink*. | f	a	n	g	
24	Final blend: *ng*	**Breaking Words**	Write *sang* on the easel and tell students to take the letters off their trays to make the word. Students break the word at the onset and rime *(s-ang)* and read it. Tell them to change the *s* to *b*. Students break and read the word *bang*. Write the word *rang* on the easel. Students read the word.
25	Final blends: *nd, nt, pt*	**Making Words**	Students remove the following letters from their trays: d e n p s t w Dictate these words for students to make: *send, sent, went, wept*. Have students check each word and then break apart the word at the onset and rime.
26	Final blends: *mp, nt, st*	**Sound Boxes** (4 boxes)	Distribute Sound Boxes, dry-erase markers, and erasers. Dictate the following words for students to write: *last, rent, pump, lint*. | l	a	s	t	

27	Final blend: *nd*	**Breaking Words**	Write *bend* on the easel and tell students to take the letters off their trays to make the word. Students break the word at the onset and rime *(b-end)* and read it.
			Tell them to change the *b* to *l*. Students break and read the word *lend*.
			Write the word *send* on the easel. Students read the word.

| 28 | Final blends: *nk* and *ng* | **Making Words** | Students remove the following letters from their trays: |

g i k n s t w

Dictate the following words for students to make: *ink, wink, wing, swing, sting*. Have students check each word and then break apart the word at the onset and rime.

| 29 | Final blends: *mp, nt, nd, ng* | **Sound Boxes** (4 boxes) | Distribute Sound Boxes, dry-erase markers, and erasers. Dictate the following words for students to write: *jump, sang, lend, went*. |

j	u	m	p

30	Final blend: *nt*	**Breaking Words**	Write *print* on the easel and tell students to take the letters off their trays to make the word. Students break the word at the onset and rime *(pr-int)* and read it.
			Tell them to change the *pr* to *gl*. Students break and read the word *glint*.
			Write the word *stint* on the easel. Students read the word.

| 31 | Final blends: *nt, nk, st, mp* | **Sound Boxes** (4 boxes) | Distribute Sound Boxes, dry-erase markers, and erasers. Dictate the following words for students to write: *test, pant, sink, bump*. |

t	e	s	t

Early

Level G Word Study Lessons

These lessons teach digraphs, initial and final blends, and silent *e*. Make adjustments to match the needs of your students.

Lesson	Skills	Activity	Directions
32	Digraphs and blends: *sh, fl, br* Silent *e*	**Breaking Words**	Write *shake* on the easel and tell students to take the letters off their trays to make the word. Students break the word at the onset and rime *(sh-ake)* and read it. Tell them to change the *sh* to *fl*. Students break and read the word *flake*. Write the word *brake* on the easel. Students read the word.
33	Digraphs and blends: *ch, sh, tr, sm, mp, nch*	**Sound Boxes** (4 boxes)	Distribute Sound Boxes, dry-erase markers, and erasers. Dictate the following words for students to write: *champ, trash, bunch, smash*. **ch | a | m | p**
34	Initial blends: *bl, cr, sl*	**Making Words**	Students remove the following letters from their trays: **a b c k l o r s** Dictate the following words for students to make: *rock, crock, block, black, crack, slack*. Have students check each word and then break apart the word at the onset and rime.
35	Digraphs and blends: *ch, tr, str, sh, gr, scr* Silent *e*	**Analogy Chart** (2 columns)	Distribute the Analogy Charts, dry-erase markers, and erasers. Tell students to write *cap* and *cape* at the top of their chart. Underline the pattern in each word and discuss its sound. Dictate these words for students to write under the matching pattern. Have them underline the pattern after they write each word.

Analogy Chart for Lesson 35:

c<u>ap</u>	c<u>ape</u>
ch<u>ap</u>	sh<u>ape</u>
tr<u>ap</u>	gr<u>ape</u>
str<u>ap</u>	scr<u>ape</u>

Write the words *snap* and *drape* on the easel and have students read them.

| 36 | Digraphs and blends: *cr, fl, shr, nch, nk* | **Sound Boxes** (5 boxes) | Distribute Sound Boxes, dry-erase markers, and erasers. Dictate the following words for students to write: *crunch, flinch, flank, shrunk*. |

c	r	u	n	ch

| 37 | Digraphs and blends: *kn, ck, bl, sh* | **Breaking Words** | Write *knock* on the easel and tell students to take the letters off their trays to make the word. Students break the word at the onset and rime *(kn-ock)* and read it. |

Tell them to change the *kn* to *bl*. Students break and read the word *block*.

Write the word *shock* on the easel. Students read the word.

| 38 | Initial and final blends: *fl, ck*

Silent *e* | **Making Words** | Students remove the following letters from their trays: |

a   c   e   f   i   k   l   q   t   u

Dictate these words for students to make: *fat, fate, fake, flake, quake, quick*. Have students check each word and then break apart the word at the onset and rime.

| 39 | Digraphs and Initial blends: *st, tr, sp, str, th*

Silent *e* | **Analogy Chart** (2 columns) | Distribute the Analogy Charts, dry-erase markers, and erasers. |

Tell students to write *sick* and *like* at the top of their chart. Underline the pattern in each word and discuss its sound. Dictate these words for students to write under the matching pattern. Have them underline the pattern after they write each word.

<u>sick</u>	<u>like</u>
st<u>ick</u>	h<u>ike</u>
tr<u>ick</u>	sp<u>ike</u>
qu<u>ick</u>	str<u>ike</u>

Write the words *thick* and *pipe* on the easel and have students read them.

| 40 | Digraphs and blends: *sh, wh, sp*

Silent *e* | **Breaking Words** | Write *shine* on the easel and tell students to take the letters off their trays to make the word. Students break the word at the onset and rime *(sh-ine)* and read it. |

Tell students to change the *sh* to *wh*. Students break and read the word *whine*.

Write the word *spine* on the easel. Students read the word.

| 41 | Digraphs and blends: *sh, dr, pr, sl, sc*

 Silent *e* | **Analogy Chart** (2 columns) | Distribute the Analogy Charts, dry-erase markers, and erasers.

 Tell students to write *mop* and *mope* at the top of their chart. Underline the pattern in each word and discuss its sound. Dictate these words for students to write under the matching pattern. Have them underline the pattern after they write each word. |

m<u>op</u>	m<u>ope</u>
sh<u>op</u>	h<u>ope</u>
dr<u>op</u>	sl<u>ope</u>
pr<u>op</u>	sc<u>ope</u>

Write the words *slop* and *slope* on the easel and have students read them.

Level H Word Study Lessons

These lessons teach digraphs, blends, silent *e*, simple vowel patterns (*all, ar, ay, ee, ell, ill, oo, or, ow*), and inflectional endings. Make adjustments to match the needs of your students.

Lesson	Skills	Activity	Directions
42	Blends Silent *e*	**Analogy Chart** (2 columns)	Distribute the Analogy Charts, dry-erase markers, and erasers. Tell students to write *mad* and *made* at the top of their chart. Underline the pattern in each word and discuss its sound. Dictate these words for students to write under the matching pattern. Have them underline the pattern after they write each word.

m<u>ad</u>	m<u>ade</u>
h<u>ad</u>	sp<u>ade</u>
gl<u>ad</u>	gl<u>ade</u>
sl<u>ab</u>	st<u>age</u>

Write the words *plan* and *plane* on the easel and have students read them.

43	Digraphs and blends	**Making Words**	Students remove the following letters from their trays (extra *c* and *e*):
	Vowel pattern: *ee*		**c d e h p r s**
			Dictate these words for students to make: *see, seed, speed, speech, screech.* Have students check each word and then break apart the word at the onset and rime.

44	Blends	**Breaking Words**	Write *greeting* on the easel and tell students to take the letters off their trays to make the word. Students break the word at the onset, rime, and ending (*gr-eet-ing*) and read it.
	Vowel pattern: *ee*		
	Inflectional endings		Tell students to change the *gr* to *sl.* Students break and read the word *sleeting.*
			Write the word *sweeter* on the easel. Students read the word.

45	Blends	**Making Words**	Students remove the following letters from their trays:
	Vowel pattern: *ow*		**c d f l n o r w**
			Dictate these words for students to make: *down, drown, frown, crown, clown.* Have students check each word and then break apart the word at the onset and rime.

46	Blends	**Breaking Words**	Write *growled* on the easel and tell students to take the letters off their trays to make the word. Students break the word at the onset, rime, and ending (*gr-owl-ed*) and read it.
	Vowel pattern: *ow*		
	Inflectional endings		Tell them to change the *gr* to *sc.* Students break and read the word *scowled.*
			Write the word *prowler* on the easel. Students read the word.

47	Digraphs and blends	**Making Words**	Students remove the following letters from their trays (extra *l*):
	Vowel patterns: *all, ell, ill*		**a e h i l m p s t**
			Dictate these words for students to make: *mall, small, smell, shell, spell, spill, still.* Have students check each word and then break apart the word at the onset and rime.

48	Blends Vowel pattern: *ay* Inflectional endings	**Breaking Words**	Write *spraying* on the easel and tell students to take the letters off their trays to make the word. Students break the word at the onset, rime, and ending (*spr-ay-ing*) and read it. Tell them to change the *spr* to *str*. Students break and read the word *straying*. Write the word *swayed* on the easel. Students read the word.

49	Blends Vowel patterns: *ay* and *all* Inflectional endings	**Analogy Chart** (2 columns)	Distribute the Analogy Charts, dry-erase markers, and erasers. Tell students to write *day* and *ball* at the top of their chart. Underline the pattern in each word and discuss its sound. Dictate these words for students to write under the matching pattern. Have them underline the pattern after they write each word.

d<u>ay</u>	b<u>all</u>
st<u>ay</u>	st<u>all</u>
pr<u>ay</u>ed	sm<u>all</u>er
spr<u>ay</u>ing	c<u>all</u>ed

Write the words *ballpark* and *playground* on the easel and have students read them.

50	Digraphs and blends Vowel patterns: *ar* and *or* Inflectional endings	**Analogy Chart** (2 columns)	Distribute the Analogy Charts, dry-erase markers, and erasers. Tell students to write *car* and *for* at the top of their chart. Underline the pattern in each word and discuss its sound. Dictate these words for students to write under the matching pattern. Have them underline the pattern after they write each word.

c<u>ar</u>	f<u>or</u>
st<u>ar</u>	sp<u>or</u>t
h<u>ar</u>m	t<u>or</u>ch
f<u>ar</u>mer	st<u>or</u>my
sm<u>ar</u>ter	sh<u>or</u>ter

Write the words *harder* and *worn* on the easel and have students read them.

51	Blends Vowel pattern: *oo* Inflectional endings	**Breaking Words**	Write *scooped* on the easel and tell students to take the letters off their trays to make the word. Students break the word at the onset, rime, and ending (*sc-oop-ed*) and read it. Tell students to change the *sc* to *sw*. Students break and read the word *swooped*. Write the word *drooping* on the easel. Students read the word.

Level I Word Study Lessons

These lessons teach blends, silent *e*, more complex vowel patterns (*ai, ar, oi, oa, oo, ou*), and inflectional endings.

Lesson	Skills	Activity	Directions
52	Blends Vowel pattern: *ar*	**Making Words**	Students remove the following letters from their trays: a c d p r t y Dictate these words for students to make: *far, car, card, cart, part, party*. Have students check each word and then break apart the word at the onset and rime.
53	Blends Vowel pattern: *ai* Inflectional endings	**Breaking Words**	Write *trainer* on the easel and tell students to take the letters off their trays to make the word. Students break the word at the onset, rime, and ending (*tr-ain-er*) and read it. Tell students to add an *s*. Students break and read the word *strainer*. Write the word *sprained* on the easel. Students read the word.
54	Digraphs and blends Vowel patterns: *oi* and *oa*	**Analogy Chart** (2 columns)	Distribute the Analogy Charts, dry-erase markers, and erasers. Tell students to write *oil* and *boat* at the top of their chart. Underline the pattern in each word and discuss its sound. Dictate these words for students to write under the matching pattern. Have them underline the pattern after they write each word. <table><tr><td>o**i**l</td><td>b**oa**t</td></tr><tr><td>br**oi**l</td><td>thr**oa**t</td></tr><tr><td>c**oi**l</td><td>c**oa**l</td></tr><tr><td>sp**oi**led</td><td>c**oa**ting</td></tr><tr><td>p**oi**nty</td><td>r**oa**ster</td></tr></table> Write the words *boiled* and *roasting* on the easel and have students read them.
55	Blends Vowel pattern: *oa*	**Making Words**	Students remove the following letters from their trays: a b c g l o s t Dictate these words for students to make: *coat, coast, boast, boat, goat, gloat*. Have students check each word and then break apart the word at the onset and rime.

Early

56	Blends Vowel pattern: *oa* Inflectional endings	**Breaking Words**	Write *gloating* on the easel and tell students to take the letters off their trays to make the word. Students break the word at the onset, rime, and ending (*gl-oat-ing*) and read it. Tell them to change the *gl* to *fl*. Students break and read the word *floating*. Write the word *groaned* on the easel. Students read the word.
57	Blends Vowel pattern: *oi* Inflectional endings	**Making Words**	Students remove the following letters from their trays: c d e i j l n o p s Dictate these words for students to make: *join, coin, coil, soil, spoil, spoiled*. Have students check each word and then break apart the word at the onset and rime.
58	Digraphs and blends Vowel patterns: *ai* and *oo* Inflectional endings	**Analogy Chart** (2 columns)	Distribute the Analogy Charts, dry-erase markers, and erasers. Tell students to write *rain* and *cool* at the top of their chart. Underline the pattern in each word and discuss its sound. Dictate these words for students to write under the matching pattern. Have them underline the pattern after they write each word. | **r<u>ai</u>n**	**c<u>oo</u>l**
---	---
tr<u>ai</u>n	f<u>oo</u>l
f<u>ai</u>th	st<u>oo</u>l
p<u>ai</u>nter	sm<u>oo</u>thly
br<u>ai</u>ded	sc<u>oo</u>ter	 Write the words *chained* and *gloomy* on the easel and have students read them.
59	Digraphs and blends Vowel pattern: *ou*	**Making Words**	Students remove the following letters from their trays: c g h l n o r s t u Dictate these words for students to make: *shout, snout, grout, grouch, slouch*. Have students check each word and then break apart the word at the onset and rime.

60	Digraphs and blends Vowel pattern: *ou* Inflectional endings	**Breaking Words**	Write *grouchy* on the easel and tell students to take the letters off their trays to make the word. Students break the word at the onset, rime, and ending (*gr-ouch-y*) and read it. Tell them to change the *gr* to *sl*. Students break and read the word *slouchy*. Write the word *crouching* on the easel. Students read the word.
61	Blends Silent *e*	**Analogy Chart** (2 columns)	Distribute the Analogy Charts, dry-erase markers, and erasers. Tell students to write *sun* and *cute* at the top of their chart. Underline the pattern in each word and discuss its sound. Dictate these words for students to write under the matching pattern. Have them underline the pattern after they write each word.

<u>sun</u>	<u>cute</u>
sp<u>un</u>	fl<u>ute</u>
st<u>un</u>	br<u>ute</u>
dr<u>um</u>	t<u>ube</u>
str<u>um</u>	h<u>uge</u>

Write the words *rude* and *humming* on the easel and have students read them.

Early

Encourage Students to Apply Word Study Skills to Reading

As students read you will have an opportunity to help them use what they have been learning in word study to solve new words in the text. Your teaching needs to be directed at guiding students to take a useful strategic *action*. Differentiate your support based on the assessed needs of each student. Your targeted questions prompt students to attend to or use something that will help them problem-solve.

For example, if a student stumbles on the word *stay*, you might prompt, "What do you know that might help?" The student might say, *st* (a part she knows). Next, you might cover up *st* with your finger and prompt, "Do you know a word like that?" With this prompt, you are assisting her in noticing that the next part (*ay*) looks similar to *day* (a word she knows). Use the following prompts to guide students to use word-solving skills to decode unknown words.

Word-Solving Goals and Prompts	
Word-Solving Goal	**Prompts for Strategic Action**
Notices errors (monitors); cross-checks multiple sources of information to correct errors	• *You said ___. Were you right?* • *Find the tricky part.* • *Check the middle (or end) of the word.*
Uses knowledge of letter/sound relationships to initiate an action at the point of difficulty	• *Read it again and think about what makes sense and begins with those letters.* • *Do you know another word that has this part in it?*
Searches through unknown words in a left-to-right sequence; blends letters into sounds	• *Say it slowly like when you write it.* • *Look through the word.* • *Say the first part. Now say more of the word.*
Takes apart simple unknown word parts/patterns	• *Use your finger or a card to break the word.* • *What do you know that can help?*
Reads high frequency words quickly, fluently, and automatically	• *Find ___. That's a word you know. Read it quickly.*

As you confer with students, you will need to make moment-by-moment decisions about how much or how little assistance to provide. Too much help can lead to student overdependence. Too little can lead to student frustration. The following chart offers a scale of help to use when prompting for student independence (Clay, 2016).

Prompts for Strategic Action		
	Teacher/Student Interaction	**Teacher Prompts**
LESS SUPPORT ↑	Student solves the word independently.	• *You worked that out!* • *How did you know it said _____?*
	Teacher prompts to a known part.	• *Do you know a word that starts/ends with those letters?* • *What do you know that might help?*
	Student divides the word with his/her finger.	• *Use your finger to break apart the word and look for a part that might help you.*
	The teacher says a part of the word and the student locates that part.	• *Show me _____.* • *What can you hear that might help?* • *Find the part that says* ow.
	The teacher divides the word with a finger.	• *Do you know a word like that?* • *Look at this part.*
MORE SUPPORT	The teacher writes the word or word part.	• *Take it apart like this. You know this part.* • *If we change this part, we can make the new word _____.* (rumble – stumble)

A goal of every guided reading lesson is to teach students how to use their newly acquired word study skills while they are reading and writing. Through explicit demonstrations and prompts, you can help your students take words apart and use analogies to monitor and self-correct.

Monitor Progress

It is important to monitor the progress students are making when learning letters, sounds, patterns, and words. The following formative assessments can help you determine when they are ready to tackle texts and skills at a higher level. The assessments can be administered during your guided reading lessons.

Guiding Questions	Assessment Tool	When to Administer
• Which sight words can students write? • Which words do they know partially that need to be reviewed during the Sight Word Review? • Which words should I teach next?	Sight Word Assessment (Appendix D, page 206) 	Every day. Have students write three familiar words from the sight word list. Record progress by checking off words the student writes without prompting.
• What skills are students using to notice errors (monitoring)? • What skills are they using to try to solve unknown words? • Are they applying the skills I have taught them?	Running Records 	During the familiar reading component of each Day 2 lesson. Take a short running record on one student.
• Which high frequency words can students spell correctly? • Which words do they partially know that need to be reviewed? • What sounds can they hear and record when writing unknown words? What sounds do I need to teach? • Are students applying the skills I have taught them?	Writing 	During the guided writing component of each Day 2 lesson. Take anecdotal notes on individual students.

Firm Up Knowledge During Independent Practice

During independent practice, students should be engaged in developmentally appropriate activities that help them practice the skills you have taught in guided reading. They should *always* reread the books they have read during guided reading. Reading familiar books will improve their fluency and help them internalize the decoding strategies you have taught them. Students should also be encouraged to write on their own. They could write about one of the books you read aloud during whole-class instruction, or they could write stories about personal experiences. If writing workshop is part of your literacy curriculum, students will be eager to write on their own while you teach other guided reading groups. Below are some other word study activities they could do during independent work time.

- **Digraph Board Game** Make a simple board game that has digraphs printed in the squares. Students each get a set of picture cards that begin with a digraph. (Do not print words on the picture cards.) When students roll the dice and land on a digraph, they give up a picture that begins with that digraph. The first student to end up with no cards wins the game. (This game also can also be done with blends.)

- **Word Building** Provide picture cards and magnetic letters. The students take a picture card and use the magnetic letters to make the word. This activity can be self-checking if you write the word on the back of the picture card. (For example, if you are working on digraphs you can use the following pictures: *ship*, *chip*, and *chin*.)

- **Adding Endings** Provide word cards with simple verbs such as *go*, *look*, *play*, and *jump*. Then provide ending cards such as *ed*, *ing*, and *s*. Have students write new words by adding an ending to one of the words.

- **Partner Analogy Charts** Prepare word cards with long and short vowels and attach them to a metal ring. Student A reads a word on the ring, and Student B selects the column—long vowel or short vowel—to fill in on the chart.

- **Partner Sound Boxes** Place a Sound Box template inside a plastic sleeve. Prepare 12 word cards with CCVC words on each one (e.g., *clip, snap, grab*). Place the cards on a large metal ring. Student A reads a word on the ring. Student B uses the Sound Box template to write the word. This game could also be done using CVCC and CCVCC words.

The Next Step Forward in Word Study and Phonics

Decades of research make clear that children grow the most when they read text that can be read with approximately 95 percent accuracy (Allington, 2006; Betts, 1946; Swanson & Hoskyn, 1998). What's more, Freddy Hiebert's (2008) research demonstrates that this boost is even stronger when children engage in repeated readings of the text. As Gretchen Owocki (2007) reminds us, "Consistent reading of 'too hard' text does little to support children's confidence or development" (p. 17).

SUPPORTING STRIVING READERS

In this section we discuss typical challenges in working with striving early readers and offer advice on overcoming them.

Challenge: Students are making the first sound of a blend and appealing for help at difficulty. Use your finger to show the student the initial blend or digraph. When the student comes to another word with an initial blend or digraph, ask the student to use his or her finger to show you the first part of that word.

Challenge: During guided writing, students misspell words you have taught. Encourage students to find the misspelled word and practice writing it correctly on the top of the journal. Provide a model if needed.

Challenge: Students are reading accurately but don't understand what they have read. Tell them to stop at the end of each page, cover the words and tell themselves what they have read. They can use the picture if they can't remember.

Challenge: Students are making slow progress and falling behind their classmates. Good first teaching starts in the classroom, but some children may need more intensive instruction. The RISE framework, which is described in *The Next Step Forward in Reading Intervention* (Richardson & Lewis, 2018), is an intensive, short-term, targeted intervention based on Jan's carefully scaffolded lesson plan. Each day students receive 45 to 60 minutes of comprehensive literacy instruction at four stations: Read a New Book, Word Study and Phonics, Reread Yesterday's Book, and Guided Writing. After only 6 to 8 weeks of intervention, students gain the confidence, proficiency, and skills they need to excel as readers and exit long-term intervention.

JAN RICHARDSON & ELLEN LEWIS

THE NEXT STEP FORWARD IN READING INTERVENTION

The RISE Framework

SCHOLASTIC

QUESTIONS TEACHERS ASK ABOUT EARLY WORD STUDY

I have students who stumble on some high frequency words I have already taught. Should I reteach the word using the sight word routines? Yes. Use all four steps in order on Day 1 and Day 2. Some high frequency words may need more than two days. Don't introduce a new word until students are able to write the previous word without support. Review tricky words at the beginning of the next several lessons. During reading if students struggle on a word you have taught them, ask them to write it on the table with their finger. Writing often triggers their memory of the word. During writing, if a student misspells a sight word you have taught, write it at the top of his or her journal and have the student practice writing it several times. Prompt him or her to write it quickly. Do not allow students to spell the word or segment each sound. You want them to learn the word as a complete unit. Send home some magnetic letters and a list of sight words you have taught. Ask the parent to say a word on the list for their child to make out of magnetic letters. The student should mix it and fix it.

I have some students who make errors but keep reading without correcting them.
Your students need to monitor their reading. Use prompts such as, "Were you right? Did it look right and make sense?" Direct them to look through the word. During your word study lessons, teach the word parts they have been ignoring.

I have students who are reading at Level F but don't know the digraphs.
Most students reading at text Level F already know digraphs and initial blends. If your students need to learn digraphs, use some of the lessons at Level D. Once they learn the digraphs and transfer that skill to reading and writing, teach the next skill they need to learn.

I have been using the guided reading sight words for spelling lessons. Is that enough? It's a great idea to use your guided reading sight words for weekly spelling assignments. We suggest that you assign spelling words by the students' guided reading group. That way the students can work on developmentally appropriate spelling words. You might also add a few words with the digraphs, blends, or vowel patterns you have taught in guided word study. See Appendix CC for an example of a weekly spelling program based on guided reading text levels.

Early

CHAPTER 6

Word Study for the Transitional Reader: Levels J–P

"As readers mature, they are able to recognize common letter patterns and have a store of known words they are able to read by sight. Therefore, instead of reading words sequentially in a letter-by-letter fashion, they recognize common letter chunks and, when reading unfamiliar words, blend chunks together."

—Janice F. Almasi and Susan King Fullerton (2012)

As the name suggests, transitional readers are making the transition from the early stage to the fluent stage. They quickly recognize a large bank of high frequency words and know many phonics elements, but they are still learning how to apply those skills to decode multisyllabic words. Instead of attempting to decode long words, some transitional readers will just mumble through them.

> ### Word Study Goals for Transitional Readers
>
> - Learn and use three-letter consonant clusters (*str-, spr-, thr-*)
> - Learn and use silent *e* and vowel patterns to read and write new words
> - Understand spelling changes when adding inflectional endings (*slam-slammed, happy-happily, country-countries*)
> - Sound the first part of the word and think about the story (*ter-rific*)
> - Break words at the onset, rime, and ending (*spr-int-ing*)
> - Break the word into syllables (*ten-ta-cles*)
> - Break the word at the affix (*im-polite*)
> - Break compound words (*water-proof*)
> - Use analogies (*boy-voyage*)
> - *Always* check for meaning

TEXT CONSIDERATIONS FOR TRANSITIONAL READERS

Texts for transitional readers contain complex sentence structures, unfamiliar content, and new vocabulary. They should provide plenty of opportunities to problem-solve new words, especially words with multiple syllables and complex vowel patterns. Most of those words will be in the students' listening vocabulary. Students should be able to gain an approximate pronunciation by following phonics rules, but they will need to check that pronunciation against the meaning of the word as it is used in the sentence. For example, a student might say, *The deer ran a great dis-tance* (short *a* as in *dance*). However, she should immediately recognize that her pronunciation is incorrect.

A World of Worms (Level K) by Michèle Dufresne is an example of a transitional text with complex vowel patterns (<u>ea</u>rth, <u>bu</u>ried), multisyllabic words to decode (*protect, quickly, earthworm*), and new vocabulary supported by the illustrations (*cocoons*) (see sample pages on the next page).

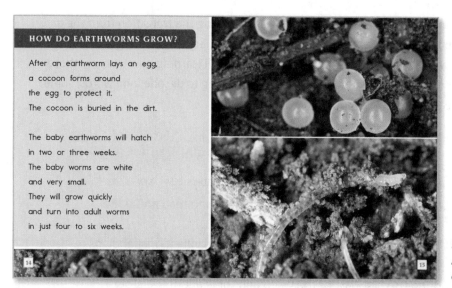

Pages from A World of Worms

Oki and the Polar Bear (Level N) by Michèle Dufresne is an example of a text that supports readers in the construction of meaning, but also challenges them to extend word-solving strategies (see sample pages at left). It contains new vocabulary (*lance, lumbered*) that requires students to use decoding strategies and contextual clues to solve the words. There are also multisyllabic words to decode (*delicious, continued*).

Pages from Oki and the Polar Bear

Working With Transitional English Learners

Inflectional endings appear more frequently in texts for transitional readers. Some English learners may drop the endings when they read because of language-related approximations. If it appears that a student is not looking through the word, say, "Look all the way to the end." Include words with inflectional endings in Breaking Words and Make a Big Word activities (pages 40 and 46).

THE ASSESS-DECIDE-GUIDE FRAMEWORK

Use this framework to plan and carry out instruction.

Assess: Determine your transitional readers' word study strengths and needs

Use formal assessments and daily observations during guided reading lessons to identify the skills your students know and those they need to learn. Let these questions guide your observations and assessments:

- Which sight words do my students misspell?
- Do they struggle to decode words with consonant clusters?
- Which vowel patterns do they mispronounce when reading?
- Do they break apart unfamiliar words while reading?
- When writing a multisyllabic word, do they listen for and record each syllable?
- Do they attempt the necessary spelling changes when adding inflectional endings?
- Do they use familiar word parts to decode compound words?
- Do they attend to prefixes and suffixes?
- Are they transferring the phonics skills they have learned to their reading and writing?

We recommend two assessments for this stage: Transitional Word Study Inventory (Appendix I) and Sight Word Assessment (Appendix D). The Transitional Word Study Inventory is appropriate for all transitional readers. The Sight Word Assessment is optional for students who still struggle to spell sight words correctly.

Transitional Assessments for Planning		
Assessment	**What it tells you**	**How to use it to plan lessons**
Transitional Word Study Inventory (J–P)	• The sounds the student can hear and record	• Decide which skills to teach next • Decide which word study activity to use • Expect students to apply the skills they know
Sight Word Assessment (optional)	• The sight words the student continues to misspell	• Identify words the students can't spell using the Sight Word Checklists for Levels G–I (Appendix E). Then teach those words during guided reading lessons. The procedures for teaching sight words are explained in Chapter 2, pages 27–30.

Transitional Word Study Inventory (Levels J–P)

Purpose: The Transitional Word Study Inventory (Appendix I) is a carefully designed list of words for students to write. The words are arranged to help you assess 56 target skills in six categories:

- Blends (initial and final)
- Vowel patterns (e.g., silent *e*, *ight*, *ai*, *oa*)
- *r*-controlled vowels (e.g., *ar*, *er*, *ir*, *or*, *ur*)
- Adding inflectional endings (e.g., *e* drop, doubling feature, change *y* to *i*)
- Prefixes (e.g., *over*, *un*, *dis*)
- Suffixes (e.g., *less*, *ness*, *ful*, *ment*, *ous*, *tion*, *ture*)

Directions: Give each student a blank sheet of paper. Then dictate the words as a spelling test. Say, "You don't know how to spell some of these words, but I want you to try. Think about other words you know that sound similar." Be sure students cannot see one another's papers.

Analyze and Reflect: On the Transitional Word Study Inventory, circle or highlight the words the students missed. Record your observations about individual students.

APPENDIX I

Transitional Word Study Inventory (Levels J–P)

Student: Kyle   Date: 5/2

Directions: Administer the inventory at the level students are reading and one level below. Give each student a blank sheet of paper. Then say, "You don't know how to spell some of these words, but I want you to try. Think about other words you know that sound similar."

Analyze and Reflect: Use this form to record observations about individual students or groups. Circle the skills students need to learn.

	Initial blend	Final blend/ digraph	Vowel feature	Inflectional ending/suffix	Prefix	Notes
strive	str		i_e			✔
gloating	gl		oa	ing		
slouch	sl	ch	ou			
scraped	scr		a-e	ed (t sound)		
dreamy	dr		ea	y		✔
squawk	squ		aw			
growled	gr		ow	ed (d sound)		
flew	fl		ew			ue for ew
slower	sl		ow	er		✔
twirl	tw		ir			
blurted	bl		ur	ed (ed sound)		✔
brightly	br		igh	ly		✔
splitting	spl			ing (doubling)		
quaking	qu			ing (e drop)		
bunnies				es (change y to i)		
stainless	st		ai	less		
darkness			ar	ness		
overweight			eigh		over	✔
unhelpful				ful	un	✔
payment			ay	ment		✔
fabulous				ous		
portion			or	tion		
dispute			u-e		dis	
moisture		st	oi	ture		

Word study needs: vowel patterns, doubling, change y to i and suffixes.

The Next Step Forward in Word Study and Phonics © 2019 by Jan Richardson & Michèle Dufresne, Scholastic Inc.   213

Appendix I, page 213

Level N/O   5-2 Kyle
1. Sttire   15. bunnys
2. gloating   16. Staihies
3. Slach   17. Qarknes
4. Scraches   18. overweight
5. Dreamy   19. unhelpful
6. Squke   20. Paymment
7. growed   21. falbeies
8. flue   22. Purshin
9. Slower   23. disbeit
10. thorl   24. musher
11. blurted
12. brightly
13. Splitting
14. Quvaking

You can also use the Transitional Word Study Inventory to summarize the word study needs of each guided reading group. Circle or highlight the skills at least one student in the group missed. If other students missed the same skill, put a tally mark on the inventory next to that skill. You will be able to identify quickly which skills most of the students need to learn.

APPENDIX I

Transitional Word Study Inventory (Levels J–P)

Student Group: Lyvia, Bralynn, Oscar, Sonia, Jamel, Ty   Date: 10/1

Directions: Administer the inventory at the level students are reading and one level below. Give each student a blank sheet of paper. Then say, "You don't know how to spell some of these words, but I want you to try. Think about other words you know that sound similar."

Analyze and Reflect: Use this form to record observations about individual students or groups. Circle the skills students need to learn.

	Initial blend	Final blend/ digraph	Vowel feature	Inflectional ending/suffix	Prefix	Notes
strive	(str) I		(i_e) I			
gloating	gl		(oa) IIII	ing		
slouch	sl	ch	(ou) II			
scraped	(scr) II		a-e	ed (t sound)		
dreamy	dr		ea	y		
squawk	(squ) HHI		(aw) I			Need qu + squ
growled	gr		ow	(ed (d sound)) I		
flew	fl		ew			
slower	sl		ow	er		
twirl	tw		(ir) II			
blurted	bl		(ur) II	ed (ed sound)		r-controlled vowels
brightly	br		(igh)	ly		
splitting	spl			(ing (doubling)) HHI		Adding inflectional
quaking	(qu) III			(ing (e drop)) HHI		endings — ALL
bunnies				(es (change y to i)) HHI		
stainless	st		(ai)	less		
darkness			ar	ness		
overweight			(eigh) II		over	
unhelpful				ful	un	
payment			(ay)	ment		
fabulous				(ous) III		Suffixes ous, tion, ture
portion			or	(tion) IIII		
dispute			u-e		dis	
moisture		st	(oi) I	(ture) IIII		

The Next Step Forward in Word Study and Phonics © 2019 by Jan Richardson & Michèle Dufresne, Scholastic Inc.   213

Transitional

Decide: Determine a skill focus and word study activity

Use information gained from the Transitional Word Study Inventory to plan the word study portion of your guided reading lesson. Choose the skill focus that your students need most.

Level	Skill Focus
J–K	• Silent *e* • Vowel patterns • *r*-controlled vowels • Inflectional endings with spelling changes • Compound words
L–M	• Vowel patterns • *r*-controlled vowels • Inflectional endings with spelling changes • Compound words • Prefixes • Suffixes
N–P	• Vowel patterns • Inflectional endings with spelling changes • Prefixes • Suffixes

Once you've chosen a skill focus, choose an activity: Breaking Words, Analogy Charts, Make a Big Word, or Writing Big Words. The following chart summarizes the purpose of each activity.

Activity	Purpose	Where to Find Teaching Guidelines
Breaking Words	• To attend to parts in words • To learn inflectional endings, prefixes, and suffixes	Chapter 2, page 40
Analogy Charts	• To notice patterns in known words in order to read and write unknown words	Chapter 2, page 43
Make a Big Word	• To see and hear syllable breaks • To learn inflectional endings, prefixes, and suffixes	Chapter 2, page 46
Writing Big Words	• To learn common vowel patterns, prefixes, and suffixes	Chapter 2, page 47

The following chart summarizes the skill focus and typical words taught for each activity.

Skill Focus	Breaking Big Words	Analogy Charts		Make a Big Word	Writing Big Words
• Vowel patterns • *r*-controlled vowels	*tr ain ing* *st ain ing* *spr ain ed*	**oil** toil spoil boiler	**rain** train sprain strainer	*container*	*exclaiming* *maintain* *painless*
Compound words	*over come* *over all*	N/A		*understand*	*underbrush* *keyboard*
Inflectional endings with spelling changes	*car ried* *mar ried* *un mar ried*	**cry** try puppy story	**cries** tries puppies stories	*countries*	*happiest* *silliest* *funniest*
Suffixes	*fr ight ful* *de light ful*	**care** hope power grace	**careful** hopeful powerful graceful	*wonderful*	*regretful* *pocketful* *masterful*
Prefixes	*dis charge* *dis ap prove*	**like** able obey prove	**dislike** disable disobey disprove	*discovered*	*dismay* *disdain* *disgust*

Guide: Teach word study in an integrated lesson framework

Word study should be part of a guided reading lesson that:

1. allows for developmental and explicit instruction not only in word study, but also in reading and writing.

2. invites students to use their newly acquired word study skills immediately, while they're engaged in reading and writing.

Transitional

LESSON WALK-THROUGH

The following transitional guided reading plan has been annotated to show how word study skills can be taught and practiced throughout a lesson. The plan is based on the book *The Little Red Fort* by Brenda Maier.

Pages from The Little Red Fort

① Book Introduction (Days 1 and 2)

Write the challenging words on an easel and underline the parts.

② Read With Prompting (Days 1 and 2)

Prompt students to take words apart when they get stuck (e.g., *How would you break that word? Is there a part you know?*).

③ Discussion Prompt

Encourage students to use the new vocabulary you introduced.

④ Follow-Up Teaching Points (Days 1 and 2)

Show students how to break apart big words (e.g., *ad – ven – ture*). Point out affixes.

⑤ Word Study (Day 2)

Have students write words that contain the affix you taught during the teaching point on Day 1.

⑥ Guided Writing (Day 3)

As students write about the story, prompt them to use the skills you have taught them.

Transitional Guided Reading Plan: *The Little Red Fort*

Transitional Guided Reading Plan (Levels J–P)

Students: Lyvia, Bralynn, Oscar, Sonia, Jamel, Ty	Date: 10/3-5	Title/Level: The Little Red Fort/ Level L
Word Study Focus	**Strategy Focus**	**Comprehension Focus**
Inflectional endings	Take words apart	Analyzing characters
Day 1	**Day 2**	**Day 3**

	Reading 12-15 minutes	**Writing** 20 minutes

6

1 **Introduce and Read a New Text**
Synopsis:
Ruby asks her brothers to help her build a fort, but they are too busy. Find out what happens when her fort is finished!

New vocabulary:
  clutched, satisfied

Model strategy (if necessary):
Cover the ending to take apart big words.

Continue Reading the Text
Reread and put a sticky note on a page that describes Ruby. Write a character trait for Ruby.

New vocabulary:
Introduce character trait words: lazy, fair, confident, helpful, positive, etc.

Writing Prompt
Write about Ruby and the kind of person she is. Use examples from the story.

Sentence stems for ELs:
Ruby is _____. For example,....

Provide choices if needed: smart, fair, confident

2 *Students read the book with prompting (use backside for recording observations and prompts)*

Plan With Key Words
Put a sticky flag on two pages that describe Ruby's character.

3 Discussion Prompts:
What does this story remind you of? How is Ruby like the Little Red Hen?

Discussion Prompts:
Which traits describe Ruby? Her brothers? Her parents? Who changed in this story? Why?

Write
Goals/Observations
Lyvia: Include periods.
Bralynn: Use word wall.
Oscar: Rehearse each sentence before writing.
Sonia: Clap big words.
Jamel: Capitalize first word in each sentence.
Ty: Use handwriting paper.

4 **Follow-Up Teaching Points** (choose 1 or 2 each day)
☐ Monitor for meaning ☐ Check middle (or end) ☒ Break words apart
☐ Reread and sound the first part ☐ Use analogies ☐ Use known parts
☒ Inflectional endings ☐ Use vocabulary strategies
☐ Read with phrasing, expression, and punctuation

Teaching Point for Day 1	**Teaching Point for Day 2**
Break words apart: com-plete, pre-tend-ed	Spelling change: y to i satisfy – satisfied supply - supplies

5 **Word Study Activity for Day 2** 3-5 minutes

☐ Breaking Words
☒ Analogy Charts
☐ Make a Big Word
☐ Writing Big Words

cry	cries
try	tries
supply	supplies
hurry	hurried

Teaching Point for Day 3
Reread your writing and point to each word with your eraser. Did you remember to use capital letters for names?

Next Steps	Text: Select a Level L-fiction with conversation	Goals: Reading: Fluency Word study: y to i Writing: Topic sentence	Students to Assess: Ty and Sonia

The Next Step Forward in Word Study and Phonics © 2019 by Jan Richardson & Michèle Dufresne, Scholastic Inc.

241

Transitional

See Appendix GG, page 241, for the lesson plan template.

APPENDIX GG

Teacher Notes and Observations for Transitional Readers (Levels J–P)

Monitoring and Word-Solving Prompts
☐ Does that make sense? Reread.
☐ Say the first part. Now say more.
  Think about the story.
☐ Check the middle (or end) of the word.
☐ Find a part you know.
☐ Show me the parts in that word.
☐ Do you know another word that looks like that?
☐ What can you try? How can you figure out
  that word?
☐ Can you say this part of the word?

Fluency and Comprehension Prompts
☐ Can you read it quickly?
☐ Read it like the character would say it.
☐ What did you read? What's happened so far?
☐ What have you learned?
☐ Why did the character do (or say) that?
☐ What was important on this page? Why?
☐ What caused _____? What was the effect of?
☐ How are _____ and _____ similar (or different)?

Anecdotal notes, running records, observations, and teaching points	Next Steps
Student: __Lyvia__ *Can you read it quickly? How would Ruby say that? Read the punctuation.* *"clutched" (meaning). Why did her brothers clutch their sides?*	☐ Monitor ☐ Word Solving ☒ Fluency ☐ Vocabulary ☐ Retell ☐ Other:
Student: __Bralynn__ *What happened at the beginning? What did Ruby say to her brothers?* *Who helped Ruby build her fort?*	☐ Monitor ☐ Word Solving ☐ Fluency ☐ Vocabulary ☒ Retell ☐ Other:
Student: __Oscar__ *Satisfied (appealed for help) T: Break the word. What does it mean?* * gather T: Run your finger under the word. Check the end.* *gathered*	☐ Monitor ☒ Word Solving ☐ Fluency ☐ Vocabulary ☐ Retell ☐ Other:
Student: __Sonia__ *what T: Are you right? Reread and make it make sense.* *when* *prevented T: Check the middle. What would look right and* *pretended make sense?*	☒ Monitor ☐ Word Solving ☐ Fluency ☐ Vocabulary ☐ Retell ☐ Other:
Student: __Jamel__ *"shrugged" I like how you broke that word apart. Do you know what the word means? Why did Ruby shrug?* *S: cr-ea-tion T: Does that sound right? Break the word like this: cre-a-tion. What was Ruby's creation? Why was it her creation?*	☐ Monitor ☐ Word Solving ☐ Fluency ☒ Vocabulary ☐ Retell ☐ Other:
Student: __Ty__ *Why didn't the boys help their sister?* *Why did Grandma help Ruby hammer the nails?* *Which characters changed in this story? What caused them to change?*	☐ Monitor ☐ Word Solving ☐ Fluency ☐ Vocabulary ☐ Retell ☒ Other: *Inferring*

242   *The Next Step Forward in Word Study and Phonics* © 2019 by Jan Richardson & Michèle Dufresne, Scholastic Inc.

Word Study Lessons

In this section, you'll find three series of lessons for the transitional stage—for Levels J–K, L–M, and N–P. Teach these lessons during the last three to five minutes of your guided reading lesson.

There is no need to teach every lesson at each level range. Choose the ones that best meet the needs of your students as identified by your assessments. Use the chart on this book's inside front cover to pinpoint specific lessons, based on your findings. We have grouped the lessons by skill focus so you can quickly find the ones that will benefit your students most. If your students need more lessons on a specific skill, use our model to plan another lesson. Most students should move up a text level every eight to nine weeks.

Levels J-K Word Study Lessons

These lessons teach silent *e*, vowel patterns (*ea*, *ai*, *ow*), *r*-controlled vowels, and inflectional endings with and without spelling changes. Adjust the lessons to meet the needs of your students.

Lesson	Skills	Activity	Directions
1	Silent *e*	Analogy Chart (2 columns)	Distribute the Analogy Charts, dry-erase markers, and erasers. Tell students to write *hop* and *hope* at the top of their chart. Underline the pattern in each word and discuss what the silent *e* does to the vowel sound. Dictate these words for students to write under the matching vowel sound.
2	Silent *e* Compound words	Make a Big Word	Students remove the following letters from their trays: a d e i r v w y Have them clap the word *driveway* and make it. Then have them break the word into parts (*drive-way*) and read it.

Within Lesson 1 Directions:

h**op**	h**o**p**e**
crop	drone
slob	grove
plot	those
broth	phone

Write the words *drove* and *flop* on the easel and have students read them.

| 3 | Silent *e* | **Analogy Chart** (2 columns) | Distribute the Analogy Charts, dry-erase markers, and erasers. Tell students to write *sick* and *side* at the top of their chart. Underline the pattern in each word and discuss what the silent *e* does to the vowel sound. Dictate these words for students to write under the matching vowel sound. |

<u>si**ck**</u>	<u>si**de**</u>
trick	pride
dock	stroke
snack	flame
speck	scribe

Write the words *crack* and *stripe* on the easel and have the students read them.

| 4 | Vowel pattern: *ea*

Inflectional endings | **Make a Big Word** | Students remove the following letters from their trays:

a c e g i k n r

Have them clap the word *creaking* and make it. Then have them break the word into parts (*creak-ing*) and read it. |

| 5 | Vowel pattern: *ea*

Inflectional endings | **Breaking Words** | Write *dreaming* on the easel and tell students to take the letters off their trays to make the word. Students break the word at the onset, rime, and ending (*dr-eam-ing*) and read it.

Tell students to change the *dr* to *str*. Students break and read the word *streaming*.

Write the word *screamer* on the easel. Students read the word. |

| 6 | Vowel pattern: *ea* and *ea*

Inflectional endings | **Analogy Chart** (2 columns) | Distribute the Analogy Charts, dry-erase markers, and erasers. Tell students to write *mean* and *head* at the top of their chart. Underline the pattern in each word and discuss the vowel sounds. Dictate these words for students to write under the matching vowel sound. |

m**ea**n	h**ea**d
steam	bread
cleaned	breath
preacher	spread
meaning	dread

Write the words *stream* and *bread* on the easel and have the students read them.

7	Vowel pattern: *ea* Inflectional endings	**Writing Big Words**	Distribute dry-erase boards, markers, and erasers. Write *head* on the easel and discuss the vowel sound. Dictate the following words for students to write. Have them underline the *ea* in each word: *threading, ahead, breaded.*
8	Vowel pattern: *ai* Inflectional endings	**Breaking Words**	Write *strained* on the easel and tell students to take the letters off their trays to make the word. Students break the word at the onset, rime, and ending (*str-ain-ed*) and read it. Tell them to remove the *s*. Students break and read the word *trained*. Write the word *draining* on the easel. Students read the word.
9	Vowel pattern: *ai* Inflectional endings	**Writing Big Words**	Distribute dry-erase boards, markers, and erasers. Write *rain* on the easel and discuss the vowel sound. Dictate the following words for students to write. Have them underline the *ai* in each word: *mermaid, reclaim, exclaimed.*
10	*r*-controlled vowels: *or* Inflectional endings	**Make a Big Word**	Students remove the following letters from their trays (extra *c*): c g h i n o r s Have them clap the word *scorching* and make it. Then have them break the word into parts (*scorch-ing*) and read it.
11	*r*-controlled vowels: *ir* and *or* Inflectional endings	**Analogy Charts** (2 columns)	Distribute the Analogy Charts, dry-erase markers, and erasers. Tell students to write *bird* and *corn* at the top of their chart. Underline the vowel pattern in each word and discuss the vowel sounds. Dictate these words for them to write under the matching vowel sound. See chart below.

b**ir**d	c**or**n
girl	worn
first	thorny
thirsty	snorted
squirted	scornful

Write the words *squirmy* and *sporting* on the easel and have the students read them.

12	*r*-controlled vowels: *ir*	**Breaking Words**	Write *flirting* on the easel and tell students to take the letters off their trays to make the word. Students break the word at the onset, rime, and ending (*fl-irt-ing*) and read it.
	Inflectional endings		Tell them to change the *fl* to *squ*. Students break and read the word *squirting*.
			Write the word *twirling* on the easel. Students read the word.

13	*r*-controlled vowels: *or*	**Make a Big Word**	Students remove the following letters from their trays (extra *t*):
			a i m n o p r t
			Have them clap the word *important* and make it. Then have them break the word into parts (*im-por-tant*) and read it.

14	*r*-controlled vowels: *ar* and *ur*	**Analogy Charts** (2 columns)	Distribute the Analogy Charts, dry-erase markers, and erasers. Tell students to write *car* and *fur* at the top of their chart. Underline the vowel pattern in each word and discuss the sounds. Dictate these words for students to write under the matching vowel sound. Have them underline the vowel pattern.
	Inflectional endings		

c<u>ar</u>	f<u>ur</u>
st<u>ar</u>ted	c<u>ur</u>ly
h<u>ar</u>mful	sp<u>ur</u>t
ch<u>ar</u>ming	ch<u>ur</u>ch
sm<u>ar</u>tly	h<u>ur</u>tful

Write the words *marching* and *murky* on the easel and have the students read them.

15	*r*-controlled vowels	**Make a Big Word**	Students remove the following letters from their trays (extra *r*):
			a b e g h m r u
			Have them clap the word *hamburger* and make it. Then have them break the word into parts (*ham-burg-er*) and read it.

16	Vowel pattern: *ow*	**Breaking Words**	Write *snowy* on the easel and tell students to take the letters off their trays to make the word. Students break the word at the onset, rime, and ending (*sn-ow-y*) and read it.
	Inflectional endings		Tell them to change the *sn* to *sh*. Students break and read the word *showy*.
			Write the word *growing* on the easel. Students read the word.

17	Vowel pattern: *ow* *r*-controlled vowels: *or* Compound words	**Writing Big Words**	Distribute dry-erase boards, markers, and erasers. Write *snow* on the easel and discuss the vowel sound. Dictate the following words for students to write. Have them underline the *ow* in each word: *blowtorch, overthrow, tomorrow.*
18	Inflectional endings with spelling changes: *e* drop	**Analogy Chart** (2 columns)	Distribute the Analogy Charts, dry-erase markers, and erasers. Tell students to write *bake* and *baking* at the top of their chart. Explain that you drop the silent *e* when you add an ending that begins with a vowel. Dictate these words for students to write under the matching pattern.

bake	baking
skate	skating
shake	shaking
scrape	scraping
graze	grazing

Write the words *hope* and *hoping* on the easel and have the students read them.

19	Inflectional endings with spelling changes: *e* drop	**Analogy Chart** (2 columns)	Distribute the Analogy Charts, dry-erase markers, and erasers. Tell students to write *joke* and *joked* at the top of their chart. Explain that you drop the silent *e* when you add an ending that begins with a vowel. Dictate these words for students to write under the matching pattern.

joke	joked
vote	voted
close	closed
slope	sloping
stroke	stroking

Write the words *smoke* and *smoky* on the easel and have the students read them.

Transitional

Levels L–M Word Study Lessons

These lessons teach vowel patterns (*aw, igh, ow, ew*), r-controlled vowels, inflectional endings with and without spelling changes, compound words, prefixes (*over, un*), and suffixes (*ship, ful, ly, ness, less, ous*). Adjust the lessons to meet the needs of your students.

Lesson	Skill Focus	Activity	Directions
20	Vowel pattern: *ow* Inflectional endings	Make a Big Word	Students remove the following letters from their trays (extra *l*): **e f l o p r u w y** Have them clap the word *powerfully* and make it. Then have them break the word into parts (*pow-er-ful-ly*) and read it.
21	Vowel pattern: *ow* Inflectional endings	Breaking Words	Write *growled* on the easel and tell students to take the letters off their trays to make the word. Students break the word at the onset, rime, and ending (*gr-owl-ed*) and read it. Tell students to change the *gr* to *pr*. Students break and read the word *prowled*. Write the word *scowling* on the easel. Students read the word.
22	Vowel pattern: *ow* Inflectional endings Compound words	Writing Big Words	Distribute dry-erase boards, markers, and erasers. Write *cow* on the easel and discuss the vowel sound. Dictate the following words for students to write. Have them underline the *ow* in each word: *uncrowded, crowned, downtown*.
23	Inflectional endings with spelling changes: *e* drop	Analogy Chart (2 columns)	Distribute the Analogy Charts, dry-erase markers, and erasers. Tell students to write *like* and *liking* at the top of their chart. Explain that you drop the silent *e* when you add an ending that begins with a vowel. Dictate these words for students to write under the matching pattern. | like	liking | |---|---| | close | closing | | prune | pruning | | shine | shining | | blame | blaming | Write the words *strive* and *striving* on the easel and have the students read them.

24	Inflectional endings with spelling changes: *e* drop	**Analogy Chart** (2 columns)	Distribute the Analogy Charts, dry-erase markers, and erasers. Tell students to write *love* and *loving* at the top of their chart. Explain that you drop the silent *e* when you add an ending that begins with a vowel. Dictate these words for students to write under the matching pattern.

love	loving
wide	wider
scale	scaling
scope	scoped
probe	probing

Write the words *slide* and *slider* on the easel and have the students read them.

25	Inflectional endings with spelling changes: *e* drop	**Analogy Chart** (2 columns)	Distribute the Analogy Charts, dry-erase markers, and erasers. Tell students to write *take* and *taking* at the top of their chart. Explain that you drop the silent *e* when you add an ending that begins with a vowel. Dictate these words for students to write under the matching pattern.

take	taking
choke	choked
strike	striking
smile	smiled
graze	grazer

Write the words *paste* and *pasting* on the easel and have the students read them.

26	*r*-controlled vowels: *ar* Suffix: *ship*	**Make a Big Word**	Students remove the following letters from their trays (extra *r* and *p*): a e h i n p r s t Have them clap the word *partnership* and make it. Then have them break the word into parts (*part-ner-ship*) and read it.

27	Vowel pattern: *ow* *r*-controlled vowels: *ar* Compound words	**Writing Big Words**	Distribute dry-erase boards, markers, and erasers. Write *car* on the easel and discuss the vowel sound. Dictate the following words for students to write. Have them underline the *ar* in each word: *graveyard, postcard, flowchart.*

Transitional

28	*r*-controlled vowels: *ar* Suffix: *ship* Compound words	**Breaking Words**	Write *hardship* on the easel and tell students to take the letters off their trays to make the word. Students break the word (*hard-ship*) and read it. Write the word *landmark* on the easel. Students read the word.
29	Vowel pattern: *ew* *r*-controlled vowels: *or* Compound words	**Make a Big Word**	Students remove the following letters from their trays (extra *c* and *r*): c e k o r s w Have them clap the word *corkscrew* and make it. Then have them break the word into parts (*cork-screw*) and read it.
30	Vowel pattern: *ew* Compound words	**Writing Big Words**	Distribute dry-erase boards, markers, and erasers. Write *new* on the easel and discuss the vowel sound. Dictate the following words for students to write. Have them underline the *ew* in each word: *newcomer, withdrew, screwball.*
31	Vowel pattern: *aw* Prefix: *un* Suffix: *ful*	**Make a Big Word**	Students remove the following letters from their trays (extra *l* and *u*): a f l n u w Have them clap the word *unlawful* and make it. Then have them break the word into parts (*un-law-ful*) and read it.
32	Vowel pattern: *aw* Inflectional endings	**Breaking Words**	Write *crawling* on the easel and tell students to take the letters off their trays to make the word. Students break the word at the onset, rime, and ending (*cr-awl-ing*) and read it. Tell students to change the *cr* to *spr*. Students break and read the word *sprawling.* Write the word *squawked* on the easel. Students read the word.
33	Vowel pattern: *igh* Suffix: *ly*	**Make a Big Word**	Students remove the following letters from their trays (extra *l*): i g h l s t y Have them clap the word *slightly* and make it. Then have them break the word into parts (*slight-ly*) and read it.

34	Vowel pattern: *igh* Suffixes: *ful* and *ness*	**Breaking Big Words**	Write *rightful* on the easel and tell students to take the letters off their trays to make the word. Students break the word at the onset, rime, and ending (*r-ight-ful*) and read it. Tell students to add an *f* to the beginning of the word. Students break and read the word *frightful*. Write the word *brightness* on the easel. Students read the word.
35	Inflectional endings with spelling changes: doubling	**Make a Big Word**	Students remove the following letters from their trays (extra *n* and *e*): **b e g i n r** Have them clap the word *beginner* and make it. Then have them break the word into parts (*be-gin-ner*) and read it.
36	Inflectional endings with spelling changes: doubling	**Analogy Chart** (2 columns)	Distribute the Analogy Charts, dry-erase markers, and erasers. Tell students to write *sum* and *summer* at the top of their chart. Explain that you double the last consonant in a CVC word when adding *er*, *ed*, or *ing*. <table><tr><th>sum</th><th>summer</th></tr><tr><td>run</td><td>runner</td></tr><tr><td>grin</td><td>grinning</td></tr><tr><td>splat</td><td>splatter</td></tr><tr><td>crop</td><td>cropped</td></tr></table> Write the words *slop* and *sloppy* on the easel and have the students read them.
37	Inflectional endings	**Breaking Big Words**	Write *shimmering* on the easel and tell students to take the letters off their trays to make the word. Students break the word at the onset, rime, and endings (*sh-im-mer-ing*) and read it. Tell them to change the *sh* to *gl*. Students break and read the word *gl-im-mer-ing*. Write the word *simmered* on the easel. Students read the word.
38	Suffix: *ous*	**Make a Big Word**	Students remove the following letters from their trays (extra *u*): **c i o r s u** Have them clap the word *curious* and make it. Then have them break the word into parts (*cur-i-ous*) and read it.

39	Suffix: *ous*	**Writing Big Words**	Distribute dry-erase boards, markers, and erasers. Write *ous* on the easel and discuss the sound it makes at the end of a word. Dictate the following words for students to write. Have them underline the *ous* in each word: *fabulous, joyous,* and *enormous*.
40	Suffix: *ous*	**Breaking Big Words**	Write *generous* on the easel and tell students to take the letters off their trays to make the word. Students break the word apart (*gen-er-ous*) and read it. Write the word *hazardous* on the easel. Students read the word.
41	Suffixes: *ly, ful, less, ness*	**Analogy Chart** (2 columns)	Distribute the Analogy Charts, dry-erase markers, and erasers. Tell students to write *love* and *lovely* at the top of their chart. Explain that you do NOT drop the silent *e* when adding an ending that begins with a consonant. <table><tr><td>**love**</td><td>**lovely**</td></tr><tr><td>joy</td><td>joyful</td></tr><tr><td>home</td><td>homely</td></tr><tr><td>bright</td><td>brightness</td></tr><tr><td>pain</td><td>painless</td></tr></table> Write the words *fright* and *frightful* on the easel and have the students read them.
42	Prefix: *over* Compound words	**Make a Big Word**	Students remove the following letters from their trays (extra *e* and *r*): c d e i o p r v Have them clap the word *overpriced* and make it. Then have them break the word into parts (*over-priced*) and read it.
43	Prefix: *over* Compound words	**Writing Big Words**	Distribute dry-erase boards, markers, and erasers. Write *over* on the easel. Dictate the following words for students to write. Have them underline the *over* in each word: *overspend, overcrowded, overboil*.

Levels N–P Word Study Lessons

These lessons teach inflectional endings with and without spelling changes, vowel patterns (*eigh*, *oi*), prefixes (*dis*, *com*, *pre*), and suffixes (*tion*, *ture*, *less*, *ment*). Adjust the lessons to meet the needs of your students.

Lesson	Skill Focus	Activity	Directions
44	Prefix: *dis* Suffix: *tion*	Make a Big Word	Students remove the following letters from their trays (extra *i* and *t*): **a c d i n o r s t** Have them clap the word *distraction* and make it. Then have them break the word into parts (*dis-trac-tion*) and read it.
45	Suffix: *tion*	Writing Big Words	Distribute dry-erase boards, markers, and erasers. Write *action* on the easel and discuss the sound for *tion*. Dictate the following words for students to write: *vacation*, *nation*, and *pollution*.
46	Prefix: *com* Suffix: *tion*	Breaking Big Words	Write *commotion* on the easel and tell students to take the letters off their trays to make the word. Students break the word apart (*com-mo-tion*) and read it. Write the word *completion* on the easel. Students read the word.
47	Prefix: *pre* Suffix: *tion*	Make a Big Word	Students remove the following letters from their trays (extra *e* and *n*): **e i o n p r t v** Have them clap the word *prevention* and make it. Then have them break the word into parts (*pre-ven-tion*) and read it.
48	Suffix: *ture*	Make a Big Word	Students remove the following letters from their trays (extra *r* and *u*): **e f i n r t u** Have them clap the word *furniture* and make it. Then have them break the word into parts (*fur-ni-ture*) and read it.
49	Suffix: *ture*	Writing Big Words	Distribute dry-erase boards, markers, and erasers. Write *picture* on the easel and discuss the sound for *ture*. Dictate the following words for students to write: *creature*, *adventure*, and *capture*.
50	Suffix: *ture*	Breaking Big Words	Write *moisture* on the easel and tell students to take the letters off their trays to make the word. Students break the word apart (*mois-ture*) and read it. Write the word *feature* on the easel. Students read the word.

51 | Vowel pattern: *eigh* | **Make a Big Word** | Students remove the following letters from their trays (extra *e* and *s*):

e g h i l s t w

Have them clap the word *weightless* and make it. Then have them break the word into parts (*weight-less*) and read it.

Suffix: *less*

---

52 | Suffix: *less* | **Breaking Big Words** | Write *aimless* on the easel and tell students to take the letters off their trays to make the word. Students break the word apart (*aim-less*) and read it.

Write the word *bottomless* on the easel. Students read the word.

---

53 | Inflectional endings without spelling changes and with: *e* drop | **Analogy Charts** (3 columns) | Distribute the 3-column Analogy Charts, dry-erase markers, and erasers. Have students copy the headings on the chart. Explain when you do and do not drop the silent *e*. Dictate the following words for students to write on their charts.

word	drop *e*	don't drop *e*
wide	wider	widely
tame	taming	tames
stroke	stroking	strokes
love	loved	lovely

Write the words *hoped* and *hopping* on the easel and have the students read them.

---

54 | Inflectional endings without spelling changes and with: *e* drop | **Analogy Charts** (3 columns) | Distribute the 3-column Analogy Charts, dry-erase markers, and erasers. Have students copy the headings on the chart. Explain when you do and do not drop the silent *e*. Dictate the following words for students to write on their charts.

word	drop *e*	don't drop *e*
shame	shaming	shameful
glide	glided	glides
hope	hoping	hopeless
shape	shaped	shapely

Write the words *taped* and *tapping* on the easel and have the students read them.

| 55 | Vowel pattern: *oi* Suffix: *ment* | **Make a Big Word** | Students remove the following letters from their trays (extra *n* and *t*):

e i n o t m

Have them clap the word *ointment* and make it. Then have them break the word into parts (*oint-ment*) and read it. |
| 56 | Suffix: *ment* | **Writing Big Words** | Distribute dry-erase boards, markers, and erasers. Write *moment* on the easel and discuss the sound for *ment*. Dictate the following words for students to write: *argument*, *ornament*, and *basement*. |
| 57 | Suffix: *ment* | **Breaking Big Words** | Write *amazement* on the easel and tell students to take the letters off their trays to make the word. Students break the word apart (*a-maze-ment*) and read it.

Write the word *amusement* on the easel. Students read the word. |
| 58 | Inflectional endings without spelling changes and with: doubling | **Analogy Charts** (3 columns) | Distribute the 3-column Analogy Charts, dry-erase markers, and erasers. Have students copy the headings on the chart. When adding an ending (*ed*, *ing*, *le*, *est*, *er*) to a word with a two-letter rime and a short vowel, you double the final consonant. Dictate the following words for students to write on their charts. |

word	double	don't double
spot	spotting	
train		training
grab	grabbed	
track		tracker

Write the words *slipping* and *sliding* on the easel and have the students read them.

Transitional

59	Inflectional endings with spelling changes: changing *y* to *i*	**Analogy Charts** (2 columns)	Distribute the 3-column Analogy Charts, dry-erase markers, and erasers. Tell students to write *baby* and *babies* at the top of their chart. Explain that you change the *y* to *i* when you add an ending that begins with a vowel. Dictate the following words for students to write on their charts.

baby	**babies**
happy	happily
hurry	hurries
marry	married
silly	silliest

Write the words *carry* and *carried* on the easel and have the students read them.

60	Inflectional endings with spelling changes: changing *y* to *i*	**Make a Big Word**	Students remove the following letters from their trays (extra *i* and *e*):

d e f i l n r s t

Have them clap the word *friendliest* and make it. Then have them break the word into parts (*friend-li-est*) and read it.

61	Prefix: *dis*	**Make a Big Word**	Students remove the following letters from their trays (extra *s*):

d e i h n o s t

Have them clap the word *dishonest* and make it. Then have them break the word into parts (*dis-hon-est*) and read it.

62	Prefix: *dis*	**Writing Big Words**	Distribute dry-erase boards, markers, and erasers. Write *dislike* on the easel and discuss the meaning of *dis*. Students write the following words and underline the prefix: *disagree, disappear, distrust*.

Discuss their meanings.

63	Prefix: *dis*	**Breaking Big Words**	Write *disgusted* on the easel and tell students to take the letters off their trays to make the word. Students break the word apart (*dis-gust-ed*) and read it.

Write the word *disappointed* on the easel. Students read the word.

Encourage Students to Apply Word Study Skills to Reading

Teaching students how to use word-solving skills to solve unknown words while they read is one of the most difficult parts of strategy instruction. Differentiate your support based on the assessed needs of each student. For example, if a student stumbles on the word *announce*, you might prompt, "What part do you know that might help?" The student will probably say *an* (a part he knows). Then you would cover *an* with your finger and prompt, "*Do you know a word that looks like this part?*" (*nounce* looks similar to *bounce*, a word he knows). Use the following prompts to guide students to apply word study skills as they read.

Word-Solving Goals and Prompts	
Word-Solving Goal	**Prompts for Strategic Action**
Use an analogy to solve unknown words	• *Do you know a word like that?* • *Do you know a word that starts with those letters?* • *Does this word (or word part) look like another word you know?*
Break apart multisyllabic words	• *Is there a part you know?* • *Cover the ending. What do you see that can help?* • *Use your finger to show me a part you know.* • *Sound the first part and think what would make sense.*
Use a variety of vocabulary strategies to understand the meaning of unknown words	• *Reread the sentence and look for clues.* • *Read on and think of what would make sense.* • *Use the picture or visualize.* • *Use a known part in the word.* • *Make a connection to other words you know.* • *Substitute a word that makes sense.* • *Use the glossary.*

Transitional

Monitor Progress

It is important to monitor the progress students are making. The following formative assessments can help you determine when they are ready to tackle texts and skills at a higher level. They can be administered during your guided reading lessons.

Guiding Questions	Assessment Tool	When to Administer
• What skills are students using to notice errors (monitoring)? • What skills are they using to try to solve unknown words? • Are they applying the skills I have taught them?	Running Records 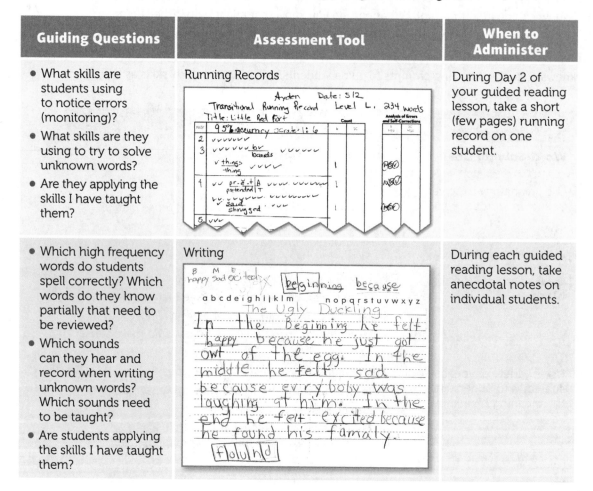	During Day 2 of your guided reading lesson, take a short (few pages) running record on one student.
• Which high frequency words do students spell correctly? Which words do they know partially that need to be reviewed? • Which sounds can they hear and record when writing unknown words? Which sounds need to be taught? • Are students applying the skills I have taught them?	Writing	During each guided reading lesson, take anecdotal notes on individual students.

Firm Up Knowledge During Independent Practice

Create a love for reading by knowing your students' reading interests. Each day students should read books they select themselves. While you are teaching guided reading, other students should read, write, or practice word study skills. Here are some activities to consider.

- **Roll, Read, and Write** Make a cube with six endings (e.g., *-ed, -ly, -er, -est, -y, -ing*). Prepare cards with root words that work with some of those endings (e.g., *slow, loud, short*). Select a word card and roll the dice. If the ending cannot be used with the root word, the student rolls the dice again until a workable ending appears. That student writes the word with the ending on a sheet of paper.

  This activity can also be used for spelling changes that occur when adding an ending, such as *e* drop (*coming*), doubling (*sloppy*), and changing the *y* to *i* (*happier*).

- **Breaking Words** After you have taught a prefix or suffix, write words containing that prefix or suffix on cards and place the cards in a plastic bag, along with magnetic letters for making those words. Students choose a card, make the word with magnetic letters, and break it apart. Then each student uses the word in a sentence.

- **Vowel Team Connect 4** Make a game board with six by six squares filled with vowel patterns (e.g., *ee*, *ea*, *oa*). Prepare two sets of 20 cards, in two different colors, with words that contain the vowel patterns on the board (e.g., *greeter*, *bleating*, *gloated*). In pairs, students take turns picking a word card, reading it, and placing it on the board's matching vowel pattern. The first player to get four cards in a row wins the game.

SUPPORTING STRIVING READERS

In this section we discuss typical challenges in working with striving transitional readers and offer advice on overcoming them.

Challenge: Students find it difficult to read multisyllabic words. Use your finger or a small strip of paper to show them a known part of the word. Then on another word, ask the students to use their finger to show you a part they know.

Challenge: Students find it difficult to spell multisyllabic words. Have them clap the word parts before they write a big word. As they write, they should say each part of the word to themselves.

Challenge: Students are reading accurately but aren't understanding what they read. It's not uncommon for students to proficiently decode words but not understand what they mean, especially as the texts increase in difficulty. Teach students to use strategies for determining word meanings. The most effective strategies are as follows:

- Reread (or read on) and look for clues.
- Use the picture or visualize.
- Use a known part.
- Make a connection.
- Substitute a word that makes sense.
- Use the glossary.

QUESTIONS TEACHERS ASK ABOUT TRANSITIONAL WORD STUDY

I have some students who still stumble on high frequency words. Should I add the sight word routines to my lesson? Yes. Some high frequency words may need more teaching. If students are misreading or stumbling on a high frequency word, reteach it. You may not need to do all four steps for teaching a sight word. Instead have the students get a good look at the tricky word in the book. Have them close their eyes and

"see" it in their head. Then ask them to write it. Review the word at the beginning of the next lesson and over the next several days. Also look for misspelled words in their writing. Teach those words using the sight word procedures described on pages 27–30. During guided writing, give students the High Frequency Word Wall (Appendix Y). It contains the most frequently misspelled words.

My school requires me to have a spelling program. Is there a way to use the skills I am teaching in word study in a spelling program? Yes! Assign words for each guided reading group based on the skill they are learning in word study. For example, if you are using the vowel patterns *ai* and *oa* in word study, give students six to ten spelling words that contain those patterns. You will find a list of words by pattern in Appendix X. For help on creating a small-group spelling program, see pages 11–12.

I have some students who make mistakes and keep reading without correcting them. This means your students are not monitoring (not noticing errors). Use prompts such as, "Were you right? Can you find the tricky word?" When they find their mistake, direct them to look more closely at the part they missed: "Check the ending [or middle]." You can incorporate the word parts they missed into your word study lessons.

The word study lessons in this chapter are too difficult for some of my students. What lessons should I use? We have suggested lessons that are appropriate for most transitional readers, but if these lessons are too difficult, use the early word study lessons in Chapter 5. Always use your assessments to identify the skills your students are ready to learn.

CHAPTER 7

Word Study for the Fluent Reader: Levels Q–Z

"As students mature as readers and writers, they learn vocabulary from written language that they have not heard in oral language."
—Donald Bear, Marcia Invernizzi, Shane Templeton, and Francine Johnston (2016)

Fluent readers recognize words automatically and can read aloud effortlessly. Because they have few decoding challenges, they are able to focus more of their attention on comprehension. At this stage, readers add polysyllabic words to their working vocabulary and begin to use the meanings of affixes to discern the meanings of unknown words.

The word study lessons in previous chapters focus primarily on phonemes (i.e., a unit of sound) and syllables. At the fluent stage, word study lessons focus on morphemes, the building blocks of English words. For example, the word *act* is one morpheme, but it has three phonemes (/a/ /c/ /t/). The word *reaction* contains three morphemes: the root *act*, the prefix *re-*, and the suffix *-ion*.

Studies show that, beginning at the third grade, approximately 60 percent of the words students read contain affixes (Nagy & Anderson, 1984). Some of the affix words are explicitly defined in the text or a glossary, but others require the reader to access background knowledge, make connections to known words, or search for implied meanings. Informational texts at this stage often contain technical words and specialized vocabulary. Even if students are able to decode the unfamiliar words, they may not understand what those words mean. As such, they will benefit from word study that focuses on learning the meanings of common word parts (i.e., affixes and roots) and how to use those parts to decode unknown words strategically and infer their meanings. That process is called morphological analysis.

Word Study Goals for Fluent Readers

- Break a polysyllabic word into syllables (*de – reg – u – late*) or morphemes (*de – regulate*).
- Recognize meaningful units that will help define words.
  - Identify an affix (*de* in *deregulate*).
  - Use the meaning of an affix to figure out the meaning of a word (*de* means *opposite* so *deregulate* means the opposite of *regulate*).
- Learn the meanings of common affixes.
- Make connections between words with similar morphemes (*deregulate, deconstruct, dehumanize*).
- Use morphological analysis and the context of the word/ sentence to determine meaning.
- Spell polysyllabic words by hearing and recording syllables and parts.

Scott, Skobel, and Wells (2008) remind us that "Words are not isolated units. They are multidimensional, with connections to other sets of both semantic and linguistic knowledge" (p. 8). As an example, they ask us to consider the word *erupt*; immediately, we may think of all the morphological connections such as *eruption, erupted*, and *rupture*. But it also calls to mind words such as *volcanoes* and *geysers*. In sum, as our students become more confident readers and encounter many more words through their wide reading, the more information they accrue about the words and the meaning the words represent. Nagy and Scott (2000) maintain that the more times we encounter a word, the more information we gather—creating a "word schema" for each concept.

TEXT CONSIDERATIONS FOR FLUENT READERS

Texts for fluent readers are more complex and more cognitively demanding in terms of vocabulary and comprehension. When selecting texts for fluent readers, look for articles or short stories that have challenging words to problem-solve. If students can't define those words using text features or strategies, discuss them with the students before they read.

Beneath the Ocean Waves (Level V) by Michèle Dufresne is an example of a text students might encounter at the fluent stage (see sample pages below). It contains several challenging words that may be unfamiliar, such as *nonthreatening* and *unsuspecting*. If students know how to break these words apart, and if they understand the meanings of the affixes *non-* and *un-*, they will be able to use the context and their word study skills to define the challenging words and understand the passage.

Pages from Beneath the Ocean Waves

THE ASSESS-DECIDE-GUIDE FRAMEWORK

Use this framework to plan and carry out instruction.

Assess: Determine your fluent readers' word study strengths and needs

Use formal assessments and daily observations during guided reading lessons to identify the skills your students know and those they need to learn. Let these questions guide your observations and assessments:

- Do students struggle to decode polysyllabic words?
- Can they break words at the affix and root?
- When writing a polysyllabic word, do they hear and record each syllable?
- Do they know the meanings of common affixes?
- Do they use context clues and affixes to infer the meanings of unfamiliar words?
- Do they make connections between words with similar roots or affixes?

Although most fluent readers are good spellers, some still struggle to spell words with complex vowel patterns and inflectional endings. If that describes your fluent readers, use the Transitional Word Study Inventory to identify phonics skills that need to be taught. Then teach the appropriate transitional word study lessons in Chapter 6. The word study lessons in this chapter, on pages 183–194, focus on affixes and how they affect the meanings of words.

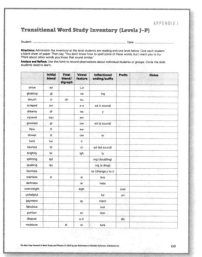

Appendix I, page 213

Fluent Word Study Inventory (Levels Q–Z)

Purpose: The Fluent Word Study Inventory assesses students' knowledge of 36 affixes, using the cloze technique. Each text level range (Q–R, S–T, U–V, W–X, Y–Z) assesses six affixes.

Directions: Have students read each sentence. Then have them think of what they know about the suffix, prefix, and root word to select the word that best fits in the blank.

Analyze and Reflect: We have found this assessment to be especially beneficial as a posttest after you teach the affix word study lessons.

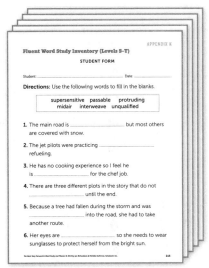

Appendices J–O, pages 214–219

Decide: Determine a skill focus and word study activity

The affixes listed in the chart below are appropriate for elementary students (Manyak, Baumann, & Manyak, 2018) and commonly appear in texts at Levels Q–Z. We have grouped them by text level range.

Skill Focus/Affix	Definition	Example
High Frequency Affixes		
Affixes for Levels Q–R		
-ist	person who	artist
-less	without	hopeless
-ment	result of an action	agreement
-tion	result of an action	information
-ous	full of	famous
post-	after, later	postgame
Affixes for Levels S–T		
-able	can be, able to be	reliable
mid-	middle	midyear
un-	not, opposite of	unknown
inter-	between or together	interaction
pro-	for, forward	proceed
super-	over, high, extreme	superstar

Fluent

Affixes for Levels U–V		
sub-	under, below	submarine
de-	remove, reverse	defrost
in-	not, opposite	inactive
under-	below, too little	underwater
re-	again, backwards	return
im-	not, opposite	impossible
Affixes for Levels W–X		
anti-	against	antifreeze
en-	to cause, to be	enlarge
auto-	self	autograph
fore-	before	foresee
counter-	against, opposite	counterattack
micro-	small	microchip
Affixes for Levels Y–Z		
ir-	not, opposite	irregular
-ity	state or condition of	activity
hyper-	over, exaggerated	hyperactive
mal-	evil, bad, wrong	maltreat
trans-	through, across, change	transformer
pre-	before	preschooler

When selecting an affix to teach, first look for one that appears in your current guided reading text. Although some students may already know the affix you choose, they may not be using their knowledge of it when encountering unfamiliar words. A second option is to choose an affix that students missed on the Fluent Word Study Inventory (Appendices J–O).

The ultimate goal of fluent word study lessons is to equip students to comprehend complex texts. Take a few minutes at the end of each guided reading lesson to do one of the following hands-on, engaging activities: Make an Affix Word, Write an Affix Word, or Read an Affix Word. They are designed to teach students to decode polysyllabic words, learn the meanings of commonly occurring affixes, and use strategies to infer the meanings of unfamiliar affix words.

Activity	Description	Example	Where to Find Teaching Guidelines
Make an Affix Word	Have students use magnetic letters to make a word that contains the target affix.	• *Take the following letters off your tray: b, e, i, l, n, o, p, r, s. I will give each of you an extra e, i, r, and s. Now make the word irresponsible.* • *Clap it and break it into syllables.* • *Now break it at the prefix, root, and suffix.*	Chapter 2, page 48
Write an Affix Word	Dictate one or two words that contain the target affix for students to write.	• *I'm going to say a word. I want you to say it in parts as you write it on your dry-erase boards. Write the word irregular. What does it mean? Who can use it in a sentence?*	Chapter 2, page 48
Read an Affix Word	Distribute word cards from scholastic.com/NSFWordStudy that contain the affix you taught on Day 1 and Day 2.	• Students take turns reading their word, defining it, and using it in a sentence.	Chapter 2, page 48

Guide: Teach word study in an integrated lesson framework

Word study should be part of a guided reading lesson that

1. allows for developmental and explicit instruction not only in word study, but also in reading and writing.

2. invites students to use their newly acquired word study skills immediately, while they're engaged in reading and writing.

Fluent

LESSON WALK-THROUGH

The following fluent guided reading plan has been annotated to show how affixes can be taught and practiced throughout a lesson. The plan is based on the book *When Marian Sang: The True Recital of Marian Anderson* by Pam Muñoz Ryan.

Pages from When Marian Sang

1 Book Introduction (Day 1)

Write the challenging words on an easel and underline the parts. Clarify any affixes and explain how they affect the meaning of the word.

2 Read With Prompting (Days 1 and 2)

Prompt students to use affixes and the context to infer the meanings of unfamiliar words.

3 Word Study (Day 1)

Have students write words that contain the affix you taught during the teaching point on Day 1.

4 New Word List (Day 2)

Discuss the meanings of two challenging words, and have students write those words in their reading notebooks. We call this section of the notebook the "New Word List."

5 Guided Writing (Day 3)

Encourage students to include the affix words in their writing. Guide them to use the index to find affix words.

Fluent Guided Reading Plan: *When Marian Sang*

Fluent Guided Reading Plan (Levels Q–Z)

Students: Elias, Mina Lucille, Ashley, Kaitlin	Date: 2/18–21	Title/Level: When Marian Sang/R
Word Study Focus	**Comprehension Focus**	
Take words apart Affix: pro-	Asking Questions: Literal and Inferential (Green Questions and Red Questions)	

Day 1	**Day 2** (and 3, if needed)	**Day 3**
Reading 12–15 minutes		**Writing** 20 minutes

① Introduce and Read a New Text

Synopsis: Learn how Marian Anderson, an exceptional singer, achieved her dreams despite racial discrimination.

New vocabulary:
terminal—train station
tuition—payment for school
Model strategy (if necessary):

Green Question (p. 1) What song did Marian and her sister sing?

Red Question (p. 2) Why was no one surprised that Marian loved to sing?

Continue Reading the Text

Write questions about key events and answer them.

Support students who need help asking or answering questions.

New vocabulary:

humiliation—embarrassment
opulent—rich
trepidation—fear

Writing Prompt

Who helped Marian achieve her dream (her church, her mother, Giuseppe Boghetti, and President Roosevelt)?

Use sticky flags to mark illustrations that provide evidence and details.

---

② *Students read the book with prompting (use back side for recording observations and prompts)*

Discussion Prompts:
Students take turns asking and answering each other's questions.
What challenges did Marian face?

Discussion Prompts:
What were the most important events in Marian's life?
Why does the author include the words to some songs? What inferences can you make about the lyrics?

Plan With Key Words

Write the names of three people who influenced Marian.

Write With Support
Goals/Observations
Elias—organization
Mina—reread for meaning
Lucille—transition words
Ashley—spelling
Kaitlin—add details

Follow-Up Teaching Points (choose 1 or 2 each day)
☒ Solve big words   ☐ Use vocabulary strategies   ☒ Affixes

Teaching Point for Day 1

Write "passionate" on the easel and model how to break it apart. Make connections (passion, compassion)

Teaching Point for Day 2

Write "professional" on the easel and explain the meaning of the prefix "pro-" (for). Generate a list of words with the affix "pro-."

---

③ Word Study Activity

Affix: ___pro-___

☐ Make an Affix Word
☒ Write an Affix Word
☐ Read an Affix Word

Dictate these words for students to write:
    protective, professional

④ New Word List

Word: ___passionate___

Definition: ___emotional___

Word: ___trepidation___

Definition: ___fear___

Teaching Point for Day 3

Find a place in your essay to add a direct quote from the book.

Model how to use quotation marks correctly.

Next Steps	Text: Biography	Goals: Identify V.I.P.s (Very Important Parts)	Students to Assess: Ashley

The Next Step Forward in Word Study and Phonics © 2019 by Jan Richardson & Michèle Dufresne, Scholastic Inc.   243

See Appendix HH, page 243, for the lesson plan template.

APPENDIX HH

Teacher Notes and Observations for Fluent Readers (Levels Q–Z)

Prompts
- ☐ What are you thinking? What are you noticing? Tell me more about that.
- ☐ Was there something you didn't understand? How can you help yourself?
- ☐ Is there a word you don't understand? Reread the sentence and substitute a word that makes sense.
- ☐ What is the main idea? What are the important details? Use your heading and illustration.
- ☐ What are the key words in this part? Use the words to summarize what you read.
- ☐ What questions can you ask yourself? What is a good green (red or yellow) question?
- ☐ What is similar (or different) about _____ and _____? What caused....? What was the effect of...?
- ☐ How is the character feeling? Why did the character say (or do) that?
- ☐ What traits best describe the character? Describe the relationship between _____ and _____.
- ☐ What inferences are you making? What conclusion can you draw?

Anecdotal notes, running records, observations, and teaching points	Next Steps/Strategy
Student: _____ Elias _____ Wrote a good literal (green) question. Needed support answering it. Missed the very important part of the story (V.I.P.).	Asking and answering green questions V.I.P.
Student: _____ Mina _____ Needed support with English structure. Asked and answered literal questions. Missed the important part of the story (V.I.P.).	Asking and answering inferential (red) questions V.I.P.
Student: _____ Lucille _____ Wrote good literal and inferential questions and was able to answer them. Missed the important part of the story (V.I.P.).	Asking and answering yellow questions V.I.P.
Student: _____ Ashley _____ Wrote good literal and inferential questions and was able to answer them. Has difficulty decoding big words. Guesses at the word using the first and last syllables. Sometimes substitutes a non-word.	Asking and answering yellow questions Break big words
Student: _____ Kaitlin _____ Wrote good literal and inferential questions and was able to answer them. Missed the important part of the story (V.I.P.).	Asking and answering yellow questions V.I.P.
Student: _____	

Word Study Lessons

On Day 1, spend the final three to five minutes of your guided reading lesson teaching an affix your students need to learn. You can design your own affix lessons using the word lists in Appendices Z–BB or select lessons from this section. We have grouped the lessons by text level ranges Q–R, S–T, U–V, W–X, and Y–Z. Although you should feel free to select a lesson from any set, we have arranged them by difficulty based on research and field testing with upper-elementary students. We've found that even if a student knows the meaning of a specific affix, he or she will benefit from these lessons, which go beyond having students memorize an affix. They guide students to use the affix to infer the meanings of unknown words.

There are three lessons for each affix. After you teach three affixes (i.e., nine lessons), teach a review lesson, which is also included. We have found that these lessons engage students and pique their interest in studying big words. For maximum impact, guide students to determine the meanings of challenging words that contain the target affix, and help them use those words in their writing and conversations.

Levels Q–R Word Study Lessons

Go to scholastic.com/NSFWordStudy for affix word cards.

Lesson	Skills	Activity	Directions
1	Suffix: *ist*	Make an Affix Word	Discuss the meaning of *ist* (person who). Give an example: *artist*. Students make the word *guitarist*. From there, they break the word by syllable and then by affix. Letters needed (extra *i* and *t*): **a g i r s t u**
2	Suffix: *ist*	Write an Affix Word	Review the meaning of *ist*. Dictate the following words for students to write: *alarmist, tourist*.
3	Suffix: *ist*	Read an Affix Word	Review the meaning of *ist*. Give an affix word card to each student to read, define, and use in a sentence: *nutritionist, motorist, terrorist, chemist, colonist, loyalist*.
4	Suffix: *less*	Make an Affix Word	Discuss the meaning of *less* (without). Give an example: *hopeless*. Students make the word *breathless*. From there, they break the word by syllable and then by affix. Letters needed (extra *e* and *s*): **a b e h l r s t**
5	Suffix: *less*	Write an Affix Word	Review the meaning of *less*. Dictate the following words for students to write: *senseless, worthless*.
6	Suffix: *less*	Read an Affix Word	Review the meaning of *less*. Give an affix word card to each student to read, define, and use in a sentence: *weightless, motionless, bottomless, emotionless, thoughtless, penniless*.

7	Suffix: *ment*	**Make an Affix Word**	Discuss the meaning of *ment* (result of an action). Give an example: *agreement*. Students make the word *argument*. From there, they break the word by syllable and then by affix. Letters needed:
			a e g m n r t u
8	Suffix: *ment*	**Write an Affix Word**	Review the meaning of *ment*. Dictate the following words for students to write: *amazement, amendment*.
9	Suffix: *ment*	**Read an Affix Word**	Review the meaning of *ment*. Give an affix word card to each student to read, define, and use in a sentence: *achievement, advancement, advertisement, announcement, replacement, discouragement*.
10	Affixes: *ist, less, ment*	**Review Lesson**	Give each student one affix word card that contains either *ist, less*, or *ment*. Have students draw or act out their word. Other students determine the affix word.
11	Suffix: *tion*	**Make an Affix Word**	Discuss the meaning of *tion* (result of an action). Give an example: *information*. Students make the word *exclamation*. From there, they break the word by syllable and then by affix. Letters needed (extra *a*):
			a c e i l m n o t x
12	Suffix: *tion*	**Write an Affix Word**	Review the meaning of *tion*. Dictate the following words for students to write: *expectation, cooperation*.
13	Suffix: *tion*	**Read an Affix Word**	Review the meaning of *tion*. Give an affix word card to each student to read, define, and use in a sentence: *extermination, declaration, destination, manipulation, installation, complication*.
14	Suffix: *ous*	**Make an Affix Word**	Discuss the meaning of *ous* (full of). Give an example: *famous*. Students make the word *glamorous*. From there, they break the word by syllable and then by affix. Letters needed (extra *o*):
			a g l m o r s u
15	Suffix: *ous*	**Write an Affix Word**	Review the meaning of *ous*. Dictate the following words for students to write: *hazardous, wondrous*.
16	Suffix: *ous*	**Read an Affix Word**	Review the meaning of *ous*. Give an affix word card to each student to read, define, and use in a sentence: *adventurous, miraculous, numerous, prosperous, mischievous, ridiculous*.

Lesson	Skills	Activity	Directions
17	Prefix: *post*	**Make an Affix Word**	Discuss the meaning of *post* (after or later). Give an example: *postgame*. Students make the word *postponed*. From there, they break the word by syllable and then by affix. Letters needed (extra *p* and *o*): d e n o p s t
18	Prefix: *post*	**Write an Affix Word**	Review the meaning of *post*. Dictate the following words for students to write: *posttreatment, postproduction*.
19	Prefix: *post*	**Read an Affix Word**	Review the meaning of *post*. Give an affix word card to each student to read, define, and use in a sentence: *postoperative, postponement, posthypnotic, postgraduate, postelection, posttraumatic.*
20	Affixes: *tion, ous, post*	**Review Lesson**	Give each student one affix word card that contains either *tion, ous,* or *post*. Have students work with a partner to use both words in one sentence.

Levels S–T Word Study Lessons
Go to scholastic.com/NSFWordStudy for affix word cards.

Lesson	Skills	Activity	Directions
21	Suffix: *able*	**Make an Affix Word**	Discuss the meaning of *able* (can be or able to be). Give an example: *reliable*. Students make the word *adorable*. From there, they break the word by syllable and then by affix. Letters needed (extra *a*): a b d e l o r
22	Suffix: *able*	**Write an Affix Word**	Review the meaning of *able*. Dictate the following words: *dependable, comfortable.*
23	Suffix: *able*	**Read an Affix Word**	Review the meaning of *able*. Give an affix word card to each student to read, define, and use in a sentence: *admirable, desirable, honorable, solvable, passable, comparable.*
24	Prefix: *mid*	**Make an Affix Word**	Discuss the meaning of *mid* (middle). Give an example: *midyear*. Students make the word *midpoint*. From there, they break the word by syllable and then by affix. Letters needed (extra *i*): d i m n o p t

Fluent

25	Prefix: *mid*	Write an Affix Word	Review the meaning of *mid*. Dictate the following words for students to write: *midwinter, midsection*.
26	Prefix: *mid*	Read an Affix Word	Review the meaning of *mid*. Give an affix word card to each student to read, define, and use in a sentence: *midstream, midrange, midair, midweek, midfielder, midsummer*.
27	Prefix: *un*	Make an Affix Word	Discuss the meaning of *un* (not, opposite). Give an example: *unfriendly*. Students use magnetic letters to make the word *ungracious*. From there, they break the word by syllable and then by affix. Letters needed (extra *u*): **a c g i n o r s u**
28	Prefix: *un*	Write an Affix Word	Review the meaning of *un*. Dictate the following words for students to write: *unfavorable, unpopulated*.
29	Prefix: *un*	Read an Affix Word	Review the meaning of *un*. Give an affix word card to each student to read, define, and use in a sentence: *unassuming, unqualified, unproductive, unfashionable, unacceptable, unexceptional*.
30	Affixes: *able, mid, un*	Review Lesson	Put six affix word cards faceup on the table. Give students a clue for one of the words—for example, *I'm thinking of a word that has five syllables and means "out of style."* Once other students guess the word, add another affix word card. Invite other students to play the role of the "thinker."
31	Prefix: *inter*	Make an Affix Word	Discuss the meaning of *inter* (between or together). Give an example: *interaction*. Students use magnetic letters to make the word *interrupt*. From there, they break the word by syllable and then by affix. Letters needed (extra *r* and *t*): **e i n p r t u**
32	Prefix: *inter*	Write an Affix Word	Review the meaning of *inter*. Dictate the following words for students to write: *interference, interception*.
33	Prefix: *inter*	Read an Affix Word	Review the meaning of *inter*. Give an affix word card to each student to read, define, and use in a sentence: *interweave, interchangeable, interconnection, international, intercoastal, interplanetary*.
34	Prefix: *pro*	Make an Affix Word	Discuss the meaning of *pro* (forward, for). Give an example: *proceed*. Students use magnetic letters to make the word *projector*. From there, they break the word by syllable and then by affix. Letters needed (extra *o* and *r*): **c e j o p r t**

35	Prefix: *pro*	**Write an Affix Word**	Review the meaning of *pro*. Dictate the following words for students to write: *protection, progressive*.
36	Prefix: *pro*	**Read an Affix Word**	Review the meaning of *pro*. Give an affix word card to each student to read and define, and use in a sentence: *prosecutor, promotion, projectile, protrusion, proactive, protagonist*.
37	Prefix: *super*	**Make an Affix Word**	Discuss the meaning of *super* (over, high, extreme). Give an example: *superstar*. Students use magnetic letters to make the word *supervision*. From there, they break the word by syllable and then by affix. Letters needed (extra *i* and *s*): e i n o p r s u v
38	Prefix: *super*	**Write an Affix Word**	Review the meaning of *super*. Dictate the following words for students to write: *supertanker, supersonic*.
39	Prefix: *super*	**Read an Affix Word**	Review the meaning of *super*. Give an affix word card to each student to read, define, and use in a sentence: *superhighway, supercharged, supernatural, supersaturated, supersensitive, superabundant*.
40	Affixes: *inter, post, super*	**Review Lesson**	Give each student one affix word card that contains *inter, pro*, or *super*. Have students work with a partner to draw or act out one of their words.

Levels U–V Word Study Lessons

Go to scholastic.com/NSFWordStudy for affix word cards.

Lesson	Skills	Activity	Directions
41	Prefix: *sub*	**Make an Affix Word**	Discuss the meaning of *sub* (under, below). Give an example: *submarine*. Students use magnetic letters to make the word *subtraction*. From there, they break the word by syllable and then by affix. Letters needed (extra *t*): a b c i n o s t r u
42	Prefix: *sub*	**Write an Affix Word**	Review the meaning of *sub*. Dictate the following words for students to write: *subcontractor, subdivision*.
43	Prefix: *sub*	**Read an Affix Word**	Give an affix word card to each student to read and define: *subconscious, subnormal, subpopulation, subtropical, sublease, substructure*.

Fluent

44	Prefix: *de*	**Make an Affix Word**	Discuss the meaning of *de* (remove or reverse). Give an example: *defrost*. Students use magnetic letters to make the word *destabilize*. From there, they break the word by syllable and then by affix. Letters needed (extra *i* and *e*):
			a b d e i l s t z
45	Prefix: *de*	**Write an Affix Word**	Review the meaning of *de*. Dictate the following words for students to write: *deportation, deactivate*.
46	Prefix: *de*	**Read an Affix Word**	Review the meaning of *de*. Give an affix word card to each student to read, define, and use in a sentence: *decriminalize, depersonalize, dehumanize, deconstruct, deregulate, dehydration*.
47	Prefix: *in*	**Make an Affix Word**	Discuss the meaning of *in* (not, opposite). Give an example: *inactive*. Students use magnetic letters to make the word *inexcusable*. From there, they break the word by syllable and then by affix. Letters needed (extra *e*):
			a b c e i l n s u x
48	Prefix: *in*	**Write an Affix Word**	Review the meaning of *in*. Dictate the following words for students to write: *invisible, incognito*.
49	Prefix: *in*	**Read an Affix Word**	Review the meaning of *in*. Give an affix word card to each student to read, define and use in a sentence: *inconspicuous, inedible, invalid, independent, intolerant, inexperienced*.
50	Affixes: *sub, de, in*	**Review Lesson**	Give each student one affix word card that contains *sub, de,* or *in*. Have students work with a partner to use both words in one sentence.
51	Prefix: *under*	**Make an Affix Word**	Discuss the meaning of *under* (below, too little). Give an example: *underwater*. Students use magnetic letters to make the word *underweight*. From there, they break the word by syllable and then by affix. Letters needed (extra *e*):
			d e g h i n r t u w
52	Prefix: *under*	**Write an Affix Word**	Review the meaning of *under*. Dictate the following words for students to write: *underhanded, underfunded*.

53	Prefix: *under*	**Read an Affix Word**	Review the meaning of *under*. Give an affix word card to each student to read, define, and use in a sentence: *undervalued, underprivileged, underachiever, underutilize, underestimated, undernourished.*
54	Prefix: *re*	**Make an Affix Word**	Discuss the meaning of *re* (again, backwards). Give an example: *return*. Students use magnetic letters to make the word *reclassify*. From there, they break the word by syllable and then by affix. Letters needed (extra *s*): a c e f i l r s y
55	Prefix: *re*	**Write an Affix Word**	Review the meaning of *re*. Dictate the following words for students to write: *rechargeable, rearrange.*
56	Prefix: *re*	**Read an Affix Word**	Review the meaning of *re*. Give an affix word card to each student to read, define, and use in a sentence: *reconfigure, redistribute, reinvestigate, rededicate, recondition, renegotiate.*
57	Prefix: *im*	**Make an Affix Word**	Discuss the meaning of *im* (not, opposite). Give an example: *impossible*. Students use magnetic letters to make the word *impatient*. From there, they break the word by syllable and then by affix. Letters needed (extra *i* and *t*): a e i m n p t
58	Prefix: *im*	**Write an Affix Word**	Review the meaning of *im*. Dictate the following words for students to write: *immature, immortal.*
59	Prefix: *im*	**Read an Affix Word**	Review the meaning of *im*. Give an affix word card to each student to read, define, and use in a sentence: *imbalanced, impartial, impenetrable, improper, imperfect, impractical.*
60	Affixes: *under, re, im*	**Review Lesson**	Put six affix word cards faceup on the table. Give students a clue for one of the words—for example, *I'm thinking of a word that has three syllables and describes a three-year-old child*. Once students guess the word, add another affix word card. Invite other students to play the role of the "thinker."

Fluent

Levels W–X Word Study Lessons

Go to scholastic.com/NSFWordStudy for affix word cards.

Lesson	Skills	Activity	Directions
61	Prefix: *anti*	**Make an Affix Word**	Discuss the meaning of *anti* (against). Give an example: *antifreeze*. Students use magnetic letters to make the word *antiwrinkle*. From there, they break the word by syllable and then by affix. Letters needed (extra *i* and *n*): a e i k l n r t w
62	Prefix: *anti*	**Write an Affix Word**	Review the meaning of *anti*. Dictate the following words for students to write: *antislavery, antibiotic*.
63	Prefix: *anti*	**Read an Affix Word**	Review the meaning of *anti*. Give an affix word card to each student to read, define, and use in a sentence: *antibacterial, antisocial, anticompetitive, anticorruption, antiperspirant, antidiscrimination*.
64	Prefix: *en*	**Make an Affix Word**	Discuss the meaning of *en* (to cause, to be). Give an example: *enlarge*. Students use magnetic letters to make the word *encourage*. From there, they break the word by syllable and then by affix. Letters needed (extra *e*): a c e g n o r u
65	Prefix: *en*	**Write an Affix Word**	Review the meaning of *en*. Dictate the following words for students to write: *encountering, endangerment*.
66	Prefix: *en*	**Read an Affix Word**	Review the meaning of *en*. Give an affix word card to each student to read, define, and use in a sentence: *enrichment, entangled, enlistment, enlighten, entitled, enchanting*.
67	Prefix: *auto*	**Make an Affix Word**	Discuss the meaning of *auto* (self). Give an example: *autograph*. Students use magnetic letters to make the word *automatic*. From there, they break the word by syllable and then by affix. Letters needed (extra *a* and *t*): a c i m o t u
68	Prefix: *auto*	**Write an Affix Word**	Review the meaning of *auto*. Dictate the following words for students to write: *automotive, autobiography*.
69	Prefix: *auto*	**Read an Affix Word**	Review the meaning of *auto*. Give an affix word card to each student to read, define, and use in a sentence: *autohypnosis, autopilot, autofocus, autonomous, automation, autocorrecting*.
70	Affixes: *anti, en, auto*	**Review Lesson**	Assign an affix to each student. Ask each student to think of a word with that affix and use it in a sentence.

71	Prefix: *fore*	Make an Affix Word	Discuss the meaning of *fore* (before). Give an example: *foresee*. Students use magnetic letters to make the word *forecaster*. From there, they break the word by syllable and then by affix. Letters needed (extra *e* and *r*):
			a c e f o r s t
72	Prefix: *fore*	Write an Affix Word	Review the meaning of *fore*. Dictate the following words for students to write: *foreshadowed, foreclosure*.
73	Prefix: *fore*	Read an Affix Word	Review the meaning of *fore*. Give an affix word card to each student to read, define, and use in a sentence: *foreground, forefathers, foreknowledge, forefront, forethought, foreseeable*.
74	Prefix: *counter*	Make an Affix Word	Discuss the meaning of *counter* (against or opposite). Give an example: *counterattack*. Students use magnetic letters to make the word *counterspies*. From there, they break the word by syllable and then by affix. Letters needed (extra *e* and *s*):
			c e i n o p r s t u
75	Prefix: *counter*	Write an Affix Word	Review the meaning of *counter*. Dictate the following words for students to write: *countersign, counteroffer*.
76	Prefix: *counter*	Read an Affix Word	Review the meaning of *counter*. Give an affix word card to each student to read, define, and use in a sentence: *counterterror, counterpunch, counterpart, counterassault, counterculture*.
77	Prefix: *micro*	Make an Affix Word	Discuss the meaning of *micro* (small). Give an example: *microchip*. Students use magnetic letters to make the word *microphone*. From there, they break the word by syllable and then by affix. Letters needed (extra *o*):
			c e h i m n o p r
78	Prefix: *micro*	Write an Affix Word	Review the meaning of *micro*. Dictate the following words for students to write: *microbiologist, microscopic*.
79	Prefix: *micro*	Read an Affix Word	Review the meaning of *micro*. Give an affix word card to each student to read, define, and use in a sentence: *microculture, micromanage, microcosmic, microreader, microfilm, microsurgery*.
80	Affixes: *fore, counter, micro*	Review Lesson	Place six affix word cards facedown on the table. Students take turns picking a card to read and define. As cards are read and defined, add more cards to the table.

Fluent

Levels Y–Z Word Study Lessons

Go to scholastic.com/NSFWordStudy for affix word cards.

Lesson	Skills	Activity	Directions
81	Prefix: *ir*	**Make an Affix Word**	Discuss the meaning of *ir* (not, without). Give an example: *irregular*. Students use magnetic letters to make the word *irresponsible*. From there, they break the word by syllable and then by affix. Letters needed (extra *e, i, r, s*): b e i l n o p r s
82	Prefix: *ir*	**Write an Affix Word**	Review the meaning of *ir*. Dictate the following words for students to write: *irreplaceable, irregular.*
83	Prefix: *ir*	**Read an Affix Word**	Review the meaning of *ir*. Give an affix word card to each student to read, define, and use in a sentence: *irretrievable, irreversible, irresistible, irredeemable, irreproachable, irremovable.*
84	Suffix: *ity*	**Make an Affix Word**	Discuss the meaning of *ity* (state or condition of). Give an example: *activity*. Students use magnetic letters to make the word *maturity*. From there, they break the word by syllable and then by affix. Letters needed (extra *t*): a i m r t u y
85	Suffix: *ity*	**Write an Affix Word**	Review the meaning of *ity*. Dictate the following words for students to write: *hostility, deformity.*
86	Suffix: *ity*	**Read an Affix Word**	Review the meaning of *ity*. Give an affix word card to each student to read, define, and use in a sentence: *regularity, immaturity, disability, similarity, tranquility, monstrosity.*
87	Prefix: *hyper*	**Make an Affix Word**	Discuss the meaning of *hyper* (over, exaggerated). Give an example: *hyperactive*. Students use magnetic letters to make the word *hypercautious*. From there, they break the word by syllable and then by affix. Letters needed (extra *u*): a c e h i o p r s t u y
88	Prefix: *hyper*	**Write an Affix Word**	Review the meaning of *hyper*. Dictate the following words for students to write: *hypersensitive, hyperextended.*

89	Prefix: *hyper*	**Read an Affix Word**	Review the meaning of the affix *hyper*. Give an affix word card to each student to read, define, and use in a sentence: *hyperefficient, hyperthermia, hyperinflated, hypercritical, hyperconscious, hyperaggressive*.
90	Affixes: *ir, ity, hyper*	**Review Lesson**	Give each student one affix word card that contains *ir, ity,* or *hyper*. Have students work with a partner to define their words and use them in a sentence.
91	Prefix: *mal*	**Make an Affix Word**	Discuss the meaning of *mal* (evil, bad, wrong). Give an example: *maltreat*. Students use magnetic letters to make the word *malformed*. From there, they break the word by syllable and then by affix. Letters needed (extra *m*): a d e f l m o r
92	Prefix: *mal*	**Write an Affix Word**	Review the meaning of *mal*. Dictate the following words to write: *maladjusted, malnutrition*.
93	Prefix: *mal*	**Read an Affix Word**	Review the meaning of *mal*. Give an affix word card to each student to read, define, and use in a sentence: *malfunction, malpractice, maldistribution, maltreatment, malodorous, malcontented*.
94	Prefix: *trans*	**Make an Affix Word**	Discuss the meaning of *trans* (through, across, change). Give an example: *transformer*. Students use magnetic letters to make the word *translucent*. From there, they break the word by syllable and then by affix. Letters needed (extra *n* and *t*): a c e l n r s t u
95	Prefix: *trans*	**Write an Affix Word**	Review the meaning of *trans*. Dictate the following words for students to write: *transcontinental, transformation*.
96	Prefix: *trans*	**Read an Affix Word**	Review the meaning of *trans*. Give an affix word card to each student to read, define, and use in a sentence: *transparent, transplanted, transmit, translator, transaction, transferring*.

Fluent

97	Prefix: *pre*	Make an Affix Word	Discuss the meaning of *pre* (before or prior to). Give an example: *preschooler*. Students use magnetic letters to make the word *prehistoric*. From there, they break the word by syllable and then by affix. Letters needed (extra *i* and *r*):
			c e h i o p r s t
98	Prefix: *pre*	Write an Affix Word	Review the meaning of *pre*. Dictate the following words for students to write: *preparation, premonition*.
99	Prefix: *pre*	Read an Affix Word	Review the meaning of *pre*. Give an affix word card to each student to read and define: *predestined, preadolescent, premeditated, precondition, predetermine, preoccupied*.
100	Affixes: *mal, trans, pre*	Review Lesson	Place six affix words faceup on the table. Students choose a word to read and define for the group.

Have Students Keep a New Word List

Have students create a section in their reading notebooks to record vocabulary they have learned. During Day 2 of the guided reading lesson, choose two challenging words from the text they are reading and discuss their meanings. Have students write the words on the New Word List at the back of their reading notebooks. Encourage them to use the new words as they discuss the text and write about it. Students can review these words with a partner during independent practice. Every week or two, test students on the words they learned most recently.

Monitor Progress

Use the Fluent Word Study Inventory (Appendices J–O) to monitor student progress. If you teach the lessons in sequence, use the sentences that correspond to each text level range. If you select the lessons based on your guided reading books, choose the sentences that contain the affixes you have taught. We recommend assessing students after you have taught about six affixes. Then decide if you need to reteach any of those affixes before you move to the next set of lessons. If you design your own affix lessons, create cloze sentences for each affix you teach. Again, assess the students after you have taught about six affixes.

Firm Up Knowledge During Independent Practice

While you work with a small group of students, the rest of the class should be engaged in reading independently, writing about the books they read, and discussing books in small groups. Students can also work with the affixes you have taught them. Here are some ideas for independent word study practice.

- **Affix Word Wall** Create a wall chart that lists the affixes you have taught, grouped by their meaning. For example, *im-*, *un-*, and *ir-* would be grouped together because they all mean *not*. Challenge students to find words in their independent reading book that include these affixes. They can write the words on a sticky note and post them under the correct affix. As you teach a new affix, add it to the chart.

Prefixes that mean "not"	Prefixes that show position	Prefixes that represent numbers	Suffixes that refer to a person
dis-, un-, im-, mis-	over-, super-, mid-, sub-, post-	uni-, bi-, tri-, mono-	-er, -or, -ist
disagree		unicycle	guitarist
misunderstand	postgame	monorail	inventor

- **Review Affix Words** Make a copy of the affix word cards at scholastic.com/NSFWordStudy that you have used in your lessons. Have students work with a partner to define the words and create sentences with them.

- **Build Affix Words** Create three sets of cards—one with suffixes written on the cards, one with prefixes written on them, and one with roots written on them. Use a different color for each set of cards to help students organize the cards. Students work with a partner to see how many combinations of prefixes, suffixes, and roots they can create that result in real words. Have them write the words they are able to make. Be sure they have access to a traditional or digital dictionary so they can check to see if they have created a real word.

- **Affix Word Hunt** Have students locate examples of affix words in various texts, including newspapers, advertisements, books, manuals, and brochures. Have them write down the words and group the ones that contain a common morpheme (affix or root). This will help students develop an awareness and understanding of morphemes.

- **Make and Break Affix Words** Give students magnetic letters and a list of affix words. Have them make a word on the list and break it in two ways:
  1. by syllable and read it (e.g., *un – be – liev – a – ble*).
  2. by affix and root and use it in a sentence (e.g., *un-believ-able*).

- **Word Trees** Draw a tree on chart paper and laminate it. Each week, use a dry-erase marker to write an affix or root at the bottom of the trunk. Have students write words that contain that affix or root on the branches.

- **Affix Charades** On individual index cards, copy 12 to 18 words that contain the affixes you have taught a guided reading group. Have students from that group work together. First, they lay six words faceup. Then they take turns drawing or acting out one of the affix words. They can use gestures and pictures, but no spoken words. The others guess the affix word. Once a word is guessed correctly, students remove that card and replace it with a new affix word.

- **Guess the Affix Word** Give students from the same guided reading group a set of affix word cards that contain affixes you have taught. After the dealer shuffles the cards, he or she places six of them faceup on the table. One student chooses a word secretly and says, "I'm thinking of a word that means . . . [definition]." Other students try to guess the word from the cards showing on the table. A variation of this game is for a student to think of a word and the other students to ask questions such as: How many syllables does it have? Does the prefix mean "not"? Is it a verb?

SUPPORTING STRIVING READERS

In this section we discuss typical challenges in working with striving fluent readers and offer advice on overcoming them.

Challenge: Students are having difficulty decoding multisyllabic words with prefixes and suffixes. Ask the student to show you the affix. If the student needs help, point to the suffix or prefix. Prompt the student to find a part he or she knows.

Challenge: Students do not understand what they have read. Ask, *What part is confusing you? Is there a word you don't know?* Help students use affixes and the context to define the challenging word.

Challenge: Students need to learn more vocabulary strategies. Using the affix and base word to determine the meanings of unfamiliar words is a great strategy for fluent readers, but it doesn't always work. Students need to apply a variety of vocabulary strategies when they come to an unknown word. As you confer, take every opportunity to teach the following strategies:

- Reread (or read on) and look for clues.
- Use the illustration.
- Use a known part.
- Make a connection to a word that looks similar.
- Substitute a word that makes sense.
- Use the glossary.

Challenge: Students are struggling to spell multisyllabic words. Have them clap the syllables and say each part as they write it.

Challenge: Students are struggling with vowel patterns. Administer the Transitional Word Study Inventory (Appendix I) to identify the skills they still need to learn. Then use the word study lessons that teach those skills.

QUESTIONS TEACHERS ASK ABOUT FLUENT WORD STUDY

Where should I begin? Begin with the first affix lesson for text Levels S–T, or choose a lesson that targets an affix found in the guided reading text. There are three short lessons for each affix. Teach each lesson on a separate day.

I have students who can read almost any word, but they don't understand what they are reading. How can I help them? Sometimes fluent readers glide along on their decoding skills but do not stop to think about the text or use strategies to make inferences. Ask them to stop after they read a page and tell you what they read. Be sure to cover the text with your hand to force them to use their own words to paraphrase. If a page is too much to paraphrase, have them stop after each paragraph. During your conferences, ask them to explain the meanings of important vocabulary words and use them as they paraphrase the passage. *The Next Step Forward in Guided Reading* (Richardson, 2016) contains 29 modules for teaching 12 primary comprehension strategies. Those modules can be taught during whole-class and small-group lessons.

How can I hold students accountable for remembering new vocabulary? Select a couple of words from each guided reading book to discuss and define with the group. After students practice using the new words in a sentence, they can record them in a section of their reading notebooks. Administer a vocabulary test on these words every week or two.

CLOSING REMARKS

Writing this book together has given us an amazing opportunity to explore, read, discuss, observe, and think about how students learn to make sense of the world of print. One of our final tasks in writing this book was picking the photograph for the cover. We love the one we chose because it reflects the joy and excitement your students will experience as they learn about how words work. Learning to read does not need to be drudgery. The biggest message we want to leave you with is that learning should be joyful. As you work with your students, we hope you discover the same pleasure and success we have experienced in our work with teaching children to be better readers. We also hope we have provided you with useful tools to support you in helping your students become joyful, engaged readers.

—Jan and Michèle

REFERENCES

Allington, R. (2006). *What really matters for struggling readers: Designing research-based programs*. Boston: Pearson.

Allington, R. (2011), What at-risk readers need. *Educational Leadership, 68*(6).

Almasi, J. F., & Fullerton, S. K. (2012). *Teaching strategic processes in reading (2nd ed.)*. New York: Guilford Press.

Ascenzi, L., & Espinosa, C. (in press). *Diversity in a balanced literacy classroom*. New York: Scholastic.

Bear, D. R., Invernizzi, M., Templeton, S., & Johnston, F. (2016). *Words their way: Word study for phonics, vocabulary, and spelling instruction (6th ed.)*. Boston: Pearson.

Betts, E. (1946). *Foundations of reading instruction, with emphasis on differentiated guidance*. New York: American.

Blevins, W. (2017). *Phonics from A to Z: A practical guide*. New York: Scholastic.

Clay, M. (1991). *Becoming literate: The construction of inner control*. Portsmouth, NH: Heinemann.

Clay, M. (2005). *Literacy lessons designed for individuals: Part two: teaching procedures*. Auckland: Heinemann.

Clay, M. (2016). *Literacy lessons designed for individuals (2nd ed.)*. Auckland: Heinemann.

Cunningham, A., & Zibulsky, Z. (2014). *Book smart: How to develop and support successful, motivated readers*. New York: Oxford University Press.

Doyle, M. A. (2018). Communicating the power of Reading Recovery and literacy lessons instruction for dyslexic learners: An ethical response. *The Journal of Reading Recovery, 17*(2), 35–50.

Dufresne, M. (2002). *Word solvers: Making sense of letters and sounds*. Portsmouth, NH: Heinemann.

Hiebert, E. (2008). *Reading more, reading better*. New York: Guilford Press.

Hurry, J., & Fridkin, L. (2018). The impact of Reading Recovery ten years after intervention London: UCL Institute of Education. Available at https://home.kpmg/content/dam/kpmg/uk/pdf/2018/12/the_impact_of_reading_recovery_ten_years_after_intervention_hurry_and_fridkin.pdf.

Manyak, P., Baumann, J., & Manyak, A. (2018). Morphological analysis instruction in the elementary grades: Which morphemes to teach and how to teach them. *The Reading Teacher, 72*(3), doi:10.1002/trtr.1713

Moustafa, M. (1996). *Beyond traditional phonics: Research discoveries and reading instruction*. Portsmouth, NH. Heinemann.

Myers, C. (1978). Reviewing the literature on Fernald's technique of remedial reading. *The Reading Teacher, 31*(March), 614–619.

Nagy, W., & Anderson, R. (1984). How many words are there in printed school English? *Reading Research Quarterly, 19*, 304–330.

Nagy, W., & Scott, J. (2000). Vocabulary processes. In M. L. Kamil, P. Mosenthal, P. D. Pearson, & R. Barr (Eds.), *Handbook of reading research, 3*, 269–284. Mahwah, NJ: Erlbaum.

National Institute of Child Health and Human Development. (2000). Report of the National Reading Panel. Teaching children to read: An evidence-based assessment of the scientific research literature on reading and its implications for reading instruction. (NIH Publication No. 00-4769). Washington, DC: U.S. Government Printing Office.

Owocki, G. (2007). *Literate days: Reading and writing with preschool and primary children*. Portsmouth, NH: Heinemann.

Pinnell, G. S., & Fountas, I. C. (2011). *Literacy beginnings: A prekindergarten handbook*. Portsmouth, NH: Heinemann.

Pinnell, G. S., & Fountas, I. C. (2017). *Guided reading: Responsive teaching across the grades (2nd ed.)*. Portsmouth, NH: Heinemann.

Rasinski, T., & Zutell, J. (2010). *Essential strategies for word study: Effective methods for improving decoding, spelling, and vocabulary*. New York: Scholastic.

Richardson, J. (2016). *The next step forward in guided reading: An assess-decide-guide framework for supporting every reader*. New York: Scholastic.

Richardson, J., & Lewis, E. (2018). *The next step forward in reading intervention: The RISE framework*. New York: Scholastic.

Scharer, P. (Ed.). (2018). *Responsive literacy: A comprehensive framework*. New York: Scholastic.

Scharer, P. (2019). Phonics and word study: What's the fuss? *Journal of Reading Recovery*, Spring.

Scott, J., Skobel, J., & Wells, J. (2008). *The word-conscious classroom: Building the vocabulary readers and writers Need*. New York: Scholastic.

Swanson, H. Lee; Hoskyn, M. (1998). Experimental intervention research on students with learning disabilities: A meta-analysis of treatment outcomes. *Review of Educational Research, 68*(3), 277–321.

Vygotsky, L. (1978). *Mind in society*. Cambridge, MA: Harvard University Press.

Zinke, S. (2016). *Rime magic: Phonics-powered prevention and intervention*. New York: Scholastic.

Children's Literature

Dufresne, M. (2011). *The lion and the mouse*. Northampton, MA: Pioneer Valley Books.

Dufresne, M. (2011). *The three pigs*. Northampton, MA: Pioneer Valley Books.

Dufresne, M. (2014). *Busy Clarence*. Northampton, MA: Pioneer Valley Books.

Dufresne, M. (2014). *We like sunglasses*. Northampton, MA: Pioneer Valley Books.

Dufresne, M. (2015). *Dinosaur to fossils*. Northampton, MA: Pioneer Valley Books.

Dufresne, M. (2015). *A world of worms*. Northampton, MA: Pioneer Valley Books.

Dufresne, M. (2016). *Oki and the polar bear*. Northampton, MA: Pioneer Valley Books.

Dufresne, M. (2019). *Busy dogs*. New York: Scholastic.

Dufresne, M. (2019). *Fun at the park*. New York: Scholastic.

Dufresne, M. (2019). *Looking for dinner*. New York: Scholastic.

Dufresne, M. (2019). *Playtime for Cookie and Scout*. New York: Scholastic.

Land, A. (2018). *Puffins*. New York: Scholastic.

Maier, B. (2018). *The little red fort*. New York: Scholastic.

Ryan, P. M. (2002). *When Marian sang: The true recital of Marian Anderson*. New York: Scholastic.

APPENDICES

All appendices can be downloaded from scholastic.com/NSFWordStudy.

Summary of Word Study Skills and Activities for Levels A–Z

Level	Reading Stage	Skill Focus	Picture Sorting	Making Words	Sound Boxes	Breaking Words	Analogy Charts
Pre-A		• Letter Names and Sounds	Sort pictures by their initial consonant.				
A	Emergent	• Initial Consonants • Long Vowels	Sort pictures by their initial consonant.	Change initial consonant: *can-man-pan-ran*	2 boxes: *me, go, no, he*		
B	Emergent	• Initial and Final Consonants • Short *a* and *o*	Sort pictures by their initial consonant or medial vowel.	Change final consonant: *hat-ham-had* Change initial and final consonant: *cat-can-fan-fat*	2 boxes: *at, on, am* 3 boxes: *hop, fan, mom, dad*		
C	Emergent	• All Short Vowels • CVC words	Sort pictures by their medial vowel.	Change initial, medial, and final letters: *bat-bit-big-jig-jog*	3 boxes (CVC): *pan, red, hit, hot, run*		
D	Early	• Digraphs • Onset-Rime	Sort pictures by their initial digraph.	Change initial, medial, and final letters, including digraphs. Break at onset and rime: *hop-shop-chop-chip-chin*	3 boxes (CCVC, CVCC): *this, cash, much*		
E	Early	• Initial Blends • Onset-Rime	Sort pictures by their initial blend.	Change initial, medial, and final letters, including initial blends. Break at onset and rime: *pam-spam-swam-slam-slap-flap-flop*	4 boxes (CCVC): *clam, grin, plum*	Break words with initial blends and digraphs: *sl ip, tr ip* Read: *grip*	
F	Early	• Final Blends • Onset-Rime		Change initial, medial, and final letters, including final blends. Break at onset and rime: *list-lisp-wisp-wimp-limp-lamp*	4 boxes (CVCC): *last, rent, pump, lint*	Break words with final blends and digraphs: *la st, pa st* Read: *cast*	
G	Early	• Initial and Final Blends • Silent *e* • Onset-Rime		Make words with blends and short vowels or silent *e*. Break at onset and rime: *fat-fate-gate-grate-grape-gripe*	5 boxes (CCVCC): *stunk, grasp, cramp*	Break words with blends and short vowels or silent *e*: *sn ake, fl ake* Read: *brake*	
H	Early	• Silent *e* • Vowel Patterns • Inflectional Endings		Make words with vowel patterns. Break at onset and rime: *down-drown-frown-crown-clown*		Break words with vowel patterns and inflectional endings: *gr owl ed, sc owl ed* Read: *prowler*	Write words with a short vowel and silent *e*. **sick** / **side** trick / pride slick / stride prick / slide
I	Early	• Silent *e* • Vowel Patterns • Inflectional Endings		Make words with vowel patterns. Break at onset and rime: *coat-coast-boast-boat-goat-gloat*		Break words with vowel patterns and inflectional endings: *gl oat ing, fl oat ing* Read: *bloated*	Write words with vowel patterns. Add inflectional endings. **oil** / **coal** broil / foal point / roam spoiler / throat moist / boasting

Summary of Word Study Skills and Activities for Levels A–Z

Level	Reading Stage	Skill Focus	Breaking Words	Analogy Charts	Make a Big Word	Writing Big Words	Work With Affix Words
J	Transitional	• Silent *e* • Vowel Patterns • *r*-controlled Vowels • Inflectional Endings	Break words with vowel pattern and inflectional ending: *dr eam ing* *str eam ing*. Read: *screamer*	Write words with vowel patterns. Add inflectional endings. **mean** / **head** steam / tread cleaned / breath preacher / spread	Make and break a multisyllabic word: *un-der-stand*	Write words with silent *e* or vowel pattern: *choke, joker, quake*	
K	Transitional	• Silent *e* • Vowel Patterns • *r*-controlled Vowels • Inflectional Endings With Spelling Changes • Compound Words	Break words with *r*-controlled vowel, or vowel pattern and inflectional ending: *st ain ed,* *spr ain ed* Read: *draining*	Write words with vowel patterns. Add inflectional endings. **bird** / **corn** girl / worn first / thorny thirsty / snorted squirted / scornful	Make and break a multisyllabic word: *e-norm-ous*	Write words with vowel patterns: *mermaid, reclaim, exclaimed*	
L	Transitional	• Vowel Patterns • *r*-controlled Vowels • Inflectional Endings With Spelling Changes • Compound Words	Break words with vowel patterns and inflectional endings: *h owl ed,* *pr owl ed* Read: *scowling*	Write words with vowel patterns. Add inflectional endings. **like** / **liking** close / closing prune / pruning shine / shining blame / blaming	Make and break a multisyllabic word: *pow-er-ful-ly*	Write words with vowel patterns: *uncrowded, crowned, downtown*	
M	Transitional	• Vowel Patterns • *r*-controlled Vowels • Inflectional Endings With Spelling Changes • Compound Words • Prefixes • Suffixes	Break words with inflectional endings: *sl imm er,* *gl imm er* Read: *simmering*	Write words with inflectional endings. **love** / **lovely** joy / joyful home / homeless bright / brightness gain / gainful	Make and break a multisyllabic word: *gen-er-ous*	Write words with suffixes: *fabulous, joyous, enormous*	
N	Transitional	• Vowel Patterns • Inflectional Endings With Spelling Changes • Prefixes • Suffixes	Break words with suffixes: *sta tion,* *crea tion* Read: *completion*	Write words with inflectional endings. **word** / **drop *e*** / **don't drop *e*** wide / wider / widely tame / taming / tames stroke / stroking / strokes love / loved / lovely	Make and break a multisyllabic word: *pre-ven-tion*	Write words with suffixes: *fraction, pollution, vacation*	
O	Transitional	• Vowel Patterns • Inflectional Endings With Spelling Changes • Prefixes • Suffixes	Break words with suffixes: *crea ture,* *fea ture* Read: *feature*	Write words with inflectional endings. **word** / **double** spot / spotting grab / grabbed trap / trapper skip / skipped	Make and break a multisyllabic word: *ad-ven-ture*	Write words with suffixes: *capture, torture, picture*	
P	Transitional	• Vowel Patterns • Inflectional Endings With Spelling Changes • Prefixes • Suffixes	Break words with suffixes: *pave ment,* *base ment* Read: *amusement*	Write words with inflectional endings. **baby** / **babies** happy / happily hurry / hurries marry / married silly / silliest	Make and break a multisyllabic word: *ar-gu-ment*	Write words with suffixes: *basement, ornament, ointment*	
Q–S	Fluent	• Early Affixes and Roots			Make and break a multisyllabic word: *mid-point*	Write words with affixes: *mid-midnight, midsection, midwinter*	Read and define words with affixes: *mid-midstream, midrange, midfielder*
T–V	Fluent	• Intermediate Affixes and Roots			Make and break a multisyllabic word: *pro-pos-al*	Write words with affixes: *pro-progressive, protagonist, produce*	Read and define words with affixes: *pro-protrude, prosecutor, promotion*
W–Z	Fluent	• Advanced Affixes and Roots			Make and break a multisyllabic word: *de-sta-bil-ize*	Write words with affixes: *de-deportation, deactivate, decentralize*	Read and define words with affixes: *de-decriminalize, dehumanize, deconstruct*

Letter Name/Sound Recognition Student Form

A	H	O	V
B	I	P	W
C	J	Q	X
D	K	R	Y
E	L	S	Z
F	M	T	
G	N	U	

a	h	o	v
b	i	p	w
c	j	q	x
d	k	r	y
e	l	s	z
f	m	t	
g	n	u	

Letter Name/Sound Teacher Recording Form

Directions: Place a check in the column if the student identifies the letter name or sound.

Student: _____ Date: _____

Letter	Letter Name	Letter	Letter Name	Letter Sound
A		a		
H		h		
O		o		
V		v		
B		b		
I		i		
P		p		
W		w		
C		c		
J		j		
Q		q		
X		x		
D		d		
K		k		
R		r		
Y		y		
E		e		
L		l		
S		s		
Z		z		
F		f		
M		m		
T		t		
G		g		
N		n		
U		u		

Letter-Name Score: _____ /52

Letter-Sound Score: _____ /26

Letter Name/Sound Checklist

Directions: Circle the letters and sounds each student knows.

Student: _____ Date: _____

Letters

A	B	C	D	E	F	G	H	I	J	K	L	M	N	O	P	Q	R	S	T	U	V	W	X	Y	Z
a	b	c	d	e	f	g	h	i	j	k	l	m	n	o	p	q	r	s	t	u	v	w	x	y	z

Sounds

a	b	c	d	e	f	g	h	i	j	k	l	m	n	o	p	q	r	s	t	u	v	w	x	y	z

Student: _____ Date: _____

Letters

A	B	C	D	E	F	G	H	I	J	K	L	M	N	O	P	Q	R	S	T	U	V	W	X	Y	Z
a	b	c	d	e	f	g	h	i	j	k	l	m	n	o	p	q	r	s	t	u	v	w	x	y	z

Sounds

a	b	c	d	e	f	g	h	i	j	k	l	m	n	o	p	q	r	s	t	u	v	w	x	y	z

Student: _____ Date: _____

Letters

A	B	C	D	E	F	G	H	I	J	K	L	M	N	O	P	Q	R	S	T	U	V	W	X	Y	Z
a	b	c	d	e	f	g	h	i	j	k	l	m	n	o	p	q	r	s	t	u	v	w	x	y	z

Sounds

a	b	c	d	e	f	g	h	i	j	k	l	m	n	o	p	q	r	s	t	u	v	w	x	y	z

Student: _____ Date: _____

Letters

A	B	C	D	E	F	G	H	I	J	K	L	M	N	O	P	Q	R	S	T	U	V	W	X	Y	Z
a	b	c	d	e	f	g	h	i	j	k	l	m	n	o	p	q	r	s	t	u	v	w	x	y	z

Sounds

a	b	c	d	e	f	g	h	i	j	k	l	m	n	o	p	q	r	s	t	u	v	w	x	y	z

Sight Word Assessment

Student: _____ Date: _____

Directions: Give each student a blank sheet of paper and pencil. Dictate the words at the level students are reading and one level below.

Analyze and Reflect: Use this form to record progress of individuals.

Level A	Level B	Level C	Level D	Level E	Level F	Level G	Level H	Level I
am	dad	and	day	all	came	don't	didn't	again
at	he	are	down	away	have	eat	does	because
can	in	come	into	back	help	from	every	could
go	it	for	looking	big	next	give	friend	knew
is	look	got	she	her	now	good	little	laugh
like	mom	here	they	over	one	make	know	night
me	my	not	went	this	some	of	many	very
see	on	play	where	want	then	out	new	walk
the	up	said	will	who	was	saw	were	who
to	we	you	your	with	what	why	when	would

Sight Word Checklists

Directions: Put a checkmark next to the word each time a student writes it without support.

Analyze and Reflect: Use this chart to record progress of guided reading groups.

SIGHT WORD CHECKLIST — LEVEL A						
	Student 1	Student 2	Student 3	Student 4	Student 5	Student 6
am						
at						
can						
go						
is						
like						
me						
see						
the						
to						

SIGHT WORD CHECKLIST — LEVEL B						
	Student 1	Student 2	Student 3	Student 4	Student 5	Student 6
dad						
he						
in						
it						
look						
mom						
my						
on						
up						
we						

SIGHT WORD CHECKLIST — LEVEL C						
	Student 1	Student 2	Student 3	Student 4	Student 5	Student 6
and						
are						
come						
for						
got						
here						
not						
play						
said						
you						

Sight Word Checklists *continued*

Directions: Put a checkmark next to the word each time a student writes it without support.

Analyze and Reflect: Use this chart to record progress of guided reading groups.

SIGHT WORD CHECKLIST — LEVEL D						
	Student 1	Student 2	Student 3	Student 4	Student 5	Student 6
day						
down						
into						
looking						
she						
they						
went						
where						
will						
your						

SIGHT WORD CHECKLIST — LEVEL E						
	Student 1	Student 2	Student 3	Student 4	Student 5	Student 6
all						
away						
back						
big						
her						
over						
this						
want						
who						
with						

SIGHT WORD CHECKLIST — LEVEL F						
	Student 1	Student 2	Student 3	Student 4	Student 5	Student 6
came						
have						
help						
next						
now						
one						
some						
then						
was						
what						

Sight Word Checklists *continued*

Directions: Put a checkmark next to the word each time a student writes it without support.

Analyze and Reflect: Use this chart to record progress of guided reading groups.

SIGHT WORD CHECKLIST — LEVEL G						
	Student 1	Student 2	Student 3	Student 4	Student 5	Student 6
don't						
eat						
from						
give						
good						
make						
of						
out						
saw						
why						

SIGHT WORD CHECKLIST — LEVEL H						
	Student 1	Student 2	Student 3	Student 4	Student 5	Student 6
didn't						
does						
every						
friend						
little						
know						
many						
new						
were						
when						

SIGHT WORD CHECKLIST — LEVEL I						
	Student 1	Student 2	Student 3	Student 4	Student 5	Student 6
again						
because						
could						
knew						
laugh						
night						
very						
walk						
who						
would						

209

Emergent Word Study Inventory (Levels A–C)

Student: _____

Directions: Give each student a blank sheet of paper and pencil. Then say, "I am going to say some words for you to write. If you don't know how to spell the word, say it slowly and write down the sounds you hear."

Analyze and Reflect: Record observations about individual students. Circle the sounds students need to learn. In the Reflection column, note strengths and needs, such as letter reversals, letter formation, and confusions.

a b c d e f g h i j k l m n o p q r s t u v w x y z

Level A: a b d f j m n p r s t v   Date: _____

Word	Beginning consonant	Medial vowel	End consonant	Reflection
bat	b	a	t	
jam	j	a	m	
rap	r	a	p	
sad	s	a	d	
fat	f	a	t	
van	v	a	n	

Level B: a b c g h l m o p t w x y z   Date: _____

Word	Beginning consonant	Medial vowel	End consonant	Reflection
wax	w	a	x	
hog	h	o	g	
yam	y	a	m	
cob	c	o	b	
zap	z	a	p	
lot	l	o	t	

Level C: a b c d e g h i k l m n o p r s u   Date: _____

Word	Beginning consonant	Medial vowel	End consonant	Reflection
run	r	u	n	
leg	l	e	g	
kid	k	i	d	
sob	s	o	b	
cap	c	a	p	
him	h	i	m	

Early Word Study Inventory (Levels D–F)

Student: _____

Directions: Administer the inventories at the level students are reading and one level below. Give each student a blank sheet of paper and pencil. Then say, "I am going to say some words for you to write. If you don't know how to spell the word, say it slowly and write the sounds you hear."

Analyze and Reflect: Record observations about individuals and groups. Circle the skills students need to learn. In the Reflection column, note strengths and needs, such as letter reversals, letter formation, and confusions.

Level D: initial and final digraphs; medial, short vowels

a e i o u   ch sh th   Date: _____

Word	Initial consonant/ digraph	Medial vowel	Final consonant/ digraph	Reflection
chug	ch	u	g	
shop	sh	o	p	
thud	th	u	d	
mesh	m	e	sh	
rich	r	i	ch	
bath	b	a	th	

Level E: Initial blends and digraphs; medial, short vowels

a e i o u   sh th cl cr fr gl pl sp   Date: _____

Word	Initial blend	Medial vowel	Final consonant/ digraph	Reflection
glad	gl	a	d	
spot	sp	o	t	
plush	pl	u	sh	
crib	cr	i	b	
cloth	cl	o	th	
fresh	fr	e	sh	

Level F: initial and final blends and digraphs; medial, short vowels

a e i o u   bl dr tr sw pr st nk ft nd pt nt mp   Date: _____

Word	Initial digraph/ blend	Medial vowel	Final blend	Reflection
blend	bl	e	nd	
draft	dr	a	ft	
trust	tr	u	st	
swept	sw	e	pt	
print	pr	i	nt	
stomp	st	o	mp	

Early Word Study Inventory (Levels G–I)

Student: _____ Date: _____

Directions: Administer the inventories at the level students are reading and one level below. Give each student a blank sheet of paper. Then say, "I am going to say some words for you to write. If you don't know how to spell the word, say it slowly and write the sounds you hear."

Analyze and Reflect: Record observations about individuals and groups. Circle the skills students need to learn. In the Reflection column, note strengths and needs, such as letter reversals, letter formation, and confusions.

Level G: initial and final blends, silent e, inflectional endings
br dr scr shr sl qu nk ck a-e i-e o-e u-e ing ed   Date: _____

Word	Initial blend	Vowel feature	Final blend/ digraph	Inflectional ending	Reflection
scrape	scr	a-e			
slope	sl	o-e			
brute	br	u-e			
drive	dr	i-e			
shrinking	shr		nk	ing	
quacked	qu		ck	ed	

Level H: blends, inflectional endings, simple vowel patterns
ch dr sc sp spr st all ar ay ee or ow er ed ing   Date: _____

Word	Blend/ digraph	vowel feature	Inflectional ending	Reflection
stall	st	all		
charter	ch	ar	er	
scorch	sc, ch	or		
drowned	dr	ow	ed	
speeding	sp	ee	ing	
spray	spr	ay		

Level I: blends, silent e, more complex vowel teams, inflectional endings (e.g., ai, ar, oi, oa, ou)   Date: _____

Word	Initial blend	vowel feature	Inflectional ending	Reflection
pointy		oi	y	
spout	sp	ou		
floated	fl	oa	ed	
skate	sk	a-e		
starting	st	ar	ing	
brainy	br	ai	y	

Transitional Word Study Inventory (Levels J–P)

Student: _____ Date: _____

Directions: Administer the inventories at the level students are reading and one level below. Give each student a blank sheet of paper. Then say, "You don't know how to spell some of these words, but I want you to try. Think about other words you know that sound similar."

Analyze and Reflect: Use this form to record observations about individual students or groups. Circle the skills students need to learn.

	Initial blend	Final blend/ digraph	Vowel feature	Inflectional ending/suffix	Prefix	Notes
strive	str		i_e			
gloating	gl		oa	ing		
slouch	sl	ch	ou			
scraped	scr		a-e	ed (*t* sound)		
dreamy	dr		ea	y		
squawk	squ		aw			
growled	gr		ow	ed (*d* sound)		
flew	fl		ew			
slower	sl		ow	er		
twirl	tw		ir			
blurted	bl		ur	ed (*ed* sound)		
brightly	br		igh	ly		
splitting	spl			ing (doubling)		
quaking	qu			ing (*e* drop)		
bunnies				es (change *y* to *i*)		
stainless	st		ai	less		
darkness			ar	ness		
overweight			eigh		over	
unhelpful				ful	un	
payment			ay	ment		
fabulous				ous		
portion			or	tion		
dispute			u-e		dis	
moisture		st	oi	ture		

The Next Step Forward in Word Study and Phonics © 2019 by Jan Richardson and Michèle Dufresne. Published by Scholastic Inc.

Fluent Word Study Inventory (Levels Q–R)

STUDENT FORM

Student: _____ Date: _____

Directions: Use the following words to fill in the blanks.

| victimless magnification postponed |
| thunderous allergist entanglement |

1. To look at the tiny parts of the insect, _____ is needed.

2. She was always sick in the spring when the pollen was heavy, so she went to an _____ to get help.

3. There was a _____ crash as the door was smashed in.

4. The soccer match was _____ to the following Saturday because of bad weather.

5. Many dolphins die each year from _____ in fishing nets.

6. The judge gave the thief a light sentence because no one was hurt and it was a _____ crime.

Fluent Word Study Inventory (Levels S–T)

STUDENT FORM

Student: _____ Date: _____

Directions: Use the following words to fill in the blanks.

| supersensitive passable protruding |
| midair interweave unqualified |

1. The main road is _____, but most others are covered with snow.

2. The jet pilots were practicing _____ refueling.

3. He has no cooking experience, so I feel he is _____ for the chef job.

4. There are three different plots in the story that do not _____ until the end.

5. Because a tree had fallen during the storm and was _____ into the road, she had to take another route.

6. Her eyes are _____, so she needs to wear sunglasses to protect herself from the bright sun.

Fluent Word Study Inventory (Levels U–V)

STUDENT FORM

Student: _____ Date: _____

Directions: Use the following words to fill in the blanks.

> impractical   intolerant   deregulate
> substandard   underachiever   redistribute

1. Patients at the local hospital often complain about _____ care.

2. A new law will _____ the strict rules against dumping chemicals into the rivers.

3. My teacher is very _____ of bad behaviors.

4. Billy should be getting better grades in school; he is an _____.

5. We are working to _____ the money to whom it belongs.

6. It is _____ and too expensive to fence in the whole yard.

Fluent Word Study Inventory (Levels W–X)

STUDENT FORM

Student: _____ Date: _____

Directions: Use the following words to fill in the blanks.

enlighten   forethought   automation
anticorruption   microsurgery   counterparts

1. The new governor is being praised for setting up

an _____ unit to look at wrongdoing

by government officials.

2. If you have a better explanation, please

_____ us.

3. The steelworkers have been driven into unemployment

by _____.

4. With a little _____, we can reduce

the amount of energy we waste each day.

5. The female swimmers did much better in the race

than their male _____.

6. _____ is required to repair the blood

vessels.

Fluent Word Study Inventory (Levels Y–Z)

STUDENT FORM

Student: _____ Date: _____

Directions: Use the following words to fill in the blanks.

transmit   hostility   malpractice   precondition
hypercritical   irreversible

1. The damage from pollution in the river is not

_____, but it may take years for the water

to be clean again.

2. The angry crowd was full of _____

because the concert was cancelled.

3. She grew up with _____ parents, so she

was often anxious.

4. The doctor is being accused of _____

because he did not diagnose her illness correctly.

5. Chicken pox is very easy to _____, so you

should avoid contact with people who have it.

6. They had a _____ of a ceasefire before

they would begin peace talks.

Fluent Word Study Inventory

ANSWER KEY

Levels Q–R

To look at the tiny parts of the insect, magnification is needed.

She was always sick in the spring when the pollen was heavy, so she went to an allergist to get help.

There was a thunderous crash as the door was smashed in.

The soccer match was postponed to the following Saturday because of bad weather.

Many dolphins die each year from entanglement in fishing nets.

The judge gave the thief a light sentence because no one was hurt and it was a victimless crime.

Levels S–T

The main road is passable, but most others are covered with snow.

The jet pilots were practicing midair refueling.

He has no cooking experience, so I feel he is unqualified for the chef job.

There are three different plots in the story that do not interweave until the end.

Because a tree had fallen during the storm and was protruding into the road, she had to take another route.

Her eyes are supersensitive, so she needs to wear sunglasses to protect herself from the bright sun.

Levels U–V

Patients at the local hospital often complain about substandard care.

A new law will deregulate the strict rules against dumping chemicals into the rivers.

My teacher is very intolerant of bad behaviors.

Billy should be getting better grades in school; he is an underachiever.

We are working to redistribute the money to whom it belongs.

It is impractical and too expensive to fence in the whole yard.

Levels W–X

The new governor is being praised for setting up an anticorruption unit to look at wrongdoing by government officials.

If you have a better explanation, please enlighten us.

The steelworkers have been driven into unemployment by automation.

With a little forethought, we can reduce the amount of energy we waste each day.

The female swimmers did much better in the race than their male counterparts.

Microsurgery is required to repair the blood vessels.

Levels Y–Z

The damage from pollution in the river is not irreversible, but it may take years for the water to be clean again.

The angry crowd was full of hostility because the concert was cancelled.

She grew up with hypercritical parents, so she was often anxious.

The doctor is being accused of malpractice because he did not diagnose her illness correctly.

Chicken pox is very easy to transmit, so you should avoid contact with people who have it.

They had a precondition of a ceasefire before they would begin peace talks.

APPENDIX P
Alphabet Chart

A a	B b	C c	D d	E e
F f	G g	H h	I i	J j
K k	L l	M m	N n	O o
P p	Q q	R r	S s	T t
U u	V v	W w	X x	Y y
Z z				

Verbal Directions for Teaching Letter Formation

Uppercase Letters	
A	Slant down, slant down, across
B	Down, up, around, around
C	Around like a c
D	Down, up, around
E	Down, across, across, across
F	Down, across, across
G	Around, up, in
H	Down, down, across
I	Down, across, across
J	Down, hook, across
K	Down, slant in, slant out
L	Down, across
M	Down, down, up, down
N	Down, down, up
O	Around like a c, close
P	Down, up, around
Q	Around like a c, close, slant down
R	Down, up, around, slant down
S	Around like a snake
T	Down, across
U	Down, around, up
V	Slant down, slant up
W	Slant down, up, down, up
X	Slant down, slant down
Y	Slant in, slant in, down
Z	Across, slant down, across

Lowercase Letters	
a	Around like a c, close, down
b	Down, up, around
c	Around like a c
d	Around like a c, up, down
e	Across, up, around
f	Around, down, across
g	Around like a c, down, hook left
h	Down, hump
i	Down, dot
j	Down, hook left, dot
k	Down, slant in, slant out
l	Start at the top, down
m	Down, hump, hump
n	Down, hump
o	Around like a c, close
p	Down, up, around
q	Around like a c, down, hook right
r	Down, up, over
s	Around like a snake
t	Down, across
u	Down, around, up, down
v	Slant down, up
w	Slant down, up, down, up
x	Slant down, slant down
y	Slant in, down
z	Across, slant down, across

Sound Box Template for Emergent Readers

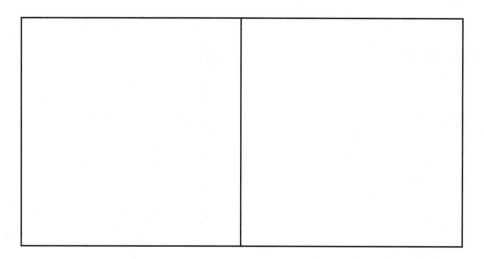

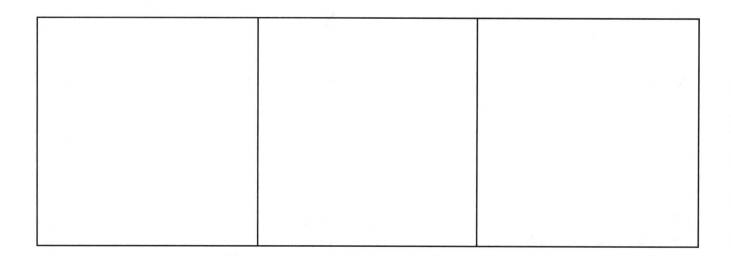

Word Lists for Emergent Readers

CVC words for Making Words and Sound Boxes	
Short *a*	
ab	cab, dab, jab, lab, nab, tab
ad	bad, dad, fad, had, lad, mad, pad, sad
ag	bag, gag, hag, jag, lag, nag, rag, sag, tag, wag
am	ham, jam, ram, yam
an	ban, can, fan, man, pan, ran, tan, van
at	bat, cat, fat, hat, mat, pat, rat, sat, tat, vat
ax	fax, tax, wax
Short *e*	
ed	bed, fed, led, red, wed
eg	beg, keg, leg, Meg, peg
em	gem, hem
en	den, hen, men, pen, ten, yen
et	bet, get, jet, let, met, net, pet, set, wet, yet
Short *i*	
ib	bib, fib, jib, rib
id	bid, did, kid, lid, rid
ig	big, dig, fig, gig, jig, pig, rig, wig
im	dim, him, rim, vim
in	bin, din, fin, gin, kin, pin, sin, tin, win
ip	dip, hip, lip, nip, rip, sip, tip, zip
it	bit, fit, hit, kit, lit, pit, sit
Short *o*	
ob	cob, gob, job, lob, mob, rob, sob
og	bog, cog, dog, fog, hog, jog, log
op	bop, cop, hop, mop, pop, top
ot	cot, dot, got, hot, jot, lot, not, pot, rot, tot
ox	box, fox, lox
Short *u*	
ub	cub, dub, hub, nub, rub, sub, tub
ud	bud, cud, dud, mud
ug	bug, dug, hug, jug, lug, mug, pug, rug, tug
un	bun, fun, nun, pun, run, sun
ut	but, cut, gut, hut, jut, nut, rut

Sound Box Template for Early Readers

Analogy Chart for Early Readers

Word Lists for Digraphs and Blends

Words for Making Words and Sound Boxes		
Digraphs (Level D Word Study)		
ch	chat, chin chip, chop, chug, much, such	
sh	cash, dash, mash, wish, dish, fish, ship, shop, shot, shed, rush, hush, shut	
th	that, than, this, then, thin, them, thud, path, math, bath, with	
Blends		
	Initial Blends	**Initial and Final Blends/Digraphs**
bl	blob, blot	black, bland, blank, blend, blink, blush
br	Brad, brag, bran, brat	brand, branch, brick, broth, brush
cl	clam, clap, clip, club	clasp, clang, clank, clamp
cr	crib, crop	crash, clash, crust, crank, crisp, crunch, crush
dr	drag, drip, drop, drum	drank, drink, draft, drift
fl	flag, flip, flop, flap, flat	flank, flunk, flash, flush
fr	frog, frap, fret, friz	fresh, frost
gl	glad, glum, glop	gland, glint
gr	grab, grin, grip	grand, grasp, grump, grunt
pl	plan, plop, plot, plug, plum, plus	plank, plant, plump
pr	prim, prom	print, prick
qu	quit, quip	quest, quack, quick
sc	scab, scum, scat, scan	scant, scamp, scrimp, script
sk	skid, skin, skip	skunk
sl	slam, slap, slip, slit, sled, slid, slim, slot	sling, slump, slung, slush
sm	smog	smash, smack
sn	snap, snug	snack, snuck
sp	spat, spot, spin, sped, spit, spun	spend, spent, splint
st	stab, stem, step, stop, stud	stamp, stand, stick, stink, stomp, stump, stung, stunt
sw	swam, swim, swum	swept, swift,
tr	trap, trim, trot	trash, trunk, trust
tw	twig, twin	twist
scr	scrub, scram	scrunch, script
shr	shrug, shred, shrub	shrink, shrunk, shrimp, shrank
str	strap, strip	strand, strong
squ	squid	squint, squish
spl	split, splat	splash
spr	sprig	spring, sprint, sprung
thr	throb	thrift, thrust
Final Blends/Digraphs		
-ck	back, sack, pack, quack, smack, black, crack, shack, snack, track, tack, stack, deck, peck, neck, check, speck, kick, lick, pick, quick, sick, tick, brick, click, slick, flick, stick, thick, trick, dock, lock, rock, sock block, duck, shock, clock, flock, stock, buck, duck, luck, puck, suck, cluck, stuck, pluck, truck, struck	
-ct	act, duct, fact, pact, strict, tact, tract	
-nd	and, band, bend, hand, send, pond, sand, send	
-lt	belt, felt, knelt, melt, quilt, tilt, welt, wilt	
-mp	bump, camp, damp, chomp, jump shrimp, slump stomp	
-ft	craft, gift, left, lift, raft, shift, soft, swift	
-nch	bench, branch, bunch, crunch, inch, lunch, pinch, punch	
-st	cost, dust, fast, lost, nest, past, pest, rest, test	
-nt	ant, bent, dent, plant, went, tent	
-nk	bank, blank, blink, chunk, drank, honk, sunk, think, trunk, plunk	
-sp	clasp, crisp, gasp, grasp, lisp, wisp	
-pt	crept, kept, script, slept, swept, wept	
-sk	ask, brisk, disk, desk, dusk, mask, risk, task	

Analogy Charts for Transitional Readers

Word Lists for Vowel Patterns

Note: Use bold words as the key words for analogy charts.

	Silent e
-ace	**face,** lace, mace, pace, race, brace, grace, place, space, trace
-ade	**made,** bade, fade, jade, wade, blade, glade, grade, shade, spade, trade
-age	**age,** cage, page, rage, wage, stage
-ake	**make,** bake, cake, fake, lake, quake, rake, take, wake, brake, flake, shake, shake, stake
-ame	**came,** fame, game, lame, name, same, tame, blame, flame, frame, shame
-ane	**cane,** lane, mane, pane, sane, vane, crane, plane
-ape	**cape,** gape, nape, tape, grape, scrape, shape
-ate	**ate,** date, fate, gate, hate, late, mate, rate, crate, grate, plate, skate, state
-ave	**gave,** cave, pave, rave, save, wave, brave, crave, grave, shave, slave
-ice	**ice,** dice, lice, mice, nice, rice, vice, price, slice, spice, twice, thrice
-ide	**hide,** ride, side, tide, wide, bride, glide, pride, slide, snide, stride
-ike	**like,** bike, dike, hike, pike, spike, strike
-ile	**smile,** mile, pile, tile, while
-ime	**time,** dime, lime, mime, chime, crime, grime, prime, slime
-ine	**nine,** dine, fine, line, mine, pine, vine, wine, shine, shrine, spine, swine, whine
-ipe	**wipe,** pipe, ripe, gripe, snipe, stripe, swipe, tripe
-ite	**bite,** kite, mite, quite, rite, site, white, write, sprite
-ive	**five,** dive, hive, jive, live, chive, drive, strive, thrive
-oke	**joke,** poke, woke, yoke, broke, choke, smoke, spoke, stoke, stroke
-ole	**hole,** mole, pole, role, stole, whole
-one	**bone,** cone, hone, lone, tone, zone, clone, crone, drone, phone, prone, shone, stone
-ope	**hope,** mope, nope, pope, rope, grope, scope, slope
-ose	**nose,** hose, pose, rose, chose, those
-ote	**note,** vote, quote, wrote
-ube	**cube,** rube, tube
-ule	**rule,** mule, yule
-une	**June,** tune, prune
-ute	**cute,** mute, brute, flute

Word Lists for Vowel Patterns *continued*

Note: Use bold words as the key words for Analogy Charts.

	Vowel Patterns
-ai	**rain,** aid, laid, maid, paid, raid, braid, lain, main, pain, brain, chain, drain, gain, grain, plain, slain, Spain, sprain, stain, strain, train, faint, paint, saint, quaint
-all	**all,** ball, call, fall, hall, mall, tall, wall, small, squall, stall
-ay	**day,** bay, hay, jay, lay, may, pay, say, way, clay, ray, gray, play, pray, slay, spray, stay, stray, sway, tray
-ar	**car,** bar, far, jar, mar, par, tar, char, scar, spar, star, arm, farm, harm, charm, yard, card, hard, bark, dark, hark, lark, mark, park, shark, spark, stark, barn, yarn, carp, harp, sharp, cart, dart, part, tart, chart, smart, start
-are	**care,** bare, dare, hare, mare, pare, rare, flare, glare, scare, share, snare, spare, square
-au	**because,** caught, cause, fault, haul, haunt, launch, sauce, taught
-aw	**paw,** caw, gnaw, jaw, law, raw, saw, claw, draw, flaw, slaw, straw, bawl, crawl, shawl, dawn, fawn, lawn, yawn, drawn
-ea	**eat,** pea, sea, tea, flea, plea, beach, each, leach, peach, reach, teach, bleach, breach, preach, beak, leak, peak, weak, creak, freak, sneak, speak, squeak, streak, tweak, deal, heal, meal, real, seal, really, zeal, squeal, steal, beam, seam, cream, dream, gleam, scream, steam, stream, team, bean, lean, mean, clean, glean, heap, leap, reap, cheap, beat, feat, heat, meat, neat, seat, cheat, cleat, pleat, treat, wheat
-ee	**bee,** fee, knee, lee, see, tee, wee, flee, free, glee, tree, beech, leech, breech, screech, speech, deed, feed, heed, kneed, need, reed, seed, weed, bleed, breed, freed, greed, speed, steed, tweed, leek, meek, peek, reek, seek, week, cheek, creek, Greek, sleek, feel, heel, keel, kneel, peel, reel, creel, steel, wheel, keen, queen, seen, teen, green, preen, screen, sheen, beep, deep, jeep, keep, peep, seep, weep, cheep, creep, sheep, sleep, steep, sweep, beet, feet, meet, fleet, greet, sheet, sleet, street, sweet, tweet
-eigh	**eight,** neigh, weigh, sleigh, weight, neighbor, freight, eighty, weightless
-ew	**new,** dew, few, hew, knew, pew, blew, brew, chew, crew, drew, flew, screw, stew, threw
-igh	**light,** high, sigh, thigh, knight, might, night, right, sight, tight, blight, bright, flight, fright, plight, slight
-ir	**bird,** fir, sir, stir, whir, third, quirk, shirk, smirk, dirt, flirt, shirt, skirt, squirt, girl, twirl, birth, squirm
-ire	**fire,** hire, tire, wire, spire, squire
-oa	**boat,** coach, poach, roach, load, road, toad, soak, cloak, croak, coal, foal, goal, foam, roam, loan, moan, groan, boast, coast, roast, toast, boat, coat, goat, moat, oat, bloat, gloat, float, throat
-oi	**oil,** boil, coil, foil, soil, toil, spoil, broil, coin, join, loin, joint, ointment, point, hoist, moist
-oo	**zoo,** boo, coo, goo, moo, too, shoo, goof, roof, proof, spoof, cool, fool, pool, tool, drool, school, spool, stool, boom, doom, loom, room, zoom, bloom, broom, gloom, groom, loon, moon, noon, soon, croon, spoon, swoon, hoop, loop, droop, scoop, snoop, stoop, swoop, boot, hoot. loot, moot, root, toot, scoot, shoot, booth, smooth, tooth, food, mood
-oo	**look,** cook, hook, book, nook, took, brook, crook, shook good, hood, wood, stood
-or	**for,** porch, torch, scorch, cord, ford, lord, chord, sword, cork, fork, pork, stork, dorm, form, norm, storm, born, corn, horn, morn, torn, worn, scorn, shorn, sworn, thorn, fort, port, sort, short, snort, sport
-ore	**more,** bore, core, fore, gore, pore, sore, tore, wore, chore, score, shore, snore, spore, store, swore
-ou	**out,** about, pout, scout, shout, snout, spout, sprout, stout, trout, house, mouse, blouse, grouse, spouse, mouth, south
-our	**our,** hour, sour, flour, scour
-ow	**cow,** how, bow, now, sow, vow, brow, chow, plow, fowl, howl, jowl, growl, prowl, scowl, down, gown, town, brown, clown, crown, drown
-ow	**snow,** bow, know, mow, low, row, sow, tow, blow, crow, flow, glow, grow, show, slow, known, sown, blown, flown, grown, shown, thrown
-oy	**boy,** coy, joy, Roy, soy, toy, ploy, enjoy, destroy, annoy, joyful, loyal, oyster royal, voyage
-ue	**blue,** cue, due, hue, clue, glue, true
-ur	**fur,** blur, slur, spur, burn, turn, churn, hurt, blurt, spurt, burl, curl, furl, hurl

High Frequency Word Wall

A	B	C	D	E
about · animals afraid · another after · around again · asked always	beautiful · believe because · between before · bought beginning	called · coming care · could caught · course children · cried	decided · doesn't didn't · don't different · dropped does	even ever every excited exciting

F	G	H	I	J
favorite first found friend frightened from	getting girl give goes gone good	happy happened hear heard house how	if I'll interesting it's (it is)	jumped just

K	L	M	N	O
kept knew know	laughed learned little looked	made many middle more mother	named need new night now	of · only off · other once · our one

P	Q	R	S	T
people perfect place pretty put	quick quiet	ready really right running	said saw scared special stopped surprised	their · threw then · through there · too they · touch things · tried thought · turn

U	V	W	Wh	Y
until upon use	very	walk · went wanted · were was · with water · would	what · while when · who where · why which	year young your you're (you are)

Common Prefixes

Prefix	Meaning	Example
anti-	against	antifreeze
auto-	self	autobiography
counter-	contrary, against	counterfeit
de-	remove or reverse	defrost
dis-	not, opposite	disagree
en-, em-	cause to	encode, embrace
fore-	before	forecast
hyper-	over or exaggerated	hypersensitive
in-, im-	in	infield
in-, im-, il-, ir-	not, opposite	injustice, impossible
inter-	between or together	interact
mal-	mean, bad, wrong	maladjusted
micro-	small	microchip
mid-	middle	midway
mis-	wrongly	misfire
non-	not	nonsense
over-	over	overlook
post-	after	postgame
pre-	before or prior to	precook
pro-	forward, for	proceed
re-	again or backward	return
semi-	half	semicircle
sub-	under, below	submarine
super-	over, big, high, or extreme	superstar
tele-	to or at a distance	telescope
trans-	through, across, change	transport
un-	not	unfriendly
under-	low, too little	underwater

Common Suffixes

Suffix	Meaning	Example
-ant, -ent	one who	assistant, resident
-able, -ible	can be done	capable, gullible
-ed	past-tense verb	stopped
-en	made of	wooden
-er	one who	faster
-est	comparative	farthest
-ful	full of	careful
-ing	present participle verb form	looking
-ist	person who	artist
-ity, -ty	state of	activity
-tive	adjective form of a noun	creative
-less	without	hopeless
-ly	every	weekly
-ly	adverb	quickly
-ment	action or process	movement
-ness	state of	kindness
-ous	possessing the qualities of	joyous
-s, -es	more than one	cakes, boxes
-tion	act, process	infection
-tive	adjective form of a noun	creative
-y	characterized by	foamy

Common Roots

Root	Meaning	Example
act	do	activity
aud	hear	audible
aqua	water	aquarium
bio	life	biology
cycl	circle	cycle
dem	people	democracy
dent	tooth	dentist
dict	speak	prediction
du	two, twice	duplicate
duct	lead	conduct
form	shape	formula
geo	earth	geography
graph	write	paragraph
grat	please	grateful
hydr	water	hydroplane
ject	throw	eject
liber	free	liberate
loc	place	location
mech	machine	mechanic
meter	measuring	centimeter
min	little or small	miniature
multi	many	multitude
path	feeling	pathetic
ped	foot	pedal
phone	sound	telephone
photo	light	photograph
port	carry	portable
rupt	break	disrupt
sci	know	science
scope	see, examine	telescope
scribe	write	scribble
sens	feel	sense
sign	mark	signature
spec	see	inspect
struct	build	construction
terr	land	territory
therm	heat	thermostat
vers	turn	reverse

Weekly Spelling Program

Use the words and skills you teach during guided reading for your students' spelling program.
The chart below contains suggestions for the number and kinds of words to assign at each text level.

Level	Word Selection	Examples
A	Assign 5 words each week: 2 sight words from Level A list; 3 CVC with short *a* vowel	• *at, see* • *cat, bat, rat*
B	Assign 5 words each week: 2 sight words from Level B list; 3 CVC with short *a* and *o* vowel	• *dad, my* • *tag, hop, pop*
C	Assign 5 words each week: 2 sight words from Level C list; 3 CVC words	• *come, not* • *sit, net, but*
D	Assign 7 words each week: 2 sight words from Level D list; review 2 words from Levels A–C; 3 words that begin with a digraph	• *looking, into* • *got, play* • *ship, chip, thin*
E	Assign 8 words each week: 2 sight words from Level E list; review 2 words from Levels A–D; 4 words that start with blends	• *all, want* • *for, said* • *grill, still, spill, drill*
F	Assign 8 words each week: 2 sight words from Level F list; review 2 words from Levels C–E; 4 words that end with blends	• *came, have* • *she, this* • *camp, damp, champ, stamp*
G	Assign 8 words each week: 2 sight words from Level G list; review 2 words from Levels D–F; 4 words with silent *e*	• *eat, from* • *over, her* • *wave, brave, tape, grape*
H	Assign 8 to 10 words each week: 2 sight words from Level H list; review 2 words from Levels E–G; 4 to 6 words with vowel patterns you have taught in guided reading (*all, or, ow, ay, old*). Add some inflectional endings.	• *every, little* • *good, make* • *falling, smaller, spraying, played*
I	Assign 8 to 10 words each week: 2 sight words from Level I list; review; 2 words from Levels F–H; 4 to 6 words with vowel patterns you have taught in guided reading (*oo, oi, oa, ou*). Add some inflectional endings.	• *again, night* • *saw, next* • *boat, floating, croaked, roomy, gloomy, scooter*
J and K	Assign 8 to 10 words each week: 2 words from the word wall; review 2 words from Levels G–I; 4 to 6 words with vowel patterns you have taught in guided reading (*ea, ir, oa, ar, ur*). Add some inflectional endings.	• *always, mother* • *give, friend* • *birthday, girl, twirling, party, started, chart*
L and M	Assign 8 to 10 words each week: 2 words from the word wall; review 2 words from Levels G–K; 4 to 6 words with vowel patterns you have taught in guided reading (*igh, ew, ow, ar, ur*). Add suffixes *ful, ness, ous, ly*.	• *wanted, scared* • *because, laugh* • *lightly, brightness, frighten, lowly, prowler, scowling*
N–P	Assign 8 to 10 words each week: 2 words from the word wall; review 2 words from Levels G–M; 4 to 6 words with vowel patterns and suffixes you have taught in guided reading.	• *special, people* • *would, who* • *neighbor, weightless, moisture, capture, nature*
Q–Z	Assign 8 to 10 words each week. Include frequently misspelled words and words with affixes you have taught in guided reading.	• *awesome, fearsome, handsome, different, movement, argument, international, interruption*

Pre-A Lesson Plan (<40 letters)

Date: Students:

Components	Activity
Working With Names (2–3 minutes)	Choose one: ☐ Name Puzzle ☐ Magnetic Letters ☐ Rainbow Writing
Working With Letters (2–3 minutes)	Choose one: ☐ Match letters in the bag ☐ Match letters to an ABC chart ☐ Name letters left to right ☐ Find the letter on an ABC chart ☐ Name a word that begins with that letter ☐ Find the letter that makes that sound ☐ Name the letter that begins that word
Working With Sounds (2–3 minutes)	Choose one: ☐ Clapping Syllables ☐ Hearing Rhymes ☐ Sorting Pictures
Working With Books (5 minutes)	Title:
	Follow-Up Teaching Points (choose one or two) ☐ One-to-one matching ☐ Concept of a word ☐ First/last word ☐ Concept of a letter ☐ First/last letter ☐ period ☐ Upper/lowercase
Interactive Writing and Cut-Up Sentence (5 minutes)	Dictated Sentence: Letter Formation:

Next Steps	Letters and Names:	Sounds:
	Books:	Writing:

Teacher Notes and Observations for Pre-A Readers (< 40 letters)

Anecdotal notes, observations, and teaching points	Next Steps
Student: _____	☐ Clap Syllables ☐ Hear Rhymes ☐ Hear Initial Consonants ☐ Attend to Print ☐ One-to-One Matching ☐ Use Pictures ☐ Oral Language ☐ Other:
Student: _____	☐ Clap Syllables ☐ Hear Rhymes ☐ Hear Initial Consonants ☐ Attend to Print ☐ One-to-One Matching ☐ Use Pictures ☐ Oral Language ☐ Other:
Student: _____	☐ Clap Syllables ☐ Hear Rhymes ☐ Hear Initial Consonants ☐ Attend to Print ☐ One-to-One Matching ☐ Use Pictures ☐ Oral Language ☐ Other:
Student: _____	☐ Clap Syllables ☐ Hear Rhymes ☐ Hear Initial Consonants ☐ Attend to Print ☐ One-to-One Matching ☐ Use Pictures ☐ Oral Language ☐ Other:

Emergent Guided Reading Plan (Levels A–C)

Students: Date: Title/Level:

Word Study Focus	Strategy Focus	Comprehension Focus

Day 1	Day 2
Sight Word Review 1 minute	**Sight Word Review** 1 minute

Reading 8–10 minutes

Introduce and Read a New Book Synopsis: New Vocabulary:	**Reread Yesterday's Book** (and other familiar books) Student to Assess:
Read the book with prompting (use back side for recording observations and prompts)	*Read books with prompting (use back side for recording observations and prompts)*
Discussion Prompts:	Discussion Prompts:

Follow-Up Teaching Points (choose 1 or 2 each day)

☐ Apply one-to-one matching   ☐ Take risks   ☐ Use meaning   ☐ Monitor for meaning
☐ Use letters and sounds   ☐ Cross-check M, S, V   ☐ Use known words   ☐ Visually scan
☐ Reread to problem-solve

Teaching Point for Day 1	**Teaching Point for Day 2**

New Sight Word What's Missing? • Mix and Fix • Table Writing • Write It & Retrieve It (1–2 minutes)

Word Study (Day 1) 5–8 minutes	**Guided Writing (Day 2)** 8–10 minutes
☐ Picture Sorting ☐ Making Words ☐ Sound Boxes	☐ A: 3–5 words ☐ B: 5–7 words ☐ C: 7–10 words

Next Steps	Text: Next Goals: Students to Assess:

Teacher Notes and Observations for Emergent Readers (Levels A–C)

Monitoring and Word-Solving Prompts
☐ Point to each word. (One-to-one matching)
☐ Check the picture. What would make sense?
☐ Say the first sound. What would make sense?
☐ Show me the word _____. (Locate a sight word.)
☐ Check the word with your finger.
☐ Could it be _____ or _____? How do you know?
☐ What did you notice?
☐ What can you do to help yourself?

Fluency and Comprehension Prompts
☐ Read without pointing.
☐ Read it the way the character would say it.
☐ What did you read? Tell me about the book.
☐ What does this book remind you of?
☐ Have you ever felt like the character feels? When?
☐ What was the problem? How was it solved?
☐ What is your favorite part? Why?
☐ How is this book like another book you have read?

Anecdotal notes, running records, observations, and teaching points	Goals/Next Steps
Student: _____	☐ One-to-One Matching ☐ Use Pictures ☐ Use First Letters ☐ Cross-Check M, S, and V ☐ Visual Scanning ☐ Other:
Student: _____	☐ One-to-One Matching ☐ Use Pictures ☐ Use First Letters ☐ Cross-Check M, S, and V ☐ Visual Scanning ☐ Other:
Student: _____	☐ One-to-One Matching ☐ Use Pictures ☐ Use First Letters ☐ Cross-Check M, S, and V ☐ Visual Scanning ☐ Other:
Student: _____	☐ One-to-One Matching ☐ Use Pictures ☐ Use First Letters ☐ Cross-Check M, S, and V ☐ Visual Scanning ☐ Other:
Student: _____	☐ One-to-One Matching ☐ Use Pictures ☐ Use First Letters ☐ Cross-Check M, S, and V ☐ Visual Scanning ☐ Other:
Student: _____	☐ One-to-One Matching ☐ Use Pictures ☐ Use First Letters ☐ Cross-Check M, S, and V ☐ Visual Scanning ☐ Other:

Early Guided Reading Plan (Levels D–I)

Students: Date: Title/Level:

Word Study Focus	Strategy Focus	Comprehension Focus

Day 1	Day 2
Sight Word Review 1 minute	**Sight Word Review** 1 minute

Reading 8–10 minutes

Introduce and Read a New Book Synopsis: New Vocabulary:	**Reread Yesterday's Book** (and other familiar books) Running Record Student:
Students read the book with prompting (use back side for recording observations and prompts)	*Students read books with prompting (use back side for recording observations and prompts)*
Discussion Prompts:	Discussion Prompts:

Follow-Up Teaching Points (choose 1 or 2 each day)

☐ Use meaning   ☐ Monitor for meaning   ☐ Reread at difficulty
☐ Monitor for letters and sounds ☐ Attend to word endings   ☐ Visually scan the word   ☐ Use known parts
☐ Attend to contractions   ☐ Use analogies   ☐ Break apart words

Teaching Point for Day 1	Teaching Point for Day 2

New Sight Word What's Missing? • Mix and Fix • Table Writing • Write It & Retrieve It (1–2 minutes)

Word Study (Day 1) (5–8 minutes)	**Guided Writing (Day 2)** (8–10 minutes)
☐ Picture Sorting ☐ Making Words ☐ Sound Boxes ☐ Breaking Words ☐ Analogy Charts	☐ Dictated sentences ☐ B-M-E ☐ Problem-Solution ☐ SWBS ☐ New facts ☐ Other:

Next Steps	Text:	Next Goals:	Students to Assess:

Teacher Notes and Observations for Early Readers (Levels D–I)

Monitoring and Word-Solving Prompts
- ☐ Reread and think what would make sense.
- ☐ Say the first part. Now look through the word.
- ☐ Check the end (or middle) of the word.
- ☐ Find the tricky part. What can you try?
- ☐ Show me a part you know.
- ☐ Do you know another word that looks like that?
- ☐ Use your finger to cover the ending.
- ☐ Break the word apart.

Fluency and Comprehension Prompts
- ☐ Can you read it quickly?
- ☐ How did you sound?
- ☐ What did you read? What's happened so far?
- ☐ What have you learned?
- ☐ Why did the character do (or say) that?
- ☐ Why...?
- ☐ What are you thinking?

Anecdotal notes, running records, observations, and teaching points	Goals/Next Steps
Student: _____	☐ Monitor ☐ Word Solving ☐ Visual Scanning ☐ Fluency ☐ Retell ☐ Other:
Student: _____	☐ Monitor ☐ Word Solving ☐ Visual Scanning ☐ Fluency ☐ Retell ☐ Other:
Student: _____	☐ Monitor ☐ Word Solving ☐ Visual Scanning ☐ Fluency ☐ Retell ☐ Other:
Student: _____	☐ Monitor ☐ Word Solving ☐ Visual Scanning ☐ Fluency ☐ Retell ☐ Other:
Student: _____	☐ Monitor ☐ Word Solving ☐ Visual Scanning ☐ Fluency ☐ Retell ☐ Other:
Student: _____	☐ Monitor ☐ Word Solving ☐ Visual Scanning ☐ Fluency ☐ Retell ☐ Other:

Transitional Guided Reading Plan (Levels J–P)

Students:	Date:	Title/Level:	

Word Study Focus	Strategy Focus	Comprehension Focus

Day 1	Day 2	Day 3
Reading 12–15 minutes		**Writing** 20 minutes

Day 1	Day 2	Day 3
Introduce and Read a New Text Synopsis: New vocabulary: Model strategy (if necessary):	**Continue Reading the Text** New vocabulary:	**Writing Prompt**

Students read the book with prompting (use back side for recording observations and prompts)

Discussion Prompts:	Discussion Prompts:	**Plan With Key Words**
		Write Goals/Observations

Follow-Up Teaching Points (choose 1 or 2 each day)
☐ Monitor for meaning ☐ Check middle (or end) ☐ Break words apart
☐ Reread and sound the first part ☐ Use analogies ☐ Use known parts
☐ Inflectional endings ☐ Use vocabulary strategies
☐ Read with phrasing, expression, and punctuation

Teaching Point for Day 1	Teaching Point for Day 2	

Word Study Activity for Day 2 3–5 minutes		Teaching Point for Day 3
☐ Breaking Words ☐ Analogy Charts ☐ Make a Big Word ☐ Writing Big Words		

Next Steps	Text:	Goals:	Students to Assess:

Teacher Notes and Observations for Transitional Readers (Levels J–P)

Monitoring and Word-Solving Prompts
- ☐ Does that make sense? Reread.
- ☐ Say the first part. Now say more. Think about the story.
- ☐ Check the middle (or end) of the word.
- ☐ Find a part you know.
- ☐ Show me the parts in that word.
- ☐ Do you know another word that looks like that?
- ☐ What can you try? How can you figure out that word?
- ☐ Can you say this part of the word?

Fluency and Comprehension Prompts
- ☐ Can you read it quickly?
- ☐ Read it like the character would say it.
- ☐ What did you read? What's happened so far?
- ☐ What have you learned?
- ☐ Why did the character do (or say) that?
- ☐ What was important on this page? Why?
- ☐ What caused _____? What was the effect of it?
- ☐ How are _____ and _____ similar (or different)?

Anecdotal notes, running records, observations, and teaching points	Next Steps
Student: _____	☐ Monitor ☐ Word Solving ☐ Fluency ☐ Vocabulary ☐ Retell ☐ Other:
Student: _____	☐ Monitor ☐ Word Solving ☐ Fluency ☐ Vocabulary ☐ Retell ☐ Other:
Student: _____	☐ Monitor ☐ Word Solving ☐ Fluency ☐ Vocabulary ☐ Retell ☐ Other:
Student: _____	☐ Monitor ☐ Word Solving ☐ Fluency ☐ Vocabulary ☐ Retell ☐ Other:
Student: _____	☐ Monitor ☐ Word Solving ☐ Fluency ☐ Vocabulary ☐ Retell ☐ Other:
Student: _____	☐ Monitor ☐ Word Solving ☐ Fluency ☐ Vocabulary ☐ Retell ☐ Other:

Fluent Guided Reading Plan (Levels Q–Z)

Students:	Date:	Title/Level:

Word Study Focus	Comprehension Focus

Day 1	Day 2 (and 3, if needed)	Day 3
Reading 12–15 minutes		**Writing** 20 minutes
Introduce and Read a New Text Synopsis:	**Continue Reading the Text**	**Writing Prompt**
New vocabulary:	New vocabulary:	
Model strategy (if necessary):		
Students read the book with prompting (use back side for recording observations and prompts)		**Plan With Key Words**
Discussion Prompts:	Discussion Prompts:	
		Write With Support Goals/Observations
Follow-Up Teaching Points (choose 1 or 2 each day) ☐ Solve big words ☐ Use vocabulary strategies ☐ Affixes		
Teaching Point for Day 1	**Teaching Point for Day 2**	
Word Study Activity	**New Word List**	**Teaching Point for Day 3**
Affix: _____ ☐ Make an Affix Word ☐ Write an Affix Word ☐ Read an Affix Word Dictate these words for students to write:	Word: _____ Definition: _____ Word: _____ Definition: _____	

Next Steps	Text:	Goals:	Students to Assess:

Teacher Notes and Observations for Fluent Readers (Levels Q–Z)

Prompts

☐ What are you thinking? What are you noticing? Tell me more about that.
☐ Was there something you didn't understand? How can you help yourself?
☐ Is there a word you don't understand? Reread the sentence and substitute a word that makes sense.
☐ What is the main idea? What are the important details? Use your heading and illustration.
☐ What are the key words in this part? Use the words to summarize what you read.
☐ What questions can you ask yourself? What is a good green (red or yellow) question?
☐ What is similar (or different) about _____ and _____? What caused...? What was the effect of...?
☐ How is the character feeling? Why did the character say (or do) that?
☐ What traits best describe the character? Describe the relationship between _____ and _____.
☐ What inferences are you making? What conclusion can you draw?

Anecdotal notes, running records, observations, and teaching points	Next Steps/Strategy
Student: _____	
Student: _____	
Student: _____	
Student: _____	
Student: _____	
Student: _____	

PRINTABLE LEVELED BOOKS

In this section, you'll find the four printable leveled books mentioned in Chapters 3 and 4, ready for copying and assembly.

In addition, go to scholastic.com/NSFWordStudy to find four more leveled books to print out and assemble.

In the Forest
(Level B)

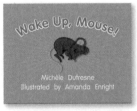

Wake Up, Mouse!
(Level C)

Cookie and Scout Together (Level B)

Nuts for Winter
(Level C)

How to Make the Books

Follow these steps to copy and assemble the books:

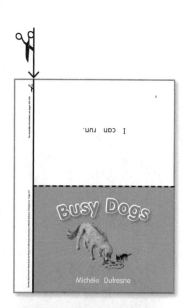

1. Remove the book pages and make single-sided copies on 8 ½-by-11-inch paper.

2. Fold each page along the dashed lines.

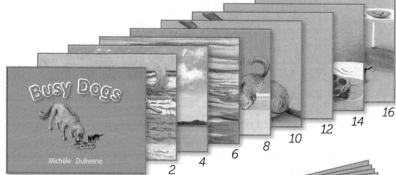

3. Place the pages in order, starting with the cover

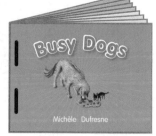

4. Staple the pages along the book's spine.

5. Glue the inside corners of each folded page together for easy page turning.

The Next Step Forward in Word Study and Phonics

For assembly instructions, see pages 245–246.

1

I can run.

Busy Dogs

Michèle Dufresne
Illustrated by Estelle Corke

I can jump.

For assembly instructions, see pages 245–246.

TM ® & © Scholastic Inc. All rights reserved. *The Next Step Forward in Word Study and Phonics* © 2019 by Jan Richardson and Michèle Dufresne. Published by Scholastic Inc.

5

I can swim.

For assembly instructions, see pages 245–246.

TM ® & © Scholastic Inc. All rights reserved. *The Next Step Forward in Word Study and Phonics* © 2019 by Jan Richardson and Michèle Dufresne. Published by Scholastic Inc. • page 249

I can hide.

7

For assembly instructions, see pages 245–246.

I can sit.

For assembly instructions, see pages 245–246.

I can beg.

For assembly instructions, see pages 245–246.

TM ® & © Scholastic Inc. All rights reserved. *The Next Step Forward in Word Study and Phonics* © 2019 by Jan Richardson and Michèle Dufresne. Published by Scholastic Inc. • page 252

I can eat.

For assembly instructions, see pages 245–246.

I can eat, too.

For assembly instructions, see pages 245–246.

TM ® & © Scholastic Inc. All rights reserved. The Next Step Forward in Word Study and Phonics © 2019 by Jan Richardson and Michèle Dufresne. Published by Scholastic Inc. • page 254

For assembly instructions, see pages 245–246.

For assembly instructions, see pages 245–246.

TM ® & © Scholastic Inc. All rights reserved. The Next Step Forward in Word Study and Phonics © 2019 by Jan Richardson and Michèle Dufresne. Published by Scholastic Inc. • page 256

1

I am a mouse.

Looking for Dinner

Michèle Dufresne

Illustrated by Amanda Enright

For assembly instructions, see pages 245–246.

3

I am a squirrel.

I am a skunk.

For assembly instructions, see pages 245–246.

I am a porcupine.

7

I am a fox.

For assembly instructions, see pages 245–246.

I am a deer.

For assembly instructions, see pages 245–246.

I am a bear.

For assembly instructions, see pages 245–246.

TM ® & © Scholastic Inc. All rights reserved. *The Next Step Forward in Word Study and Phonics* © 2019 by Jan Richardson and Michèle Dufresne. Published by Scholastic Inc. • page 262

Run! Run! Run!

For assembly instructions, see pages 245–246.

Here is my tiger.

1

Playtime for Cookie and Scout

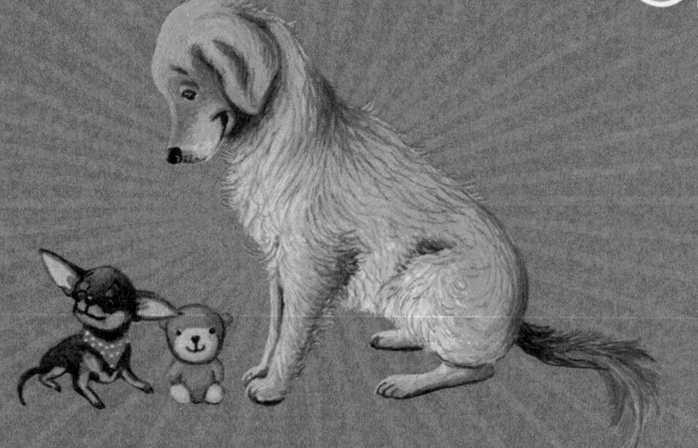

Michèle Dufresne

Illustrated by Estelle Corke

For assembly instructions, see pages 245–246.

Here is my pig.

3

For assembly instructions, see pages 245–246.

Here is my monkey.

For assembly instructions, see pages 245–246.

Here is my cat.

For assembly instructions, see pages 245–246.

Here is my rabbit.

For assembly instructions, see pages 245–246.

Here is my frog.

11

For assembly instructions, see pages 245–246.

TM ® & © Scholastic Inc. All rights reserved. The Next Step Forward in Word Study and Phonics © 2019 by Jan Richardson and Michèle Dufresne. Published by Scholastic Inc. • page 270

Here is my bear.

For assembly instructions, see pages 245–246.

Here is my ball.

For assembly instructions, see pages 245–246.

For assembly instructions, see pages 245–246.

Illustrated by Estelle Corke

Michèle Dufresne

Fun at the Park

"I like to go to the park,"
said Scout.

1

"Me, too," said Cookie.
"The park is fun!"

3

For assembly instructions, see pages 245–246.

"Here is the field," said Scout.

"I like to run in the field."

"Me, too," said Cookie.

For assembly instructions, see pages 245–246.

"Look!" said Scout.

"Here is a slide.

Can we go down the slide?"

7

"Yes," said Cookie.
"We can go down the slide!"

For assembly instructions, see pages 245–246.

"Look!" said Scout.
"Here is a house.
Can we go in the house?"

For assembly instructions, see pages 245–246.

"Yes," said Cookie.
"We can go in the house."

For assembly instructions, see pages 245–246.

TM ® & © Scholastic Inc. All rights reserved. The Next Step Forward in Word Study and Phonics © 2019 by Jan Richardson and Michèle Dufresne. Published by Scholastic Inc. • page 280

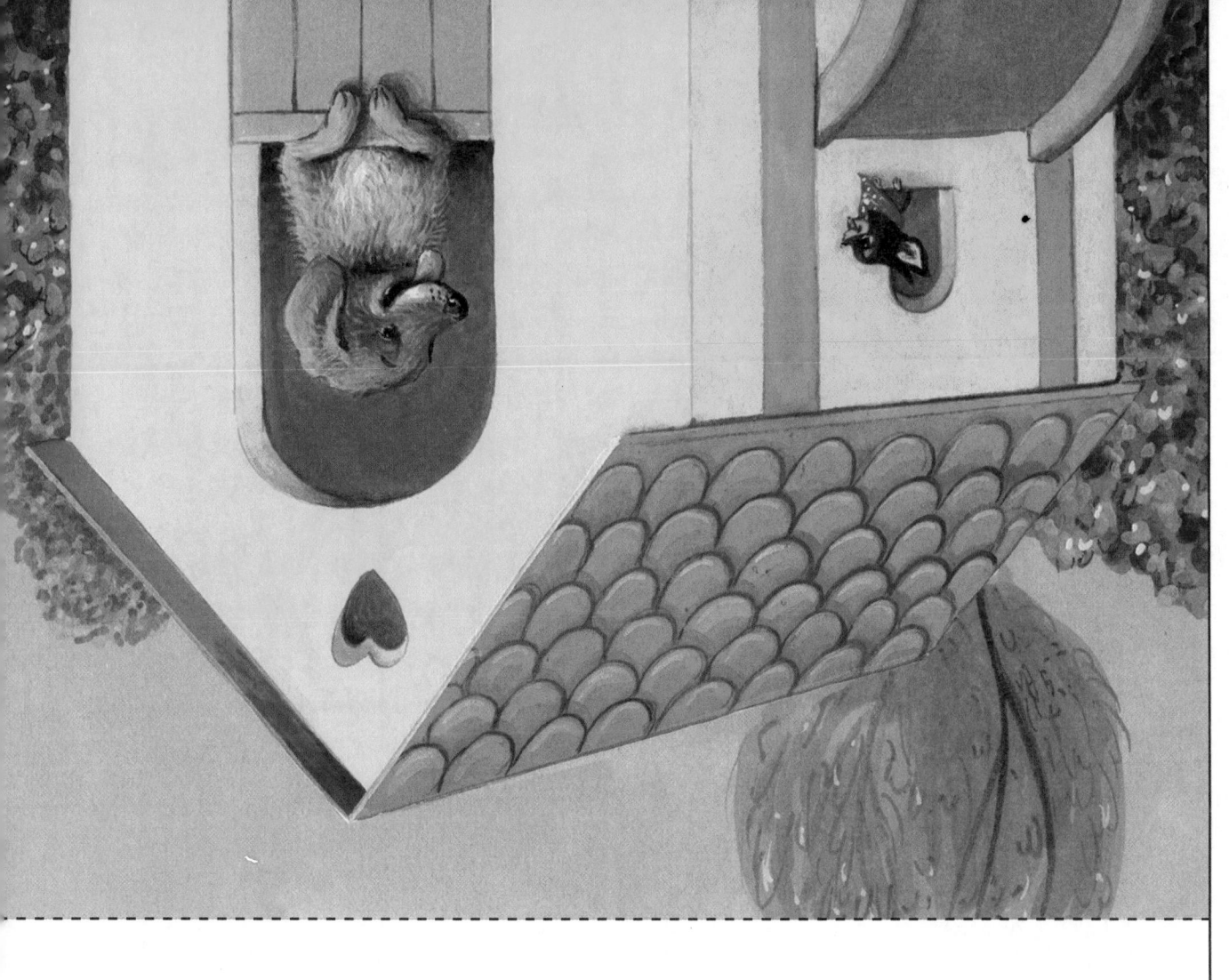

For assembly instructions, see pages 245–246.

"I like to go to the park,"
said Scout.

"I love the park," said Cookie.
"The park is fun!"

For assembly instructions, see pages 245–246.

INDEX

MAXIMIZE THE POWER OF GUIDED READING WITH JAN RICHARDSON

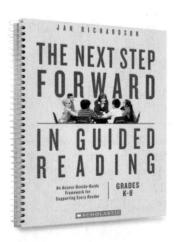

The Next Step Forward in Guided Reading: An Assess-Decide-Guide Framework for Supporting Every Reader

JAN RICHARDSON
The essential resource for teaching guided reading, K–8, organized around Jan's proven framework—with dozens of print and digital resources—to meet every reader's needs.
978-1-338-16111-3

The Guided Reading Teacher's Companion: Prompts, Discussion Starters, & Teaching Points

JAN RICHARDSON
A handy desktop reference with just-right language to use in every component of a guided reading lesson, pre-A to fluent.
978-1-338-16345-2

The Next Step Forward in Reading Intervention: The RISE Framework

JAN RICHARDSON and ELLEN LEWIS
A step-by-step handbook on RISE, a proven intervention program in which striving readers gain the confidence, proficiency, and skills they need to excel.
978-1-338-29826-0

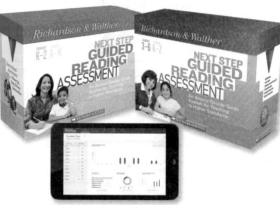

Next Step Guided Reading in Action

JAN RICHARDSON
Lead targeted lessons and accelerate the growth of readers at all stages, with the help of these step-by-step classroom videos.
Grades K–2: 978-1-338-21734-6
Grades 3 & Up: 978-1-338-21735-3

Next Step Guided Reading Assessment

JAN RICHARDSON and MARIA WALTHER
An all-in-one program to pinpoint students' reading levels and target instructional next steps with assessment data that helps move students toward reading independence.
Grades K–2: 978-1-338-54195-3
Grades 3–6: 978-0-545-44267-1